CONNECTING SINAI TO CALVARY

John C. Jeske

Northwestern Publishing House
Milwaukee, Wisconsin

Cover art: Jim Jankowski
Interior illustrations: Glenn Myers

Library of Congress Control Number: 2004101357
Northwestern Publishing House
1250 N. 113th St., Milwaukee, WI 53226-3284
www.nph.net
© 2005 by Northwestern Publishing House
Published 2005
Printed in the United States of America
ISBN-13: 978-0-8100-1653-2
ISBN-10: 0-8100-1653-2

Contents

Foreword iv

1. God Identified Himself by Name 1

2. Living under God's Covenant 15

3. A Special Homeland 29

4. A Table Set by God 43

5. Living under Law and Gospel 55

6. God's Path of Worship 69

7. Leaders Appointed by God 97

8. Custodians of God's Word..113

9. A Preview of the Promised Savior.............................. 127

10. Busy Lives 139

11. Disciplined by God... 149

12. A Song on Their Lips 167

13. A Future Life in a Better World................................ 179

    Subject Index.. 193

Foreword

The Old Testament, which makes up three-quarters of the Bible, is pretty much unexplored territory for many Christians. Twenty years of parish ministry, followed by 25 years in the Old Testament department of Wisconsin Lutheran Seminary, have convinced this writer that a lot of people have difficulty reading the Old Testament. There could be a number of reasons for that.

One is that there is so much of it. The sheer bulk of the Old Testament is intimidating—39 books, many of them much longer than most New Testament books. The time period from Abraham to Christ is 20 times longer than the entire period recorded in the New Testament. First-time readers of the Old Testament have found themselves bogged down in details of ancient history and of faraway places with strange-sounding names. College and seminary students have confessed to this writer that on many pages of the Old Testament, they find it difficult to understand what they're reading.

Another problem causing difficulty for the Old Testament reader is the wide variety of literary styles used by a couple dozen different people over ten centuries. There is *historical narrative,* usually the easiest to understand. Who could have difficulty understanding the account of creation or of the flood? But the Old Testament doesn't read like a historical novel. There is *poetry.* There are several books containing what is called *wisdom literature.* More than half of the Old Testament is *prophecy,* and many readers find this material difficult. There's the temptation to become bored when you read chapter after chapter of ancient worship regulations—unfamiliar laws about priests and animal sacrifices and festivals that God's people no longer observe.

Furthermore, the Old Testament doesn't always seem to make sense to the contemporary reader. An undisciplined, self-centered character like Samson received supernatural gifts. Solomon, a king with seven hundred wives in his harem (not to mention three hundred concubines), enjoyed extraordinary blessings from the hand of God. On the other hand, a sincere, devout child of God like Job was called upon to undergo a ghastly nightmare of suffering.

Still another stumbling block for the reader of the Old Testament is that its message often offends modern ears. As the people of Israel camped on the east bank of the Jordan River, poised to enter their new homeland, God ordered them to exterminate the Canaanite occupants of the land. To the uninformed reader, that sounds awfully much like what Adolf Hitler ordered for the Jewish citizens of Germany and the neighboring lands his armies had occupied. "Isn't that genocide?" some have asked. "How can you harmonize that with what Jesus taught us about loving our neighbor?"

For whatever reasons, three-quarters of the Bible seems strange and confusing and uninteresting to many Christians today. Many know the 23rd psalm. As children they learned some fascinating stories about how God created the world, how David killed a giant, and how Daniel survived in a den of lions. But overall knowledge of the Old Testament is fading among Christians.

The 39 books of the Old Testament were the only Bible the people of Jesus' time had. The Old Testament was the Bible Jesus read. Jesus was speaking of the Old Testament when he said: "These are the Scriptures that testify about me" (John 5:39). It simply is not true that the Old Testament is merely the story of how some courageous descendants of Abraham carved out a life for themselves in an unfriendly land.

Here is the tragedy. It isn't enough for a Christian to think of the Old Testament as a series of fascinating narratives about Adam and Eve, Abraham and Sarah, Ruth, and David. These men and women were our fathers and mothers in faith. In all of the essentials, their faith was the same as ours. For them, as for us, there was and has always been only one way to friendship and fellowship with God. That way—then as now—is through the substitute whom God sent to trade places with sinners. Page after page of the Old Testament reveals a passionate love affair between God and the people with whom he had made a covenant, a solemn contract. The connection between the Old Testament and the New Testament is both hidden and revealed in that covenant relationship, driven by the Creator's love for his wayward creatures.

People who restrict their Bible reading to the New Testament will, of course, be able to see this fundamental truth of the sinner's relationship with God, but they won't see it as clearly. Put a blindfold over your left eye and you can still see, but your perspective is distorted, your vision limited. The result will be the same for people who restrict their Bible reading to the pages of the New Testament.

Just one example. In years past, Leviticus was the first Bible book read by children in a Jewish family. Unfortunately, Leviticus is the *last* book most Christians read. At what cost? They won't be able to understand as well as they ought the comparisons between the Old Testament priest and Christ, our great High Priest. (The author of the letter to the Hebrews devotes four chapters to sketching those comparisons—chapters 7–10.) They are likely to miss all the New Testament connections to the ceremony the people of Israel witnessed each year on the great Day of Atonement. That day's high point occurred when the high priest stepped out of the sanctuary, hands red from having been dipped into a container of animal blood—at least 28 times. In plain view of all the worshipers, he wiped those bloody hands on the head of a goat, which was then led out into the desert to die. Leviticus chapter 16 gives us this graphic portrayal of Christ as the sin bearer. To overlook such details surely detracts from one's understanding of how God forgives sin.

Because so many people find the first 39 books of the Bible hard to read, knowledge of the Old Testament is fading fast among God's people. That seems especially tragic in the case of those whose lives, humanly speaking, still lie ahead of them. If adult readers find that the 13 chapters of this handbook have helped them read the Old Testament with greater understanding, that's fine. If pastors find in these chapters subject matter for Bible classes, or if Christian educators find this material helpful in preparing their Bible history lessons, those will be lovely fringe benefits. But this handbook has been written with *young* Bible readers in mind—specifically young men and women of junior high and high school ages. Here are the fathers and mothers of the next generation, the future leaders of our church, the future custodians of the truth of God's Word.

What do they know about what day-to-day life was like for a child of God during the centuries of the Old Testament? What *should* they know? When a 10th grader reads or hears about a *priest*, will he or she understand the important role God gave the priest in centuries past? Will students make the important connection to the One, who is our mediator before a holy God? Or when readers hear that God has made a *covenant* with sinners, will they recognize this as evidence of God's mercy, which is almost unbelievable? A number of brothers and sisters who teach God's Word have expressed their need for such a resource to help Bible students see the connection between the Old Testament and the New. It is the writer's hope that perhaps this handbook can begin to address that need.

It attempts to take Bible students by the hand, as it were, to let them experience day-to-day life in Old Testament times:

> To let them hear God identify himself to Abraham's descendants, who were surrounded on all sides by the worship of false gods.
>
> To help them understand how a homeland in Canaan was an instrument God used to train his people to trust him to provide for all their needs.
>
> To let them observe how God prepared his people for Messiah's coming.
>
> To let them experience, if only indirectly, what difference it made to live as God's people during the centuries of the Old Testament.

The writer acknowledges with gratitude the help offered by a number of people who helped make this handbook a reality. Several individuals deserve special recognition for their contributions to the finished product. Professor Forrest Bivens was meticulous in his review of the manuscript, going the extra mile by field testing a portion of it with several members of the target audience. Pastors Mark and Tom Jeske offered helpful suggestions for tightening the manuscript and making it user friendly. The writer is grateful also for the considerable help editor Kenneth Kremer offered, trying to ensure that the message of this book will reach its audience.

> Your works are wonderful,
> I know that full well.
> How precious to me are your thoughts, O God!
> Psalm 139:14,17

~ John C. Jeske

They will put my name on the Israelites,
and I will bless them.

~ Numbers 6:27

"I, even I, am the LORD, and apart
from me there is no savior. I have
revealed and saved and proclaimed—
I, and not some foreign god among you.
You are my witnesses," declares the
LORD, "that I am God. Yes, and from
ancient days I am he."

~ Isaiah 43:11-13

God Identified Himself by Name

When you start out to do something, the way you begin is important. The way you begin could very well determine whether or not you're going to accomplish what you hope to. Let's say you live somewhere in America's Midwest, and your family decides to take a trip to Washington, DC. If you drive to the interstate and head *west*, that wrong beginning guarantees that you're not going to get to Washington, DC.

Or let's say that you're building a new home, and the building contractor puts the corner stakes in the wrong place—on your neighbor's lot line. That whole building project is in trouble. When you begin something new, it's important that you have the right starting point.

Getting Started

This applies not only to taking a vacation trip or building a home. When you're connecting with God, it's important to know the right starting point. When it comes to figuring out how to have a good relationship with God, however, our human reason is blind. By ourselves, we don't have a clue about how to become friends with God.

Maybe that statement strikes you as strange. There are many things in life that you can figure out by yourself—how to build a model airplane, how to make money, how to fall in love. The human brain has discovered how to build microwaves and laptop computers and communication satellites. But on our own there's no way we can discover how to approach God. Many have tried, but they have not found peace. God must come to us and share his sacred secrets, or we'll never be able to live at peace with him.

The good news is that God has done just that. He broke the silence. He turned on the lights. From the very beginning of history, God made himself known to his highest creatures. Day by day in Old Testament times, he identified himself by name, so his human creatures could get to know him. The very first words of the Bible are "In the beginning God . . ." (Genesis 1:1).

God showed himself to us. He described himself to us, telling us what we need to know about him if we ever hope to live with him, as members of his family. From the very first pages of the Old Testament, God identified himself by name.

In a class all by himself

It's important for us to note that the Bible nowhere tries to prove the existence of God. It simply takes for granted that God exists. God is in a class all by himself. He is beyond our understanding. The prophet Isaiah once put this question to God's people: "To whom, then, will you compare God? What image will you compare him to?" (Isaiah 40:18).

If you were explaining to a very young child what an apple is, you might start out by saying, "An apple is a piece of fruit." To explain what a violin is, you could say, "It's a musical instrument." But to whom or to what can you compare God? God is in a class all by himself, and the Bible doesn't even try to explain him. It does, however, give us information we need to know about God. The Old Testament tells us a number of the names by which God made himself known to ancient Israel and, through Israel, to all the people of the world. We will look at four of those names.

Elohim, "God"

The first name God calls himself in the Old Testament is *Elohim* (el-oh-HEEM, always translated as "God"). This name is used 31 times in the creation account alone and several thousand times in the Old Testament. The origin of this Hebrew name is uncertain. Some scholars think it comes from a verb that means "to fear"; others, from a verb meaning "to be mighty."

The very first verse of the Bible uses this name to reveal God as the only one who is *eternal*. There was a beginning—a point in history before which there was absolutely nothing, except God. There was no this or that, no up or down, no here or there, no now or then—only Elohim. He is eternal. He is the one true and living God—the awesome God who brought heaven and earth into existence out of nothing. "He spoke, and it came to be; he commanded, and it stood firm" (Psalm 33:9). Throughout the creation account God uses the name Elohim to describe himself as almighty, wise, and kind. With just a word he called the universe into existence, and that includes not only matter (the building material of the universe) but time and space and energy and the forces of nature as well. "See now that I myself am He! There is no god besides me. I put to death and I bring to life" (Deuteronomy 32:39).

The Bible begins by telling us that "in the beginning God created the heavens and the earth" (Genesis 1:1). It is the Bible's answer to the age-old question of *origin*, which science is unable to answer. Lord Kelvin, famous British mathematician and physicist, said, "There is nothing in science which teaches the origin of anything at all." It was Elohim, our awesome God, who "thought up" atomic power. He threw a whole skyful of planets and stars into orbit. *National Geographic* magazine tells us that our sun is one of perhaps a billion stars in the Milky Way and that there could be at least another billion galaxies besides the Milky Way.

Elohim, the same almighty God who designed the solar system, paints the gorgeous reds and oranges of a summer sunset. He ordered 5 to follow 4 and to be half of 10. He arranged it that when a microscopic particle of matter from a father's body meets a microscopic particle from a mother's body, a baby is conceived. And 40 days later, that miniature human being has a heartbeat, fingerprints, and brain waves.

We humans can never create. We can rearrange the elements God has provided—some lumber and nails into a birdhouse or some eggs, flour, milk, and sugar into a cake. But we cannot create, as God did. Try it. Try to imagine a new primary color. Try to think up a third sex, in addition to the two God thought up.

We can't even begin to understand the majesty and the power and the wisdom of the God who put this universe together, the God who introduces himself to us in the first verse of the Bible. Our understanding is so limited. We might not even understand how a black cow can eat green grass and give white milk. When we read God's first statement to us—"In the beginning God created the heavens and the earth"—all we can do is to stand in silent awe. If God were small enough for us to understand, he would not be big enough to be worshiped. The name Elohim tells us that God is a big and an awesome God.

A plural form

It's important to note that the Hebrew name Elohim is a noun that is plural in form. Of all the languages in the Semitic language family, only Hebrew (the language in which God gave his Word to ancient Israel) has this plural form for God. That unusual name emphasizes, on the one hand, that the true God is *one*. "Hear, O Israel: The LORD *our God* . . . is *one*" (Deuteronomy 6:4).

On the other hand, that plural form allows for the fact that our great and majestic God is more than a simple, single person, as you and I are. The fact that the very first name used for God in the Bible is a plural prepares us for the Bible's truth that in the oneness of God there are three distinct persons. It would be an overstatement to say that the name Elohim teaches that the true God is triune. The truth of the Trinity is not taught explicitly in the Old Testament. But the creation account hints at this teaching several times. In the second verse of the Bible, for example, we learn that when God first created the elements—the materials from which our universe is made up—"*the Spirit of God* was hovering over the waters" (Genesis 1:2). The life-giving Spirit of God was active in the work of creation, preserving what God had created. And in Genesis 1:26, we learn that before creating the first human being, God engaged in solemn deliberation: "Let *us* make man in *our* image." Note the two plural pronouns. The New Testament spells out in greater detail that all three persons of the Holy Trinity were active in the work of creation. This is Elohim:

The *independent* Creator, who introduces himself to us on the first page of the Bible.
The *eternal* God, without beginning and without end.
The *almighty* God, who deserves to be held in reverence by all his creatures.

Adonai, "the Lord"

When God identified himself to us, he made it very clear that the relationship between him and us is not a relationship between equals. It's a *master-and-servant* relationship. This becomes immediately clear when we look at a second Old Testament name for God. The Hebrew word *'adhon* (ah-DOHN) means "master." *Adonai* (ah-doh-NYE) is a plural form of that word and emphasizes the truth that God is *the absolute Master*, under whom we live.

The messages God sends to us through that name Adonai are humbling ones: God is Lord and we are his servants. God designed us to live *under* him, not *alongside* him as equals with the right to argue or to disagree with him. "Tremble, O earth, at the presence of the Lord" (Psalm 114:7).

When Abraham was pleading with God to show mercy to the inhabitants of the city of Sodom, his prayer shows that he was conscious of the master-servant relationship between himself and God. God had threatened to destroy the wicked city but promised that if he could find 50 believers in Sodom, he would spare it. Note how humbly Abraham prayed to Adonai, theMaster under whom he lived as a servant:

> "Now that I have been so bold as to speak to the *Lord*, though I am nothing but dust and ashes, what if the number of righteous is five less than fifty? Will you destroy the whole city because of five people?" . . . Then [Abraham] said, "May the *Lord* not be angry, but let me speak. What if only thirty can be found there?" . . . Abraham said, "Now that I have been so bold as to speak to the *Lord*, what if only twenty can be found there?" . . . Then [Abraham] said, "May the *Lord* not be angry, but let me speak just once more. What if only ten . . . ?" (Genesis 18:27-32)

Five hundred years later, in his farewell address to the people of Israel, Moses, the humble servant of a heavenly Master, described Adonai as "*Lord* of lords, the great God, mighty and awesome, who shows no partiality and accepts no bribes" (Deuteronomy 10:17).

God appeared to Joshua, Moses' successor, to give him instructions for capturing the city of Jericho. Although Joshua was the commander in chief of the armies of Israel, he humbly fell facedown to the ground and asked Adonai, "What message does my *Lord* have for his *servant*?" (Joshua 5:14).

Turning the Master's plan upside down

It's humbling to realize that I'm not my own boss, but that's the way God designed this world. I cannot redesign the world and assign myself a new position in it. I cannot make fire to be cold either. I cannot pass a new law of nature that says "From now on water will run uphill!" God's Old Testament name Adonai (the Lord) reminds me that my position in life is that of a servant living under the heavenly master.

God will not allow my sinful pride to assign myself a new position alongside him. That's what sin is. Sin isn't so much what you do with your *hands* as it is what goes on *between your ears*. Sin is turning God's plan for our lives upside down. Instead of asking, "How can my body and life serve *God* and *people* around me?" we ask: "How can I make God and people *serve me? *How can I use them to make me happy?" The essence of sin is not that it harms another person or that it creates problems in society. The reason why God hates sin is that it defies his good and perfect will.

It's God's nature to hate sin, just as a bright light destroys darkness and an antiseptic kills germs. God is angry when his creatures rebel against him because he knows that disobedience always results in self-destruction. The one principle of hell is "I am my own boss!" What kind of father would sit by and watch his child hurt himself? What kind of God would do the same? Deny the Lord his right to control your life—consider yourself "liberated" to do what you please—and God promises you a life that is really empty and, worse yet, a future that is an absolute nightmare.

The question is not "How could a God of love be angry at sin?" but rather "How could a holy and loving God *not* be angry at sin?" God created us to live under him. We're here to follow his wise will and to bring honor to him by our thoughts and our talk and our deeds. That's what God tells us when he identifies himself as Adonai, the Lord.

Yahweh, "the Lord"*

The most common Old Testament name for God, a name used more than five thousand times, is the name *Yahweh* (YAH-weh). Actually it's a form of the Hebrew verb "to be." When at the burning bush God called Moses to deliver the people of Israel from slavery, Moses foresaw a difficulty. "Suppose I go to the Israelites and say to them, 'The God of your fathers has sent me to you,' and they ask me, 'What is his name?' Then what shall I tell them?" (Exodus 3:13).

Listen to the way in which God answered by explaining his name Yahweh: "God said to Moses, 'I AM WHO I AM. This is what you are to say to the Israelites: "I AM has sent me to you." . . . This is my name forever, the name by which I am to be remembered from generation to generation'" (Exodus 3:14,15).

Twenty times in the first several chapters of Genesis, Moses joins the name Yahweh to the name Elohim. God calls himself by the double name, "the Lord God." By so doing, he makes it clear that Yahweh is the same God whom we've learned to know as Elohim—the eternal, almighty, and all-wise Creator of the universe. But the name Yahweh had special meaning for the chosen people of God. There was a double reason why God said this would be the name by which he would be "remembered from generation to generation."

Yahweh: God of absolute independence

God himself defined the name Yahweh as "I AM." He alone can say of himself: "I AM WHO I AM." In contrast, you and I exist because God gave us life. God exists because he's God.

He is a God of *absolute independence.* God is not bound by any law of nature. He is independent of the law of gravity, for example, or of the law that says you can be in only one place at any one time. When, on God's calendar, the time came to send the Savior in human form, God again showed that he is absolutely independent. He was not bound by the law that says "Life is passed on from generation to generation by a union of male and female."

Yahweh is independent not only in his existence; his love is also independent. Why do we love another person? We love our mothers because of all they have done for us. A husband loves his wife because he finds her attractive, because she's a hard worker,

Most English Bible translations spell the name Yahweh as Lord, spelled with all capital letters. This is helpful to the reader. It's done to distinguish this covenant name from Adonai, which is a name for God that describes him as Lord and Master.

because she has returned his love. There's something selfish about human love, isn't there? Now compare that with God's love. It's totally *independent* of us. Why does God love? Day by day in Old Testament times, God himself answered that question: "I will have mercy *on whom I will have mercy*, and I will have compassion *on whom I will have compassion*" (Exodus 33:19).

Yahweh: God of absolute faithfulness

At the burning bush, God identified a second reason for identifying himself as Yahweh, the great "I AM." God explained that name by pointing to the fact that in pure mercy he had established a covenant with Abraham, Isaac, and Jacob. He identified himself as Yahweh, "the God of Abraham, the God of Isaac and the God of Jacob," and added "This is my name forever" (Exodus 3:15). Yahweh is God's Old Testament Savior name.

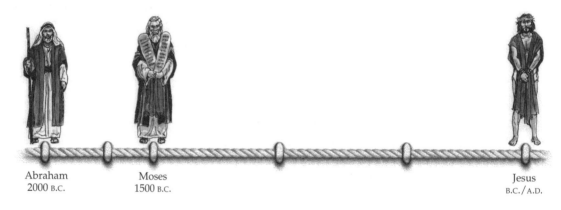

Abraham
2000 B.C.

Moses
1500 B.C.

Jesus
B.C./A.D.

Five hundred years before Moses stood at the burning bush, God had given Abraham a solemn promise. He had told him: "Through your descendants I will *carry out my plan to save the world*." In other words, one of Abraham's descendants would be the great Champion, who would free God's people from Satan's control. While the people of Israel were suffering under the whip of Egyptian slave masters, they may have wondered whether God had forgotten his promise to Abraham. At the burning bush, however, God announced that by calling Moses, he was moving to keep his promise. Delivering Israel from slavery was God's first step in carrying out his good plan for his people. At the burning bush he identified himself as Yahweh to reassure the faith of his people and to revive their hope. Day by day in Old Testament times, whenever God used his Old Testament Savior name, the LORD, it's primarily in connection with his saving plan.

Yahweh: God's covenant name

We call Yahweh God's covenant name. An independent God is under no obligation to his rebellious creatures, *unless he voluntarily puts himself under obligation*. This is precisely what God did when he made a covenant—a solemn, binding contract—with Abraham that one of Abraham's descendants would be the world's Savior.

Yahweh is serious about his covenant promise. His love is faithful, but it's not flabby. The God who has called us into his family doesn't go away for the weekend, leaving a note on the door that reads: "Whatever turns you on . . ." At Mount Sinai God announced, "I, the LORD your God [Yahweh], am a *jealous* God, *punishing* the children for the sin of the fathers to the third and fourth generation of those who hate me, but *showing love* to a thousand generations of those who love me and keep my commandments" (Exodus 20:5,6). Yahweh will not permit anyone to trample on his grace.

To summarize, then: Yahweh is the God of *absolute independence* but also the God of *absolute faithfulness*.

Yahweh is the God of free and faithful love.

God uses specific names

Genesis chapters 1 and 2—When you read the Old Testament, be sure to pay attention to the specific name God uses to identify himself, and you will gain valuable insight into Bible truth. In Genesis chapter 1, for example, God (Elohim), the eternal, almighty, all-wise Creator, is consistently named as the one who created the universe and everything that inhabits it. In Genesis chapter 2, however, we read that *"the LORD God* [Yahweh Elohim] made the earth and the heavens" (verse 4), "planted a garden . . . in Eden" (verse 8), and "made a woman from the rib he had taken out of the man, and he brought her to the man" (verse 22). By combining these two names, the author is telling us that God deals with his creatures not only in awesome might and majesty but also in free and faithful love.

Genesis 9:26,27—After the flood, Noah predicted what the future would hold for the only three men who had come through the earth-destroying flood with him, as well as for their descendants. Listen to several of the things he said: "Blessed be the LORD [Yahweh], the God of Shem!" (verse 26). Guided by the Spirit of God, Noah looked into the future with prophetic vision. He saw that the descendants of his son Shem would enjoy unusual blessings and that these would come from Yahweh. Noah understood that in the Garden of Eden, God had obligated himself by promising to send a Savior to rescue the sinful human race. By calling Yahweh "the God of Shem," Noah was saying that it would be through the bloodline of Shem that the blessings announced in Eden would be transmitted to the world. Noah understood that Yahweh, "the LORD," is the God of free and faithful love.

"May God [Elohim] extend the territory of Japheth" (verse 27). Here Noah next spoke about what the future held for his son Japheth, using a different name for God. He asked God to grant Japheth's descendants the blessings of territorial expansion and earthly prosperity. Notice that he properly ascribed those blessings to Elohim, the "chairman of the board" of the universe.

Jonah chapter 4—The closing chapter of the book of Jonah provides us with another example of an interesting interplay in the use of the divine names. Against his will, Jonah followed the LORD's (Yahweh's) call (Jonah 3:1) to bring God's words of judgment to people in the wicked city of Nineveh, capital of the Assyrian Empire. Jonah did so reluctantly; he considered Assyria a potential enemy of his own Jewish people. Despite Jonah's selfish attitude, God granted amazing success to the Word Jonah preached in Nineveh. We have Jesus' word for that: The people of Nineveh "*repented* at the preaching of Jonah" (Luke 11:32).

Now get set for a surprise. The selfish prophet was unhappy about the success his preaching had. Jonah resented the fact that the Savior had shown mercy to the heathen people of Nineveh and actually asked God to end his life. If we had been God, we might have granted Jonah his death wish and found ourselves a new prophet. But note how God reacted to Jonah's tantrum, and pay particular attention to the names he used for himself: "The LORD [Yahweh] replied, 'Have you any right to be angry?'" (Jonah 4:4).

The *God of free and faithful love* was concerned about Jonah's spiritual welfare. He didn't want Jonah's sinful stubbornness to come between him and his Savior, and he spoke to him about that.

But Jonah wasn't interested in what the Savior-God was saying to him. Instead, he went outside the city limits of Nineveh and built himself a shelter. There he could sit in the shade and wait for God to come to his senses and send down a firestorm to destroy the wicked city. And, when Nineveh went up in flames, Jonah wanted a front-row seat.

"Then the LORD God [Yahweh Elohim] provided a vine and made it grow up over Jonah to give shade for his head to ease his discomfort" (verse 6). The *all-powerful Creator* caused a vine to grow, although no one had planted it. At the same time, the *merciful Savior* showed undeserved kindness to his pouting, self-willed child, providing shade for him.

> But at dawn the next day *God* [Elohim] provided a worm, which chewed the vine so that it withered. When the sun rose, *God* [Elohim] provided a scorching east wind, and the sun blazed on Jonah's head so that he grew faint. He wanted to die, and said, "It would be better for me to die than to live." (verses 7,8)

The *majestic Creator* didn't appreciate the behavior of one of his redeemed human creatures who was showing shameful self-centeredness and a total lack of humility. He therefore arranged for two of his lower creations—a hungry worm and a scorching east wind—to get Jonah's attention. The Creator let Jonah know that he was aware of his rebellious attitude and was working to change it.

In the final two verses of the book (Jonah 4:10,11), Yahweh spoke to Jonah once more: "*The LORD* said, 'You have been concerned about this vine, though you did not tend it or make it grow. . . . But Nineveh has more than a hundred and twenty thousand people. . . . Should I not be concerned about that great city?'"

The *faithful Savior-God* had the last word. His love, powerful and active, reached out to reclaim and repair a stubborn, selfish child of his who was straying. And so for many generations we of the Christian church have had Jonah's personal account of this episode.

A god or the true God?

There is one more Old Testament name for God, which you should know about. The name *'el* (ALE) is sometimes used in the Bible as a generic name for "a god," even a false, heathen god. The prophet Isaiah used this name when he drew a vivid picture of an idol worshiper at work:

He cut down cedars, or perhaps took a cypress or oak. . . . It is man's fuel for burning; some of it he takes and warms himself, he kindles a fire and bakes bread. But he also fashions *a god* [*'el*] and worships it; he makes an idol and bows down to it. . . . He makes *a god* [*'el*], his idol; he bows down to it and worships. He prays to it and says, "Save me; you are my *god* [*'el*]." (Isaiah 44:14-17)

In the Old Testament, however, *'el* is most often used to refer to the true God. How is the Bible reader supposed to know that? When *'el* refers to God, it's clearly distinguished from all false gods. Whenever God used the name *'el* to identify himself, he qualified the term in one of two ways.

Sometimes God attached the definite article *the* to the name *'el*. After Jacob had been away from home for 20 years, God directed him to return to the land of Canaan. God identified himself by using the name *'el* together with the definite article:

"Go up to Bethel . . . and build an altar there *to God* [Hebrew: *the 'el*], who appeared to you when you were fleeing from your brother Esau." So Jacob said to his household . . . "Come, let us go up to Bethel, where I will build an altar *to God* [Hebrew: *the 'el*], who answered me in the day of my distress." (Genesis 35:1-3)

More often, however, God attached an adjective or a descriptive phrase to the name *'el*. The reader can sense immediately that the reference is not to some false god but to the true God. Look at some examples:

"the *Eternal* God" (Genesis 21:33)
"the *faithful* God" (Deuteronomy 7:9)
"the *great* God" (Deuteronomy 10:17)
"the God *who performs miracles*" (Psalm 77:14)
"the *holy* God" (Isaiah 5:16)
"the God *of gods*" (the supreme God) (Daniel 11:36)

El Shaddai, "God Almighty"

The divine name *'el* is used in several special combinations that deserve our attention. It will be worth our while to look at two of these.

"When Abram was ninety-nine years old, the LORD appeared to him and said, 'I am *God Almighty*. . . . I will confirm my covenant between me and you and will greatly increase your numbers. . . . Your wife Sarah will bear you a son . . . by this time next year'" (Genesis 17:1,2,19,21). The special name God used to identify himself on this special occasion is *El Shaddai* (ale-shah-DYE). As far as we know, this unusual name is from a verb that means "to display power" or "to deal violently."

To understand why God would use a name like that to identify himself, put yourself in Abraham's sandals. Twenty-four years had passed since God had given him and his beloved Sarah the promise of the Savior to come. "All peoples on earth will be blessed through you" (Genesis 12:3). Abraham and Sarah had been 75 and 65 years old, respectively, when God first gave them that promise of the Savior. Now they were 99 and 89 years old, respectively. Martin Luther once said, "It's God's way to empty a person first, before he fills him with his blessing." The apostle Paul helps us to see that "[Abraham] faced the fact that his body was as good as dead—since he was about a hundred years old—and that Sarah's womb was also dead" (Romans 4:19).

When God appeared to 99-year-old Abraham to reaffirm the promise he had made a quarter-century before, God introduced himself by an unusual name he had never used before. He called himself El Shaddai, "God Almighty," the God who can compel even nature to do what is contrary to itself. In this case, he was going to give a baby to a woman who was past menopause and to a man who no longer had the ability to father a child. The name El Shaddai means that God "calls things that are not as though they were" (Romans 4:17).

Two generations later we meet this unusual name for God again, in a prayer spoken by Abraham's son Isaac to his son Jacob. Jacob was about to leave his childhood home in southern Canaan. He was going to travel to northern Syria—a five-hundred mile journey. He'd be traveling alone, through mountainous territory unfamiliar to him and potentially dangerous. Listen to the prayer with which father Isaac sent Jacob on his way: "May *God Almighty* [El Shaddai] bless you and make you fruitful and increase your numbers. . . . May he give you and your descendants the blessing given to Abraham" (Genesis 28:3,4).

As Isaac said good-bye to his son Jacob, he said two significant things. He first placed Jacob into the care of El Shaddai—the God who can do awesome things, the only one who could protect Jacob during his difficult and dangerous journey.

But father Isaac said more. He prayed: "May [El Shaddai] . . . *make you fruitful*" and "give you . . . *the blessing given to Abraham*." Jacob was unmarried when he left home. And yet Jacob's father knew that his son was Abraham's grandson and that God's promises to Abraham included this grandson. God had made a covenant—a solemn contract—with Abraham that from his family line the Savior would be born. Jacob, still single, was about to set out on an uncharted course into an unknown and uncertain future. But that didn't change the fact that he was in Abraham's bloodline. Jacob was a bearer of God's promise. And so Isaac prayed that El Shaddai, the God who can make impossible things happen, would give Jacob children, *through whom God would keep his promise* to send the Savior.

Immanuel, "God with us"

Seven hundred years before Christ was born, the prophet Isaiah announced a prediction. This promise concerning 'el, "God," is at the very heart of the Christian faith: "The virgin will be with child and will give birth to a son, and will call him *Immanuel*" (Isaiah 7:14).

In the very first chapter of the New Testament, Saint Matthew helps us to see how important Isaiah's prophecy is for us. He describes a visit God's angel made to Joseph, Mary's fiancé. Joseph had been heartbroken when he learned that his beloved Mary was expecting a baby. What else could he think but that she had been sexually involved with another man? And so he decided to divorce her quietly.

> An angel of the Lord appeared to him in a dream and said, "Joseph son of David, do not be afraid to take Mary home as your wife, because what is conceived in her is from the Holy Spirit." . . . All this took place to fulfill what the Lord had said through the prophet: "The virgin will conceive and give birth to a son, and they will call him Immanuel"—which means, *"God with us."* (Matthew 1:20-23 TNIV)

The God-man

With this name Immanuel ("God with us"), God identifies himself more completely than he does with any of his other names. This name tells us, first of all, that the promised descendant of Abraham, the child born to Mary, is *God*. God's Old Testament spokesmen had predicted that the promised Messiah would be *God* (Psalm 45:6; Isaiah 7:14; 9:6). Christ himself claimed to be God (John 10:30). Christ's disciples recognized that he is *God* (John 20:28). The apostles declared in writing that Jesus is *God* (Romans 9:5; Hebrews 1:8).

But the miracle on which God's truth centers is that at one particular point in history, and at a specific location on the planet, the eternal God became a human being. "Beyond all question, the mystery from which true godliness springs is great: *[God] appeared in a body*" (1 Timothy 3:16 TNIV).

The difference this makes to you

You, as well as every other Christian, eventually wrestles with the question "What qualifies Jesus Christ to save anybody?" The name Immanuel, "God with us," answers the question.

Remember that the *second* half of that name Immanuel is one of the Hebrew names for "God." The *first* half is Hebrew for *"with us."* In the womb of the virgin Mary, God joined himself permanently to our human flesh and blood. God became a Jewish person who lived in a far-off corner of the Roman Empire. Do you see what difference it makes to you that Jesus Christ is both *God* and a *human being?*

When God gave his law to the human race, he spoke about two different subjects. He spoke first about *obedience*, which he demands: "Obey me and do everything I command you, and you will be my people, and I will be your God" (Jeremiah 11:4). And then he spoke about *disobedience*, which he forbids with a curse: "Cursed is the man who does not uphold the words of this law by carrying them out" (Deuteronomy 27:26).

Jesus' double assignment

As the substitute whom God sent to trade places with us sinners, Jesus had to do two things that we could not do for ourselves. First, he had to provide that perfect obedience to the will of God, which God demanded—but never got—from us. Since the Ten Commandments do not speak *to God* but only *to human beings*, the Savior whom God promised had to become a human being. The first half of his name Immanuel assures us that he is human. As a human being, he became subject to the law of God. He was now in a position *to do what we had not done.*

The other half of Jesus' assignment was *to undo what we had done.* He accepted in his holy body the punishment for sin that a holy God had announced for all who disobey his holy law. This is why the first half of that name Immanuel ("God *with us*") is so precious to us. As a true human being, Jesus Christ obeyed God's law and suffered death as our substitute.

Look now at the second half of that name Immanuel. You'll see a second reason for praising God. Nobody has difficulty recognizing that Jesus of Nazareth is a human being. Many people, however, refuse to acknowledge that the child born to Mary is *God*. The name the prophet Isaiah gave to that miracle child (Immanuel) assures you that that baby is not just a human baby, but *'el*, God in human form. That assures us that the work he did—obeying God's law and suffering God's punishment—is sufficient *for an entire world of sinners*. Because of the work Immanuel did as our substitute, holy God can pronounce the whole world of sinners "Not guilty!"

Martin Luther wrote many beautiful prayers, but none more beautiful than one incised in granite in the base of the Luther statue on the campus of Wisconsin Lutheran Seminary: "Lord Jesus, you are my righteousness; I am your sin. You became what you were not and made me to be what I was not."

A unique combination

No other religion—not Judaism, not Buddhism, not Islam—offers the unique combination announced by the name *Immanuel*: an all-powerful God, who willingly takes on the limitations, the suffering, the lostness, and the curse of his creatures.

God did not sit idly by and watch us suffer in isolation. The name Immanuel assures us that God became one of us. All religions have their gods, but only one has a God who cared enough to become a human being and lay down his life. Jewish rabbis question how a loving God could allow his Son to die innocently. The Qur'an, Islam's sacred book, teaches that God is much too generous to allow Jesus to go to the cross and must have substituted an evildoer in his place. Eastern religions direct their disciples to empty their minds, instead of filling them with facts and names of a Redeemer-God, who is above all others. These objections miss the main point of God's good news—and of the name Immanuel—that it was God himself who came to earth, lived a perfect life, and died an innocent death. God was not *up there*, watching tragic events take place *down here*. "God was reconciling the world to himself *in Christ*" (2 Corinthians 5:19).

God himself absorbed the awful pain of his world. Jesus is God's love letter in human flesh. Martin Luther said: "Whoever does not find God in Jesus Christ will never find him anywhere else."

Summary

Day by day in Old Testament times, God identified himself to his chosen people by name. Only when we have heard God speak to us in Jesus Christ will we have correct answers to questions like:

Whose world is this?

What's right for me?

What's ahead for me?

A God who in Christ Jesus has declared me "Not guilty!" is a God I *can love*.

A God who in Christ Jesus has declared me "Not guilty!" is a God I *will serve*.

I will establish my covenant . . . between me and you [Abraham] and your descendants after you for generations to come, to be your God.

~ GENESIS 17:7

The LORD your God has chosen you out of all the peoples on the face of the earth to be his people, his treasured possession.

~ DEUTERONOMY 7:6

Living under God's Covenant

The history of God's family is, from its very beginning, a love story. There are people who have the mistaken notion that during the time of the Old Testament, it was harder to get into God's family than it is today. They say that the God of the *Old* Testament was a stern God, who insisted on strict obedience, but that the God of the *New* Testament is a God of love.

Wrong. God did not choose the people of Israel because they behaved right. Nor did they become his chosen people because they were bigger and stronger than other nations of antiquity. God might have chosen the Irish or the Apaches or the Brazilians, but he chose the family of Abraham. He chose the descendants of Abraham and his wife Sarah to be the nation from which Jesus Christ would come. He had no other reason for choosing these two people than pure mercy. He chose them for no other reason than that *he loved them.*

The pagan view of God

Religious myths that have come down to us from the ancient Middle East paint a different picture. Pagan creation stories picture human beings as almost incidental. They're inferior beings made at the whim of the gods, designed to satisfy the personal needs of the gods. Did you know that the care and feeding of the gods was a perpetual obligation of Israel's heathen neighbors?

By contrast, the creation account recorded on the first page of the Bible describes man and woman as the crown of God's creation. In Genesis 1:26, we are told that when God created his highest creature he said two things that are highly significant: "Let us make man *in our image*" (Adam and Eve were not just one more species of animal; they were human replicas of what God is like) and "Let them rule . . . *over all the earth*" (God designed and equipped Adam and Eve to manage the earth for him).

The flood myth that has come down to us from ancient Babylon likewise distorts the relationship between God and people. It describes the great flood as an act of caprice on the part of the gods, who resented the fact that human rowdiness was disturbing their sleep. When the floodwaters came, the gods cowered like dogs. Two weeks later, when the surviving hero offered his sacrifice, the gods were so famished for lack of offerings that they descended on the altar like a swarm of hungry flies.

Contrast these caricatures with what the Old Testament teaches about God's relationship with the descendants of Abraham. Of all the gods we read about in ancient literature, Israel's God is the only one who stooped down to declare his love for the rebellious two-legged creatures who inhabit this planet. We wouldn't have believed it if God hadn't put it in writing. Our awesome God actually *bound himself by solemn contract* to a people he chose as his very own. He fashioned an unprecedented relationship with some very ordinary people who often failed him and who often rebelled against him. In his farewell address to the people of Israel, Moses marveled at the very thought of it:

"What other nation is so great as to have their gods near them the way the LORD our God is near us whenever we pray to him? . . . Has anything so great as this ever happened, or has anything like it ever been heard of?" (Deuteronomy 4:7,32).

Israel's heathen neighbors lived in fear of their gods, who were temperamental and unpredictable. Pagan Canaanites even offered their children as human sacrifices to appease their vengeful gods. Can you sense the reasoning behind such a gruesome sacrifice? "Great god, I've offered you my very best—my own flesh and blood! Now won't you love me?"

A covenant

In sharpest contrast to such pagan gods, the one true God negotiated a covenant with Israel. The word *covenant* is not an everyday word for most of us, but it's a word we ought to know. A covenant is a binding contract between two people or two countries. We might speak of a "real estate covenant" or of the "covenant of marriage." Isn't it a staggering thought that the Lord who put this universe together actually entered into a contract with the people of ancient Israel, creatures of dust? God is independent. He didn't need their help or their company. And yet he—who didn't owe them a nickel—placed himself under obligation to his creatures. It was primarily this fact that distinguished the religion of the Israelites from that of their pagan neighbors. Day by day in Old Testament times, the people of God were surrounded with evidence that, for the sake of the promised Messiah, they mattered to God:

> The LORD your God has chosen you out of all the peoples on the face of the earth to be his people, his treasured possession. The LORD did not set his affection on you and choose you because you were more numerous than other peoples, for you were the fewest of all peoples. But it was *because the LORD loved you* and kept the oath he swore to your forefathers. (Deuteronomy 7:6-8)

Here is the basic difference between the religion of ancient Israel and all pagan religions: Pagans worshiped a god they had invented and whose favor they had to earn, while God's chosen people believed in a God "as he is dressed and clothed in his word and promises" (as Martin Luther described it).

God's covenant with Abraham

The Old Testament speaks of two different covenants that God made with Abraham's descendants. He initiated the first covenant at the time he called Abraham. He asked him to leave his childhood home and family, to leave behind the life he knew, and to follow God to another land. It's important to note that *God* took the initiative in dealing with Abraham. He called Abraham and enabled him to follow by giving him a cluster of promises. This childless, 75-year-old husband of a 65-year-old, barren wife was told he'd become the ancestor of a great nation. This roving nomad, who shepherded his flocks in a land where he was a stranger, learned that his descendants would one day own that land. God promised Abraham a land and a child. From that miracle child would one day come the real miracle child, the Messiah, born of a virgin.

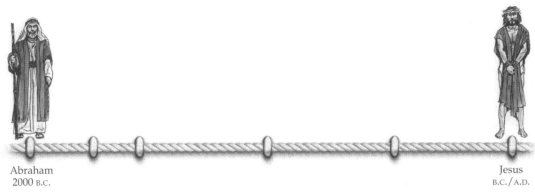

Abraham
2000 B.C.

Jesus
B.C./A.D.

The one who made all these promises is the "LORD" (in Hebrew, *Yahweh*). In the Bible of the ancient Hebrews, that's God's Old Testament Savior name. *Yahweh* is the God of absolute *independence* but also the God of absolute *faithfulness.* He is the God of free and faithful grace. By instinct and by experience, each of us feels he or she must do something to be accepted by God. But God's independent and faithful grace means there's nothing Abraham or we could do to make God love us more.

But there's more. Grace means there's nothing Abraham or we could do to make God love us *less.* The Bible tells us of one of Abraham's descendants who was an adulterer and a murderer and yet gained a reputation as the greatest king of the Old Testament. Grace is unnatural. And grace is the very essence of God's covenant with Abraham and his descendants. Grace is **G**od's **R**iches **A**t **C**hrist's **E**xpense.

Signs of God's covenant

God gave Abraham special signs of the covenant relationship between him and his people. One was circumcision. Every Jewish male wore this sign on his own body, reminding him that he belonged to God. "[Abraham] received circumcision as a sign, a seal of the righteousness that he had by faith while he was still uncircumcised" (Romans 4:11 TNIV).

Five hundred years later, when Abraham's descendants arrived at Mount Sinai, God announced another special sign of his covenant. That was the Sabbath. "[The Sabbath] will be a sign between me and you for the generations to come, so you may know that I am the LORD, who makes you holy. . . . Whoever does any work on that day must be cut off from his people" (Exodus 31:13,14).

All the pagan religions that surrounded ancient Israel announced, "You get the god's blessing *if you do* what the god requires." The God of Abraham and of Israel made a solemn contract that announced: *"Do nothing.* You don't—you can't—do anything to earn my love. My love is not for sale, and you couldn't earn it if you tried. Let the seventh day of each week be a constant sign reminding you that my covenant with you is based on absolutely nothing that *you* do. It's based on who I am and what I will do for you through the Savior, who will be born from your bloodline."

Abraham's descendants first

Does the fact that God made his covenant with Abraham and his descendants mean that God limited his love? Was there room in his family only for members of the chosen nation of Israel? (That would surely be bad news for those of us who can't trace our bloodline to Abraham.) For many centuries it may have seemed so. As the nation of Israel was about to leave Egypt, God instituted the Passover. That was a meal that reassured them of the blessings they enjoyed as his covenant people. At that time, God even added the instruction, "No foreigner is to eat of it" (Exodus 12:43).

In God's loving design, the nation of Israel was the first to receive the good news of his forgiveness in Christ. From the very beginning, God in his wisdom saw fit not to blanket the earth with his good news, but instead to give it first to the family of Abraham. In the same way, centuries later, when Jesus sent out his disciples on their first preaching assignment, he instructed them: "Do not go among the Gentiles or enter any town of the Samaritans. Go rather to the lost sheep of Israel" (Matthew 10:5,6).

Gentiles too

The Old Testament makes it very clear, however, that it was never God's plan to restrict his free and full forgiveness (grace) to the descendants of Abraham. At no time did God ever limit membership in his family to the Jewish people. The psalms repeatedly urged God's people to "make known *among the nations* what he has done" (Psalm 105:1). Through his prophets God consistently emphasized that Messiah's rule "will extend *from sea to sea*" (Zechariah 9:10). God wants the unbelievably good news of his great rescue operation to be proclaimed *"to the ends of the earth"* (Isaiah 49:6). Abraham's descendants responded: "I will praise you, O LORD, *among the nations*" (Psalm 108:3).

Perhaps the most convincing proof that God never restricted his mercy to ancient Israel is found on the very first pages of the New Testament. Here Saint Matthew gives us Jesus' family tree. In this genealogy Matthew includes the names of four women. But these are not the four famous mothers of the race (Sarah, Rebekah, Rachel, and Leah) but four of another kind. Three for sure, and maybe all four, were not even born Israelites. And they surely were not role models. Incest, prostitution, and adultery mark the careers of three of them (Tamar, Rahab, and Bathsheba). Here is evidence that the reason why God loves sinners is not that they are attractive. Sinners are attractive because God loves them. The history of God's people is not the story of human achievement but the story of God's grace. Throughout the Bible, in the Old Testament as well as the New, the truth sounds out loud and clear: "[God] wants *all people* to be saved and to come to a knowledge of the truth" (1 Timothy 2:4 TNIV).

Yahweh's covenant made a difference

What difference did Yahweh's covenant with Abraham make in the day-to-day life of a child of God in the days of the Old Testament? Well, what difference did it make to Abraham? The writer to the Hebrews tells us: "By faith [Abraham] made his home in the promised land like a stranger in a foreign country; he lived in tents. . . . For he was looking forward to the city with foundations, whose architect and builder is God" (Hebrews 11:9,10).

Yahweh's covenant with Abraham and his descendants *assured them of God's undeserved love* as they lived out their lives day by day. It held before their eyes "the Jerusalem that is above" (Galatians 4:26)—the heavenly bright country that made their lives worth living and made their deaths worth dying.

A refuge when they sinned

God's covenant with the descendants of Abraham was also their refuge when they fell into sin. Abraham himself was no spiritual superstar but a flawed human being. Genesis chapters 12 and 20 record some sleazy details of Abraham's life we wish we didn't know. On two different occasions, he asked Sarah to pretend to be his sister. It was as though he said: "Go ahead, take my wife. Disgrace her, as long as I don't get hurt." And what was the result? Sarah was taken into a king's harem. Abraham actually put the messianic promise in jeopardy. He selfishly asked Sarah to forget God's purpose for her and, instead, to sacrifice her honor and to pollute her womb. On both occasions, Yahweh, the LORD of the covenant, was faithful to his promise. He watched over the future mother of the miracle child Isaac and led Abraham to return to his identity as the promise bearer.

A source of strength for Abraham

The covenant God had made with him was Abraham's *source of strength when it seemed God had forgotten* his promise. Abraham was 75 years old, and Sarah 65, when God first promised them a child. A promise like that is hard enough to believe. Then God let them wait another 25 years before they held their miracle baby in their arms.

For almost half a century, God led Abraham through a training program, to deepen his trust. In Genesis chapter 22, we learn how successful God's training program had been. God asked him to offer up Isaac—Abraham's only link to the promised Savior—as a sacrifice to God. Would a loving father give up his dearly loved son in order to demonstrate total trust in God's promise? Reflecting on God's command, Martin Luther commented: "To Abraham's reason it must have seemed either that God's promise would fail, or else that this command must have come from the devil."

Can you imagine the thoughts that tortured the mind of this godly father all during the three-day trip to Mount Moriah? Can you feel his heartache as he contemplated the gruesome task just ahead of him? Any parent will sense instinctively that with every fiber of his being Abraham must have been tempted to say, "No, I can't do it!" Where did he find the strength—with tears streaming down his cheeks—to say, "Yes, I will"?

Years earlier, at the time Isaac was a young child, God had promised his happy parents, "It is *through Isaac* that your offspring will be reckoned" (Genesis 21:12). And now God told Abraham to take the life of that son. How did Abraham resolve this apparent contradiction?

It was God's covenant promise that made the difference. God's pledged word enabled Abraham to believe: If there's a conflict between what God has demanded and what he has promised, resolving that conflict is *God's* business, not *mine*. I'm about to offer up Isaac as a burnt offering, and several hours from now he'll be nothing but a little pile of ashes and bones. But then from those ashes and bones, God will simply have to restore Isaac to life. And not only that, but he will make Isaac a father of children. God has promised, and he cannot lie! "Abraham reasoned that God could even raise the dead, and so in a manner of speaking, he did receive Isaac back from death" (Hebrews 11:19 TNIV).

A source of strength for Abraham's descendants

The covenant of pure grace that God made with Abraham was a source of strength also for Abraham's descendants. Think of Joseph, Abraham's gifted great-grandson. Hated by his brothers, he was sold into slavery as a 17-year-old and taken to Egypt. There he was falsely accused by his master's wife and had to spend the next 13 years of his life in prison.

What was Joseph supposed to think? He knew he wasn't a slave; he was the son of a rich man. And he had done nothing to deserve a jail cell. Instead of yielding to the sexual advances of his master's wife, he had refused to use his maleness for any purpose other than the glory of God. And this is what he got for it? Joseph surely must have been tempted to become bitter—at his brothers and at God.

But during those difficult years, Joseph never forgot that he was an heir of the solemn contract God had made with Abraham. Day by day Joseph reminded himself: "God has promised to be with Abraham's descendants, and he can't go back on his word!" Even though *he* couldn't make sense out of his 13 years in prison, Joseph trusted that *God*

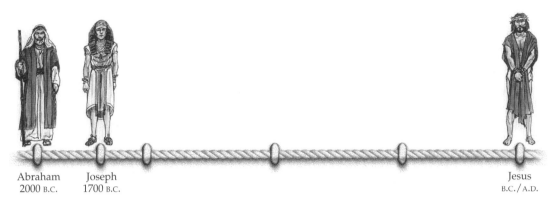

Abraham
2000 B.C.

Joseph
1700 B.C.

Jesus
B.C./A.D.

could—and would. The last ten chapters of Genesis make that clear. After 22 years in Egypt, Joseph had a reunion with the brothers who had sold him into slavery. Even then he was not bitter. "God sent me ahead of you to preserve for you a remnant on earth and to save your lives by a great deliverance" (Genesis 45:7).

And 17 years later—after their father, Jacob, had died and the brothers again begged Joseph not to take revenge—Joseph wept and said: "Don't be afraid. Am I in the place of God? You intended to harm me, but God intended it for good to accomplish what is now being done, the saving of many lives" (Genesis 50:19).

Day by day in Old Testament times, God's chosen people could remind one another: "The Lord your God is a merciful God; he will not abandon . . . you or forget the covenant with your forefathers, which he confirmed to them by oath" (Deuteronomy 4:31). God would preserve this family because he had made promises concerning Christ that absolutely had to be kept.

An unconditional covenant

God's solemn contract with Abraham reminded his descendants that the God sitting at the monitor of the universe is not distant and unapproachable. God's promise made it very clear that he had made a one-of-a-kind covenant with them. The Hebrews were special to him. They were the manger into which God the Father was going to place his Son. Throughout their history God wanted them to know he is a God they could count on. Through his prophet Isaiah he assured them:

"You descendants of Abraham my friend, . . . I have chosen you and have not rejected you. So do not fear, for I am with you; do not be dismayed, for I am your God. I will strengthen you and help you; I will uphold you with my righteous right hand." (Isaiah 41:8-10)

"Though the mountains be shaken and the hills be removed, yet my unfailing love for you will not be shaken nor my covenant of peace be removed," says the LORD, who has compassion on you. (Isaiah 54:10)

God's covenant with Abraham, which promised Israel its land and the world its Savior, asked nothing of Abraham in return. There were no strings attached to God's promise. The Abrahamic covenant was pure grace, and nothing but grace.

The Sinai covenant

Five hundred years after making that solemn covenant with Abraham, God made another covenant, a second solemn contract, with Abraham's descendants. At Mount Sinai God made a covenant that is sharply different from the one he had made with their great ancestor. Why would God do that?

Historical background

To answer that question we'll need to go back about 1,500 years before Christ was born. God's chosen people, the descendants of Abraham, were slaves in Egypt. At that critical point in their history, God did again what he had done so often before: he delivered his people.

When Adam and Eve were crushed with guilt and shame, God announced good news about a coming deliverer. When the flood wiped out a whole worldful of people, God rescued Noah and his family. Years later he snatched Abraham out of a land overrun by idolatry. He guided Joseph to Egypt, so that his father, Jacob, and his extended family could escape starvation in the land where they were living.

Centuries later, at another dark hour in his people's history, God rescued the nation of Israel from Egypt, where they had been slaves. With an awesome display of power, he forced the greatest superpower of that day to its knees. God set his people free, led them through the sea, and put them on the desert road leading to the new homeland he had promised them.

Now get set for an unpleasant surprise. The Israelites had been on the road for only three days when they began to complain. First it was the water (Exodus 15:24). And a month later, listen to them grumble about the food: "If only we had died by the LORD's hand in Egypt! . . . You have brought us out into this desert to starve this entire assembly to death" (Exodus 16:3). Israel's monumental ingratitude must have made the first months of their wilderness journey an absolute nightmare for God.

Is it any wonder that when, a couple months later, the Israelites arrived at Mount Sinai, God said: "Stop here. We've got to have a talk"? And it was quite a talk God had with the Israelites, during the 12 months they camped at Mount Sinai. The upshot of it all was that God drew up a second solemn contract with the people of Israel. At Mount Sinai he initiated the *covenant of the law* (as opposed to the *covenant of the promise*). In one of his *Table Talks* Martin Luther once remarked: "If my son John is disobedient and I give him a piece of candy instead of a spanking, I will only spoil him."

Its importance

God realized that he had a massive training job to do on those several million Israelites camped in the desert of Sinai. God saw two kinds of problems he had to deal with: On the one hand, many—very many—of Abraham's descendants did not love him and did not trust him. They were unbelievers who—in spite of their bloodline that went back to believing Abraham; in spite of the amazing mercy God had shown them; in spite of the awesome miracles he had performed to help them, in Egypt and in the desert—had no use for him. Their hearts were not loyal to him.

Centuries later, the prophet Elijah would complain to the Lord: "The Israelites have rejected your covenant, broken down your altars, and put your prophets to death with the sword. I am the only one left, and now they are trying to kill me too" (1 Kings 19:10).

Listen to God's own description of the people he had chosen for himself: "I knew how stubborn you were; the sinews of your neck were iron, your forehead was bronze" (Isaiah 48:4). The apostle Stephen would later declare that this stubborn unbelief was a national characteristic of Israel throughout its long history (Acts 7:51).

On the other hand, others of these people camping at Mount Sinai were believers, but they were immature in their faith. Both segments of this infant nation—believers and unbelievers—needed strict outward discipline. Without God's discipline they would never become the kind of people God had in mind when he formed the first human being out of the dust of the ground. Here was God's reason for initiating a second solemn contract with Israel—the Sinai covenant.

A conditional covenant

Let's revisit Mount Sinai to review what happened there. After the nation reached the desert of Sinai in the third month after leaving Egypt, God called Moses to come up to him on the mountain. He gave him this message to take back to the people:

"You yourselves have seen what I did to Egypt, and how I carried you on eagles' wings and brought you to myself. Now *if you obey me* fully and keep my covenant, then out of all nations you will be my treasured possession." (Exodus 19:4,5)

"When I brought [your forefathers] out of Egypt, . . . I said, 'Obey me and do everything I command you, and you will be my people, and I will be your God. Then I will fulfill the oath I swore to your forefathers, to give them a land flowing with milk and honey.'" (Jeremiah 11:4,5)

Note those words carefully. They speak of a *blessing* God promised to the nation of Israel but also of a *condition* God attached to his blessing. The Abrahamic covenant God had made four centuries earlier was an *unconditional* covenant, a *one-way* covenant, a covenant of pure grace. It was all promise—nothing but promise. The promise of the Abrahamic covenant pointed to the Savior, to Jesus.

The Sinai covenant was a *conditional* covenant, a *two-way covenant*, which relied on the cooperation of sinners. The demands of the Sinai covenant pointed at the sinner.

God announced, "All these *blessings* will come upon you and accompany you *if you obey* the LORD your God" (Deuteronomy 28:2). And then follows a long list of blessings.

But God went on to say, *"If you do not obey* the LORD your God and do not carefully follow all his commands . . . all these *curses* will come upon you" (Deuteronomy 28:15). And then follows a whole chapter full of frightening curses. Read Deuteronomy chapter 28, and feel a cold chill run down your spine.

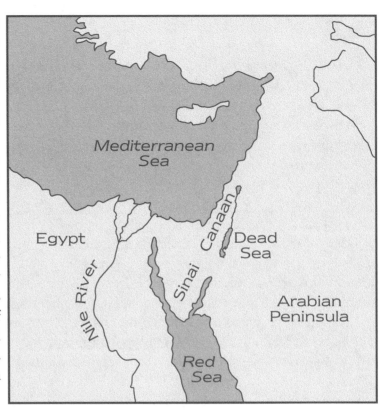

A covenant for stubborn and immature people

We must be careful not to misunderstand the Lord's words here. He did not announce his commandments at Mount Sinai so that by obeying them the Israelites might earn his favor. As descendants of Abraham living under the covenant of grace, they already enjoyed God's favor. The Sinai covenant was a necessary discipline for some stubborn and spiritually immature people, showing them how members of God's family should serve God and their neighbors, and what the results would be if they did not.

Recall the scene at Mount Sinai. Through Moses, God alerted his people:

"Be ready by the third day, because on that day the LORD will come down on Mount Sinai in the sight of all the people." On the morning of the third day there was thunder and lightning, with a thick cloud over the mountain, and a very loud trumpet blast. Everyone in the camp trembled. Then Moses led the people out of the camp to meet with God, and they stood at the foot of the mountain. Mount Sinai was covered with smoke, because the LORD descended on it in fire.

The smoke billowed up from it like smoke from a furnace, the whole mountain trembled violently, and the sound of the trumpet grew louder and louder. (Exodus 19:11,16-19)

If you had been standing in the sandals of one of those Israelites, what would you have expected to hear when God began to speak? Wouldn't you have expected him to say (in the voice of an angry top sergeant): "Now listen up, you Israelites! For the past two-and-a-half months I've heard nothing but bellyaching from you. I am sick and tired of it! If you want to find yourself another Savior, you can go to hell looking for one!" That's surely what they deserved to hear. And that's probably what they expected to hear.

But that's not what they actually did hear when God began to speak. While Mount Sinai was "ablaze with fire" (Deuteronomy 9:15), with "black clouds and deep darkness" as a backdrop (Deuteronomy 4:11), the voice of God called out, "I am the LORD your God, who brought you out of Egypt, out of the land of slavery" (Exodus 20:2).

A well-known Old Testament scholar has remarked: "There is no purer, more heart-warming gospel in the whole Scripture than this." The *conditional* covenant God announced from Mount Sinai did not annul or repeal the *unconditional* covenant God had made with Abraham. Saint Paul made that clear when, in his letter to the Galatians, he compared the two covenants:

> The law, introduced [at Mount Sinai], . . . does not set aside the [Abrahamic] covenant previously established by God and thus do away with the promise. For if the inheritance depends on the law, then it no longer depends on the promise; but God in his grace gave it to Abraham through a promise. What, then, was the purpose of the law? It was added because of transgressions . . .
> (Galatians 3:17-19 TNIV)

Without the Abrahamic covenant the religion of the Old Testament would have been essentially a different religion from that of the New Testament. (Unfortunately, many people think it is just that). We can understand the Sinai covenant correctly only in the light of the covenant of pure mercy God had made with Abraham. Remember God's opening words when he began to speak at Mount Sinai: "I am the LORD"—Yahweh—the God of free and faithful grace. With those introductory words God was restating his promise never to forget his covenant with the believing descendants of Abraham.

Role of the Sinai covenant

In view of that, what purpose did God's Sinai covenant, with its hundreds of rules and regulations (Exodus 20–40; Leviticus 1–27; Deuteronomy 5–29), serve for the people of Israel?

It was a *mirror* that helped them recognize their sinfulness and their need for the Savior whom God had promised to send. "Through the law we become conscious of our sin" (Romans 3:20 TNIV).

It was a *hedge,* or fence, to keep them separate from their heathen neighbors until Christ would come. "Do not invoke the names of other gods. . . . Do not bow down before their gods or worship them or follow their practices. You must demolish them and break their sacred stones to pieces" (Exodus 23:13,24).

It was a *foreshadowing* of the blessings the promised Messiah would bring for them. "So the law was put in charge of us until Christ came that we might be justified by faith" (Galatians 3:24 TNIV).

Introducing the Sinai covenant

The Sinai covenant was an important element in training the chosen people of Israel. God inaugurated it with a solemn ceremony, which is described for us in Exodus chapter 24. Dr. Alfred Edersheim, an outstanding Old Testament scholar who came to Christianity out of Judaism, in volume 2 of *The History of Israel and Judah*, called this "the most important transaction in the whole history of Israel." Let's review some of the details.

God announced that Moses, the mediator between a sinful people and a holy God, was to walk up Mount Sinai alone to receive the commandments from the Lord. Aaron, his two priest sons, and 70 elders represented the people of Israel "at a distance" (Exodus 24:1,2). Moses repeated to the Israelites the basic provisions of the Sinai covenant, this two-sided contract between God and them, and they accepted the responsibilities involved (verse 3). The covenant was put in writing (verse 4).

The following day the Sinai covenant was sealed and formally inaugurated by a *blood sacrifice* (verse 5), by the *sprinkling of blood* (verses 6-8), and by a *sacrificial meal* (verses 9-11).

Blood sacrifice

An altar was built at the foot of Mount Sinai and surrounded by 12 pillars, symbolizing the 12 tribes of God's covenant people. On this altar Moses offered animals as a *blood sacrifice*. This sacrifice pictured Jesus' one great sacrifice that opens up the sinner's way to the heart and the home of the heavenly Father.

Sprinkling of blood

The animal victims' blood was sprinkled—first of all *on the altar*, symbolizing that Israel had access to God only on the basis of the blood sacrifice of a substitute. The other half of the blood was sprinkled *on the people*, thereby involving them in this covenant.

Sacrificial meal

In gracious, condescending love, and as a visible pledge of his favor, God now invited the 74 leaders to be his guests at a sacrificial meal. He actually set a banquet table for them so that they could enjoy fellowship with him. Mount Sinai was surrounded by a dark cloud. At God's command those 74 men climbed up the mountain and that thick darkness was changed into pure light. Listen to Moses describe what took place:

"[The 74 guests] saw the God of Israel. Under his feet was something like a pavement made of sapphire, clear as the sky itself. But God did not raise his hand against these leaders of the Israelites; they saw God, and they ate and drank" (Exodus 24:10-11).

Because of our sin God must veil his direct presence from us. Seeing God's unveiled glory would destroy a sinner. Only in heaven will we see God face-to-face. But there on Mount Sinai, God's reconciled people were permitted to have a glimpse of blinding brightness representing God seated on his heavenly throne, with a "pavement of sapphire" as his footstool. With this impressive, three-part ceremony, God inaugurated the Sinai covenant with Israel, his covenant people.

A preliminary, preparatory message

The message God announced at Mount Sinai ("You shall . . . You shall not . . .") was not his final word to Israel. It was not the heart of his message to his people. It was only a preliminary message, to prepare his people to hear the message of his unconditional love. When God's people rebelled against his commandments, God disciplined them—often by giving them over into the hands of their enemies. When God permitted Israel to be terrified, broken, and desperate, his goal was to remind them of the words of the psalmist: "Blessed are all who take refuge *in him*"—Jesus Christ, God's anointed King (Psalm 2:12).

Then the mercy God promised in his covenant with Abraham was the Israelites' refuge. Day by day in Old Testament times, the descendants of Abraham needed to realize they could not keep the Sinai covenant. The promised Savior would do that for them.

Summary

Every other approach to God besides Christianity is a bargaining system: "If I do something good, God will notice it and be kind to me." But God does not build on what you and I bring to the bargaining table. His love, membership in his family, and a place at his side forever are given to Jews and Gentiles only as a free gift and only because of the promised Savior. Jesus Christ, born from a Jewish bloodline, traded places with us—under the demands of God and under the curse of God. Jesus is God's present to you, to assure you that you're special to him.

The cost of your sin is more than you can pay.

The gift of your God is more than you can imagine.

I will give [the land] to you as an inheritance, a land flowing with milk and honey.

~ LEVITICUS 20:24

With your hand you drove out the nations and planted our fathers. . . . It was not by their sword that they won the land. . . . It was your right hand, your arm, . . . for you loved them.

~ PSALM 44:2,3

A Special Homeland

Look at this picture of the land of Israel. Much of it is trackless desert, littered with rocks. A spine of rugged mountains bisects the narrow land, which is crisscrossed by deep valleys. Remember that this was the homeland of a people engaged primarily in farming and herding. Does this thirsty land strike you as a land "flowing with milk and honey"?

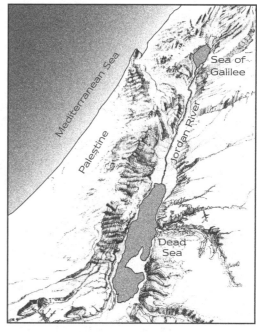

Hardly! The land God picked out for the descendants of Abraham never resembled the Great Plains of North America—with thousands of square miles of flat land, and an average of three feet of rainfall a year. That's the kind of land you want for raising crops and cattle. Yet this hilly, rocky, sandy place was the Promised Land to which God led Abraham's descendants after he freed them from slavery.

Was this land *their* choice? No. But it was *God's* choice, and for good reasons. God had a good plan for his chosen people, and he saw fit to use this land as his instrument when he carried out his plan. This land was the stage on which a fascinating drama was acted out: Jesus of Nazareth redeemed a whole history book of sinful human beings.

The Fertile Crescent

There is a settled, fertile part of the sandy, mountainous Middle East. It stretches like a half-moon, a crescent, from the Persian Gulf in the east to the Mediterranean Sea in the west and back east to the Sinai Peninsula. This huge sickle of occupied land has a *sea of salt* to the west, *mountains* to the north and east, and a *sea of sand* to the south. The geography of this important area gave it historic significance as the *Fertile Crescent*. Today this region is divided among Israel, Lebanon, Syria, Jordan, and Iraq.

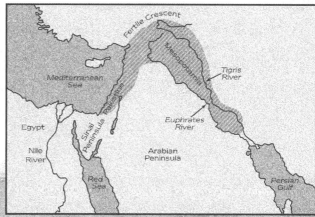

The area of the Fertile Crescent to the north and east was known as Mesopotamia, (Greek for *"the land between the rivers"*). Because this area was watered by the Tigris and the Euphrates Rivers and connecting canals, it could support a fabulous agricultural program. This was the richest section of the entire Middle East. The opposite end of the Fertile Crescent to the south and west—the land once occupied by the 12 tribes of Israel—was the poorest.

Giving the land a name

The moment we begin to talk about the land in which Abraham and Sarah and David and Mary and Joseph lived out their day-to-day lives, we bump into the problem of what to call this land. Today the names Palestine and Israel have political connotations, and that can be confusing. Let's agree up front that in this book we'll use these terms: *Palestine* for the "country of the Bible" and *Israel* for the "nation descended from Abraham."

Ocean, seas, and a river

Palestine is bordered on the west and on the east by bodies of water. To the west is the Mediterranean Sea. Merchant ships carried on a lively trade both in staples (olive oil, wine, wheat) as well as in luxury items. The Israelites, however, were not a seagoing people. The oceangoing ships that sailed the Mediterranean usually came from Phoenicia, Israel's neighbor to the north. Joppa, a city 40 miles west of Jerusalem, has a small bay that served as a harbor. When the prophet Jonah tried to run away from the Lord's call to preach in pagan Assyria, he went to Joppa and boarded a ship headed west. Just before the time of the New Testament, King Herod the Great (the "Infant Slayer") built a city along the Mediterranean coast about 35 miles north of Joppa. He named it Caesarea (in honor of his Roman boss). Caesarea had an impressive artificial harbor, with a massive breakwater 2,500 feet in circumference extending out into the sea.

Across Palestine to the east is another "sea"—this one, however, is an inland freshwater lake. This is the beautiful blue Sea of Galilee (in Hebrew *Kinnereth*, meaning *"harp-shaped"*). In Roman times it was also called the Sea of Tiberias. It's not big—only 12 miles long by about 7 miles at its widest point—and it is surrounded by hills on almost every side. When the sun sets behind those hills and the wind begins to blow, the lake can get rough in a hurry. In Bible times a dozen sizable towns stood close to its shores. Fishing was an important industry. Much of Jesus' ministry was conducted in the towns around the lake.

The Jordan River enters the Sea of Galilee from the north. Four springs of ice-cold water 25 miles farther north combine to form its headwaters. At the point where the Jordan flows south out of the Sea of Galilee, it lies 650 feet below sea level. By the time it enters the Dead Sea, 70 miles farther south, it has dropped almost 700 feet. The swift current twists and meanders through a floodplain in a series of S curves. Farther south it flows through a tangle of trees and thornbushes—once so alive with lions and other wild beasts that the prophet Jeremiah called it the jungle of the Jordan. Normally the

Jordan is not difficult to cross. The Old Testament repeatedly mentions fords, places where you could cross on foot. The river was at flood stage, however, when Israel first entered its new homeland. God miraculously opened a path for his people, so they could cross over without getting their feet wet. John the Baptist baptized our Lord Jesus in the Jordan River.

The Dead Sea is the lowest place on the earth's surface—1,300 feet below sea level at the surface, and twice that at its deepest point. It's also the saltiest body of water in the world. The Dead Sea has no outlets, and evaporation under the desert sun is responsible for the high chemical content of the water, which is poisonous to fish. Most Old Testament scholars believe that the ancient cities of Sodom and Gomorrah lie beneath what is now the shallow south end of the Dead Sea. In Bible times the Dead Sea was valued for its salt and for the bitumen which sometimes floats to the surface. (The Roman name for the sea was *Lacus Asphaltitis*, "Asphalt Lake.")

A land bridge

Geographically, Palestine was the crossroads of the ancient Middle East. Israel's Promised Land was a narrow land bridge connecting Asia and Africa. Historically, it was a corridor of land situated between two dominant river-based centers of culture: along the Tigris and Euphrates Rivers to the north and east and Egypt, the "Queen of the Nile," to the south and west

The ancient history of the land called Palestine was hopelessly entangled in the struggle between these two superpowers to control the Fertile Crescent, including that strategic land bridge. The ribbon of land that was the homeland of ancient Israel totaled less than 10,000 square miles—about the size of the state of Vermont. Most of the events recorded in the Old Testament took place in a little land, only 150 miles from north to south.

A trade route

Caravans of trade, as well as chariots of war, brought Israel into contact with its powerful neighbors to the southwest and to the northeast. In ancient times there was no shortcut across the Arabian Desert. As a result, the great trade routes that led from Asia to Africa were pressed together into a narrow funnel in Palestine. Although it was small, Palestine was an important corridor through which merchandise was carried by camel or donkey between Egypt and Mesopotamia. In times of peace, caravans loaded with grain, wine, olive oil, metal implements, fine pottery, and woolen textiles were carried along the dusty roads of Palestine. Genesis 37:25 mentions a caravan carrying spices to Egypt. First Kings chapter 10 describes King Solomon's profitable traffic with merchants and traders and all Arabian kings.

Down south, Egypt, always a major player in the power politics of the ancient Middle East, could not permit itself to be isolated. Egypt needed Palestine, not only as a buffer state, a speed bump between itself and the superpowers on the opposite end of the Fertile Crescent, but also as a communication corridor.

The most prominent highway was the *Via Maris* ("the way of the sea," Isaiah 9:1). This road followed the Mediterranean coast north from Egypt, turning eastward to Damascus, capital of Syria. From there, one branch led north, to the land of the Hittites (present-day Turkey), and another branch led north and east to Mesopotamia. Second in importance was the King's Highway that led along the edge of a high plateau east of the Jordan, along which were a string of fortresses.

An invasion corridor

In times of war there was another kind of traffic on that strip of land that was Israel's home. Throughout history the occupants of the Promised Land often heard the tramp of marching soldiers, the hooves of warhorses, and the wheels of battle chariots. From Egypt to Mesopotamia, just as in the Middle East today, armed conflict was frequent. This was true also during the 1,500 years Israel occupied Palestine. The pages of the Old Testament describe periods when hostile armies swept through Palestine, and the people of the promised Savior often fell under the control of an invading power.

The natural regions of Palestine

The land God chose as Israel's ancient homeland contains five clearly distinguishable topographical regions. From west to east, these are the areas:

A narrow coastal *plain* along the Mediterranean (the Philistine Plain and, farther north, the Sharon Plain) was once thickly forested.

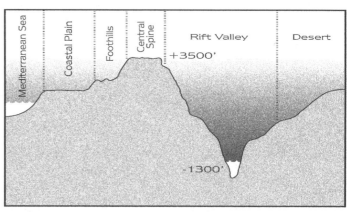

A range of *foothills* served as a buffer between the occupants of the plain (who were often hostile to Israel) and those living in the central highlands.

A central spine of *mountains,* along the crest of which many of Israel's major cities (including Jerusalem) were located, is the heartland's watershed. Rain and melted snow to the west of this line flow into the Mediterranean; whatever falls to the east flows into the Jordan. This central ridge bisecting the country drops off sharply.

A harsh and barren *desert*—without a trace of green and cut by canyons—the "wilderness of Judaea" also drops down sharply.

The *Great Rift Valley* (the "Arabah") is a deep gorge that extends all the way from Syria in the north to Africa in the south. The Jordan River cuts its way through this gorge and empties into the Dead Sea. Moses and the Israelites had to pass through this gorge on foot on their way to the Promised Land.

Transjordan

Across the Jordan to the east, the land rises sharply from the Arabah. Known in the Old Testament as Gilead and Bashan, this high plateau receives considerable rainfall. When Israel passed through this territory en route to their new homeland, several of the family tribes saw that the land was suitable for raising livestock. They asked whether they could receive their territory east of the Jordan. Those were the tribes of Reuben, Gad, and Manasseh. In the New Testament this territory is known as Perea, where Jesus conducted a brief ministry before beginning his "death journey" to Jerusalem.

The desert

Surrounding Palestine's inhabited areas to the south and east is a barren area the Israelites marched through after they left Egypt with Moses and headed for the Promised Land. The Hebrew name for this area is *midbar*, a term that is not easy to translate. The New International Version of the Bible calls it "the desert," but this is not a sand desert like the Sahara or like the interior of Arabia. This is barren wasteland. The King James Version calls it "the wilderness," but don't think of the heavily forested wilderness of Daniel Boone and Davy Crockett. The *midbar* was wilderness in the sense of "a place of wildness," a place where a person easily becomes bewildered and disoriented. The Bible describes it as "the vast and dreadful desert, that thirsty and waterless land, with its venomous snakes and scorpions" (Deuteronomy 8:15) and "a land of hardship and distress, of lions and lionesses, of adders and darting snakes" (Isaiah 30:6).

When the Israelites entered this desert land of disorder and death, it's clear from their constant complaining that they expected to die of thirst and exhaustion (Exodus 14:11,12; 16:2,3). Nature is the enemy of anyone who wanders in that desert. But the One who was leading the Israelites was in control of the desert too. He had a big promise to keep.

By the time of the New Testament, the Palestinian countryside had become more settled and more ordered. Even so, the desert was a place of terror, of hunger and thirst. Here is where the Holy Spirit led the Lord Jesus immediately after his baptism. Going without food for almost six weeks, he faced a terrible ordeal—a 40-day battle with Satan in the desert. Later, it was again in the desert that Jesus' disciples asked: "Where could we get enough bread in this remote place to feed such a crowd?" (Matthew 15:33). The desert was rough, dangerous country, which most people avoided. There wasn't enough rainfall for farming, although in a year of abundant rainfall a shepherd might lead his flock to the fringe of the desert to graze. If he did so, he risked attack by lions or bears, so he was sure to carry a club to drive off wild animals (1 Samuel 17:34-36).

West of the Jordan

West of the Jordan, the foothills, valleys, and mountains left only a limited amount of level land for farming and for sheep and goat herding. By terracing the high hills, the new settlers could plant vineyards and olive groves. They had to contend with extremes of climate. In the far north, snow-capped Mount Hermon is 10,000 feet above sea level; the smell of pine is in the air. One hundred fifty miles to the south, however, the land drops from the well-watered fields of Galilee to the stark desolation surrounding the Dead Sea.

Irrigation agriculture in Egypt

The Israelites, whom Joshua led into the Promised Land, had to get used to a different set of ground rules for farming than the ones they remembered from their stay in Egypt. In ancient Egypt the mighty Nile River flooded each spring. When those miles of floodwaters flowed into the Nile Valley, they brought with them not only snowmelt from the mountains in the interior of Africa but nutrient-rich silt, which made ancient Egypt the breadbasket of the Mediterranean. Egypt's agriculture was irrigation agriculture. Rainfall was rare, but it wasn't really needed. The Nile River was the country's life; Egyptians worshiped it as one of their gods.

Rain-fed agriculture in Palestine

In his farewell address to the people of Israel, Moses told them:
The land you are entering to take over is *not like the land of Egypt*, from which you have come, where you planted your seed and irrigated it. . . . But the land you are crossing the Jordan to take possession of is a land of mountains and valleys that *drinks rain from heaven*. . . . So if you faithfully obey the commands I am giving you today—to love the LORD your God and to serve him with all your heart and with all your soul—then I will send rain on your land in its season, *both autumn and spring rains*, so that you may gather in your grain, new wine and oil. (Deuteronomy 11:10-14)

The rainless months

In their new homeland, Israelite farmers would depend on the rain for their crops. Palestine is a land that can expect no rain for half of every year. Each May the fields turned brown, and the former tenants of Palestine, the Canaanites, believed that their god Baal—god of fertility and of the rain—had died. Half a year later, when the fall and winter rains came, they believed that Baal had come back to life. During the rainless months, there was no way an Israelite farmer could plow his land, which the prolonged summer heat and drought had left parched and powdery. "The nobles send their servants for water; they go to the cisterns but find no water. They return with their jars unfilled; dismayed and despairing, they cover their heads" (Jeremiah 14:3).

The autumn rains

Then, along about September or October, came what Israel's prophets called the *autumn rains* (or *early rains*), which broke the hot summer drought. This was the time when farmers could prepare their fields. Oxen pulled bronze-tipped plows. Families planted wheat and barley, and the autumn rains provided moisture for germination. From about December to February, Palestine gets perhaps 75 percent of its annual rainfall, often in three-day bursts, sometimes including severe thunderstorms. "[God says] to the rain shower, 'Be a mighty downpour.' . . . he stops every man from his labor. The animals take cover; they remain in their dens" (Job 37:6-8).

In the conclusion to his Sermon on the Mount, Jesus spoke of how a poorly built house collapsed in the rainy season, when "the rain came down, the streams rose, and the winds blew and beat against that house, and it fell with a great crash" (Matthew 7:27).

After the autumn rains fell, the field crops (wheat and barley) and the pasture lands were green and good.

Water and soil conservation

During the months of abundant rainfall, the Israelite farmer practiced water and soil conservation. Carefully planned watercourses would channel surplus storm water into storage pools and cisterns, later to be carried to vegetable gardens and vineyards during the dry season. After the cisterns were empty, they could be used for dry storage until the following rainy season. (The cistern into which Joseph's brothers threw him [Genesis 37:24], however, was put to a use for which it was never intended.)

The soil conservation methods so carefully practiced during the time the Israelites lived in Palestine were ignored during the centuries after they were driven out of their homeland. In the 13th century, the Mongols destroyed the carefully carved watercourses and cisterns, and the torrential downpours each fall and winter washed precious topsoil off the land. In the years before World War I, Palestine was a part of the empire of the Ottoman Turks. When they built a railroad from Turkey to Mecca (the site of Islam's holiest shrine), Palestine's trees were cut down to make railroad ties and to fuel the steam locomotives. The result was that over the centuries the constant cutting of trees for timber and for fuel laid bare the unshaded earth to the burning heat of the summer sun. Winter rains slashed away at soil no longer held by tree roots. Historical records tell of how the blue waters of the Mediterranean were often stained brown by topsoil scoured off what had once been fertile cropland. There was another unfortunate result of neglecting the carefully constructed drainage systems. By the end of the 19th century, the most fertile regions of northern Palestine had degenerated into malarial swamps, largely uninhabited. The absentee Turkish landowners were quite ready to sell such areas to European Jews who wanted to return to their ancestral homeland.

Snow

Snow is mentioned only infrequently in the Old Testament because it is rare in Palestine. In the central highlands, on average, snow falls only once a year. By contrast, 10,000-foot Mount Hermon in the far north is heavy with snow in the winter, and sometimes retains a few patches even during the hot summer months. When the Old Testament does mention snow, it may very well be referring to something unusual. We're told, for example, that Benaiah, captain of King David's bodyguard, "went down into a pit on a snowy day and killed a lion" (2 Samuel 23:20) and that God's forgiveness in Christ is as sweet and clean (and as unexpected) as snow (Psalm 51:7; Isaiah 1:18).

The spring rains

Several months after the autumn (early) rains had fallen, the fields looked green with promise. The casual viewer might have been impressed, but closer examination would show that no heads of grain had yet appeared on the wheat and barley plants. Every farmer knew that, before that could happen, the *spring rains* (sometimes referred to as the *latter rains*) were critical. April and May brought those rains, which in turn brought the field crops to harvest ripeness.

What did this unusual rainfall pattern mean for the Israelite children of God who drew their living from the soil? Day by day they realized that they were utterly dependent on the Lord, who had made a covenant with Israel. In faith the farmer planted after the autumn rains had fallen. And after the spring rains five months later, with God's blessing he harvested the crops that would feed his loved ones and his livestock for another year and provide seed for the next planting time. It was only natural that believing Israelites sang:

> How good it is to sing praises to our God, how pleasant and fitting to praise him!
> He covers the sky with clouds; he supplies the earth with rain and makes grass grow on the hills. He provides food for the cattle and for the young ravens when they call. He . . . satisfies you with the finest of wheat. (Psalm 147:1,8,9,14)

For God to withhold the spring rains, however, was looked upon as a sign of his displeasure. Eight centuries before Christ came to our planet, King Ahab's bride Jezebel brought her pagan fertility-cult religion into the marriage and the royal palace. Ahab, Jezebel, and Israel were sure Baal could provide the rain the country needed. But God's prophet Elijah issued this stinging call to repentance to the wicked king and his queen: "As the LORD, the God of Israel, lives, whom I serve, there will be neither dew nor rain in the next few years except at my word" (1 Kings 17:1). And for more than three years, neither autumn nor spring rains fell in Israel.

Several centuries later, through the prophet Jeremiah, God directed these sobering messages to the people of Judah:

> "You have defiled the land with your prostitution and wickedness. Therefore the showers have been withheld, and no spring rains have fallen. . . . They do not say to themselves, 'Let us fear the LORD our God, who gives autumn and spring rains in season, who assures us of the regular weeks of harvest.' Your wrongdoings have kept these away; your sins have deprived you of good." (Jeremiah 3:2,3; 5:24,25)

These prophetic words remind us of a remark Martin Luther once made to his generation of Christians: "God wants to eat with you, or you're not going to have anything to eat either."

The rainless summer

Once the spring rains stopped, there would be no more rainfall for almost half a year, until the autumn rains began Israel's agricultural cycle all over again. During the sunny, rainless summer, farmers harvested their field crops and, later on, their fruit crops (olives, grapes, dates, figs, and pomegranates). During the summer drought, it would be the dew (sometimes so heavy that it resembled fog) that was largely responsible for keeping the grapevines green. When Isaac blessed his son Jacob, he said, "May God give you of heaven's dew and of earth's richness—an abundance of grain and new wine" (Genesis 27:28).

A homeland in the midst of enemies

The Promised Land was hardly a farmer's dream. Anyone who makes his living from the soil would not choose a land of hills and valleys and rocks and sand. But besides that, Palestine's unique geography introduced a second factor that might have seemed to make it even less attractive as the homeland for God's people. It had no natural defenses. And it was situated right in the middle of several nations unfriendly toward Israel. God's Old Testament people were surrounded by spiritual enemies.

Enemies next door

Only 35 miles southwest of Jerusalem lived the *Philistines,* who for years (until David conquered them) frequently invaded the Israelites' heartland and made their lives miserable. (The name Palestine comes from Philistines.)

Immediately to Israel's north was *Aram* (known in New Testament times as Syria). Here was another neighbor that had no love for the little nation to the south. More than once Aram coveted Israel's territory and sent its army to occupy it.

To the east across the Jordan were the nations of *Moab* and *Ammon.* Although they

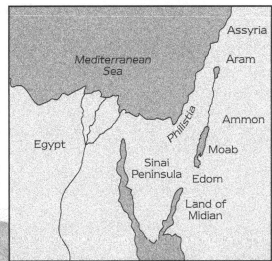

were shirttail relatives of the Israelites, they went out of their way to make trouble for them. During Israel's march to the Promised Land, and again during the period of Israel's judges, and then again during King David's reign, Moabites and Ammonites showed bitter hostility.

Finally, adjoining Israel's border south of the Dead Sea lived some other distant cousins, the nation of *Edom*. These descendants of Jacob's twin brother, Esau, were longtime enemies of the Israelites. The prophets Amos and Obadiah documented some of the vicious cruelty Edom showed its cousins to the north whenever it had an opportunity (Amos 1:11,12; Obadiah 10-14).

No matter where an Israelite lived in his ancient homeland, he and his family would be no more than 30 to 40 miles from some hostile neighbors, whose rulers had a blood lust. Satan had a strong motive for disrupting the fellowship Abraham's descendants shared around God's Word.

Enemies more distant

And those were only Israel's next-door neighbors. On opposite ends of the Fertile Crescent were the two enormous river-based superpowers, each regarding Israel as no more than a pawn in its games of international power politics. To the north and northeast was Mesopotamia, home of *Assyria* and, later, *Babylon*. And to the south was the "Queen of the Nile," *Egypt*. In their glory days these three were powerful empires, major players to be reckoned with in the politics of the Middle East. Now ask yourself: "Why would God choose to locate the home of his chosen people right in the middle of all these enemies?"

Training his people to trust him

Day by day in Old Testament times, God trained the descendants of Abraham to trust him. Agriculture in ancient Palestine was characterized by uncertainty. The soil was fertile enough, but the amount of rainfall necessary to sustain agriculture was beyond human control. If the rains failed to fall in sufficient amounts at the right times, food shortages and famine were sure to follow. The country's economy would collapse. Through this, God reminded his people, "Trust your Father to provide you with your daily bread!" As they waited for the Savior to come, the very face and nature of the land they lived in provided ongoing opportunities for the people of Israel to trust God for their daily bread. God's great promise to Abraham to send a Son was something to believe. He also promised to give Abraham a land—also something to believe. The promise of the land was braided together with the promise of the Savior.

We see a similar truth when we contemplate Israel's location on a little bridge of land in an ocean of potential enemies who could have swallowed it up. And yet, as Israel prepared to enter its new homeland, God reminded his people:

"You are now about to cross the Jordan to go in and dispossess nations greater and stronger than you. . . . But be assured today that the LORD your God is the one who goes across ahead of you. . . . [He] will drive them out before you, to accomplish what he swore to your fathers, to Abraham, Isaac and Jacob." (Deuteronomy 9:1-5)

Day by day God trained his people to trust him. An incident that occurred during the reign of good King Jehoshaphat in 850 B.C. will illustrate how the ruler of nations could defend his covenant people—even when they faced a vastly superior military force. A large army from Moab, Ammon, and Edom had invaded Israel in the area around the Dead Sea. In 2 Chronicles chapter 20, King Jehoshaphat prayed:

> "O LORD, God of our fathers, . . . they are . . . coming to drive us out of the possession you gave us as an inheritance. . . . We have no power to face this vast army that is attacking us. We do not know what to do, but our eyes are upon you." (verses 6,11,12)

God answered:

> "Do not be afraid or discouraged because of this vast army. For the battle is not yours, but God's. Tomorrow march down against them. . . . You will not have to fight this battle. Take up your positions; stand firm and see the deliverance the LORD will give you." . . . The men of Ammon and Moab rose up against the men from Mount Seir [Edom] to destroy and annihilate them. After they finished slaughtering the men from Seir, they helped to destroy one another. Then, led by Jehoshaphat, all the men of Judah and Jerusalem returned joyfully to Jerusalem, for the LORD had given them cause to rejoice over their enemies." (verses 15-17,23,27)

By giving them this particular homeland, God trained his people to trust him, not only for daily bread but also for their continued existence as a nation. Anybody who reads the history of God's people in Old Testament times with eyes open will see the hand of God at work, not only in Israel's history but even in its geography. When you see pictures of Palestine, your initial impression of the land may not be favorable. But that narrow strip of land was perfectly suited for the purposes God had in mind when he chose it as the homeland for his people. They could trust him to provide for them. They could trust him to protect them. They could also trust him to send the Savior he had promised.

Tenants, not owners

In the preceding paragraphs, ancient Palestine is repeatedly referred to as "Israel's homeland." Perhaps that term should be defined more accurately. When God called Palestine "the land the LORD your God is *giving you to possess* as your inheritance" (Deuteronomy 15:4), he was not giving Israel permanent title to the land. Throughout its history, Israel never "owned" the Promised Land. They were free to live in it and to enjoy the blessings it offered, only as long as they remained faithful to the God who had made a covenant with them. The land did not belong to them but to him. It was his to do with as he chose. At Mount Sinai, God had announced, "The land is mine and you are but aliens and my tenants" (Leviticus 25:23).

Sabbath Year

The Lord showed in a number of ways that he was the owner of the Promised Land. We see this, for example, in his regulations regarding the use of the land. At Mount Sinai, God said:

"For six years sow your fields, and . . . prune your vineyards and gather their crops. But in the seventh year the land is to have a sabbath of rest. . . . Do not sow your fields or prune your vineyards. . . . The land is to have a year of rest. Whatever the land yields during the sabbath year will be food for you." (Leviticus 25:3-6)

The Lord, the ultimate owner of the land, simply announced his plans for the land during every seventh year. The Israelites could eat the so-called *volunteer crops,* grain and fruit that had grown on their own, but they could not harvest them for sale and profit. The one who truly owned the land had spoken. During the Sabbath Year there was to be no plowing, sowing, or reaping.

Jubilee Year

God announced further: "Count off seven sabbaths of years—seven times seven years. . . . Consecrate the fiftieth year. . . . It shall be a jubilee for you; each one of you is to return to his family property. . . . The land must not be sold permanently, because the land is mine and you are but aliens and my tenants" (Leviticus 25:8,10,23).

Every 50 years the title to a particular piece of property would revert to the family to whom it had originally been awarded at the time the Israelites entered the land. If in the meantime a farmer was forced, perhaps by economic necessity, to sell his farm, the selling price would be determined by the number of years remaining until the next Jubilee Year. He was really not selling the land itself (that belonged to God). What he was really selling was the number of crops that could be harvested before the land reverted, in the Year of Jubilee, to the family of the original owner. In this way God made sure that poverty could not force a family off its homestead, make it permanently homeless, and risk a family name of Christ's ancestors to be lost.

Misguided hope for future return

Several Christian churches today teach that someday the present-day nation of Israel will return to God in repentance and faith. From this they conclude that the Israeli government is to be helped, at all costs, to reclaim its ancient homeland, with Jerusalem as its capital.

But God's plan for saving the sinful world does not have as its goal the establishment of a visible earthly kingdom, with its capital at Jerusalem. The final goal to which God wants to lead people—those descended from Abraham and those not descended from him—is not a piece of real estate in the Middle East but an eternal homeland in heaven— "the heavenly Jerusalem" (Hebrews 12:22).

Furthermore, both the Old Testament and the New Testament teach that only a remnant of Abraham's descendants ever accepted God's magnificent plan in Christ Jesus. Over the centuries, the vast majority of the people of Israel were unfaithful to the covenant that God had made with their great ancestor. As they forfeited Christ's forgiveness, they individually forfeited its blessings, including any claim on what once had been their ancient homeland.

In his solemn farewell address to the Israelites, Moses emphasized that their continued occupancy of Palestine would depend on their faithfulness to God's covenant in Christ:

> If you fully obey the LORD your God and carefully follow all his commands . . . the LORD your God will bless you in the land he is giving you. . . . However, if you do not obey the LORD your God and do not carefully follow all his commands . . . you will be uprooted from the land you are entering to possess. Then the LORD will scatter you among all nations, from one end of the earth to the other." (Deuteronomy 28:1,8,15,63,64)

The real owner of the Promised Land would permit Abraham's descendants to continue to live there only if they remained faithful to him. If, however, they were unfaithful to him and turned to other gods, they would forfeit their right to live in the land and would be driven out of it. History documents that this is exactly what happened. In regard to present-day Israelis, you will observe that the majority—at home and abroad—scorn and suppress the Word of God concerning Christ.

Summary

The history and even the geography of the "land flowing with milk and honey" show us how ideally suited it was to be the site for the Lord's training school for his covenant people. In that tiny strip of land in the ancient Middle East, God's people learned to trust him. They trusted him for their daily bread and for their continued existence as the nation from whom Christ would come. It was because of the promise of the Savior that Israel needed to be preserved during the centuries of the Old Testament.

Isn't there a truth here that not only the Israelites needed to learn, but you and I as well? What God told the descendants of Abraham as they faced the day-to-day problems of survival is essentially no different from what Jesus teaches us in the Sermon on the Mount: "Seek first [God's] kingdom and his righteousness, and all these things [*What shall we eat? What shall we drink? What shall we wear?*] will be given to you as well" (Matthew 6:33). We can understand that to mean "My children, you put me first, and I promise you will not need to worry about food and clothing and survival."

If, on the other hand, we consciously select "Toys-R-Us" as the motto of our existence, if the goal of our lives is fun, fun, fun, then God may have to teach us the hard way that life works only one way, and that's his way. There are many things God may put up with in a human heart, but second place is not one of them.

The God who loves us for his Son's sake did not design our lives to be meaningless. He had a higher goal for the day-to-day lives of Abraham's descendants than merely to pay their bills and stay out of jail. He had a different blueprint for his ancient people. It was a perfect blueprint that gave them a sense of security and brought a sense of meaning to their lives. In the little homeland he picked out for them, he trained them to live *for him* as they waited for the Messiah. For those who live in the time of the New Testament, that means "whether you eat or drink or whatever you do, do it all for the glory of God" (1 Corinthians 10:31).

The LORD your God is bringing you into a good land . . . a land with wheat and barley, vines and fig trees, pomegranates, olive oil and honey; a land where bread will not be scarce.

~ DEUTERONOMY 8:7-9

[The LORD] will bless . . . the crops of your land—your grain, new wine and oil.

~ DEUTERONOMY 7:13

A Table Set by God

All of us know that one of the basic responsibilities of parents is to provide for the physical needs of their children. The heavenly Father knows that too. He showed that by giving his ancient people of Israel a special homeland. But he was concerned also about their day-to-day needs, and he promised to provide. Day by day throughout their history—one day at a time—God set a table for his chosen people. They needed to be preserved so that God could keep the messianic promise made to Abraham. They needed to be strong so that their worship of the true God would be vibrant and attractive to outsiders.

In Egypt

God provided for his people during the hundreds of years they spent in Egypt, while they were growing from a 75-member family group into a nation numbering several million. Years later when they were marching through the desert, they fondly remembered, "[In Egypt] we sat around pots of meat and ate all the food we wanted" (Exodus 16:3). "We remember the fish we ate in Egypt at no cost—also the cucumbers, melons, leeks, onions and garlic" (Numbers 11:5).

In the desert

After God miraculously delivered his people from slavery in Egypt, he provided for them during the 40 years in the desert, while they were marching to the land of Palestine. Later on, God's people looked back over those 40 difficult years and said to him:

> Because of your great compassion you did not abandon them in the desert. By day the pillar of cloud did not cease to guide them on their path, nor the pillar of fire by night to shine on the way they were to take. For forty years you sustained them in the desert; they lacked nothing, their clothes did not wear out nor did their feet become swollen. (Nehemiah 9:19,21)

In the first few weeks after they left Egypt, the Israelites pretty well used up the food supplies they had brought along with them. When they began to complain, God made two announcements. He said, first of all: "At twilight you will eat meat. . . . That evening quail came and covered

the camp" (Exodus 16:12,13). The Israelites' dinner menu in the desert that evening was certainly unusual, humanly impossible—quail! For all!

Then after Israel had challenged God's love for them and his ability to take care of them, God asked: "Would you be impressed if I made your food fall out of the sky—out of thin air?" For their basic, day-to-day diet, God announced:

"I will rain down bread from heaven for you. The people are to go out each day and gather enough for that day." . . . In the morning there was a layer of dew around the camp. When the dew was gone, thin flakes like frost on the ground appeared on the desert floor. When the Israelites saw it, they said to each other, "What is it?" (Exodus 16:4,13-15)

When the dew had evaporated from off the ground the following morning, something sparkled like tiny pearls all over the camp of Israel. The Israelites asked the same question you would have asked: "What is it?" In Hebrew that question sounds like *"Man hu?"* And that's where the miracle food got its name: *manna*, the "what is it?" food. As Moses described it, "It was white like coriander seed and tasted like wafers made with honey" (Exodus 16:31). "The people went around gathering it, and then ground it in a handmill or crushed it in a mortar. They cooked it in a pot or made it into cakes. And it tasted like something made with olive oil" (Numbers 11:8).

A whole generation of Israelites grew up eating manna every day for 40 years. Israelite children didn't have to ask their mothers: "What's for supper tonight?" They knew without asking. A more likely question to ask their mothers might have been: "How did you fix it today, Mom?" Manna could be eaten raw (as we eat sunflower or pumpkin seeds). It could be cooked into something like oatmeal. It could be ground into flour and baked into bread. All by itself it provided a balanced diet for God's people.

Day by day for 40 years, God miraculously spread a table for his people, giving them a single day's supply of manna at a time. His instructions to his people were to gather only as much as they needed for one day. That was not only a command they were to obey; that was a promise they could trust. Day by day, one day at a time, God's people could be sure they would have the nourishment their bodies needed for one more day of travel over rocky and trackless desert. God trained them, as he trains us, to live one day at a time.

In the Promised Land

Finally their desert journey was over, and the Israelites crossed over the Jordan River into Palestine. Four days later they celebrated the Passover festival. And then "the day after the Passover, that very day, they ate some of the produce of the land: unleavened bread and roasted grain. The manna stopped the day after they ate this food from the land; there was no longer any manna for the Israelites, but that year they ate of the produce of Canaan" (Joshua 5:11,12).

In Psalm 104 the psalmist takes a tour through the wonderland of God's creation, calling on God's people to praise the Lord, the faithful covenant God. One of the reasons for praising the Lord is that "he makes grass grow for the cattle, and plants for man to cultivate—bringing forth food from the earth" (Psalm 104:14).

The calendar

In 1908, in the ruins of the city of Gezer (20 miles west of Jerusalem), archeologists uncovered a clay tablet that they identified as a school pupil's writing exercise. Known as the Gezer Calendar, the tablet enumerates the seasons, starting in fall, that determined the Israelite farmer's calendar:

The two months of [olive] harvest,
The two months of planting [grain],
The two months of late planting,
The month of hoeing up of flax,
The month of the harvest of barley,
The month of the harvest [of wheat] and storage,
The two months of vine tending,
The month of summer fruit.

Three basic food groups

Now notice in Psalm 104:15 how the poet describes the food for which he calls upon his fellow Israelites to praise God. The diet of the new occupants of the Promised Land was nourishing, but by our standards it was modest. The psalmist lists the three staple crops that dominated the agriculture of ancient Palestine: "*wine* that gladdens the heart of man, *oil* to make his face shine, and *bread* that sustains his heart."

Although he never set foot in the Promised Land, Moses assured Israel, "[The Lord] will bless . . . the crops of your land—your *grain*, new *wine* and *oil*" (Deuteronomy 7:13).

Many centuries after Moses, God's chosen people snubbed God's mercy and were indifferent toward God's Word and his worship. The prophet Joel tells us how God interrupted their food supply to let them know he did not appreciate being ignored: "The *grain* is destroyed, the new *wine* is dried up, the *oil* fails" (Joel 1:10).

Grains and herbs

The grain crops were the first to ripen. If the autumn and spring rains arrived on schedule, barley was harvested in early April; wheat, in late May. It's estimated that wheat made up perhaps half of the diet of an Israelite family, much of that in the form of bread. Barley was used mainly for animal fodder; coarse barley bread was the food of the poor. Barley or lentil porridge, a boiled dish resembling oatmeal, was common, supplemented by vegetables—beans, cucumbers, and onions. A chunk of bread and a handful of raisins or olives or a piece of fruit might be carried to the fields and eaten there about midmorning. When Ruth was gleaning in Boaz' barley field, he invited her to share in the meal his reapers were enjoying: "Have some bread and dip it in the wine vinegar" (Ruth 2:14). That, plus some roasted grain, would by our standards be a pretty skimpy lunch for workers who had already put in several hours of hard labor under the sun. On the other hand, God was taking good care of the keepers of the Savior promise.

Genesis chapter 25 records how on one occasion, when Abraham's grandson Esau had spent a day in the open country, he returned home tired and hungry. He found his twin brother, Jacob, boiling some lentils in a pot, probably for the main meal at the close of the working day. Esau was so famished that he was willing to sell his birthright—the privileges he enjoyed as the firstborn son in the family (which included the messianic promise)—for a bowl of Jacob's lentil soup! (With the exception of the forbidden fruit in the Garden of Eden, that has to be the most expensive meal anybody ever bought.)

Evidence uncovered by the archeologist's spade suggests that five thousand years ago 40 percent of Mesopotamia's grain crop may have been used for brewing purposes. The King James Version of the Bible repeatedly speaks of "strong drink" (Leviticus 10:9; Judges 13:4; Micah 2:11). The use of that term misled many KJV readers into thinking that the Bible writers were referring to what we call hard liquor. Distilled liquor was unknown to people in Bible times and is, therefore, never referred to in the Bible. But people back then certainly did know about fermented beverages made not only from grapes but also from grain. Instead of using the misleading term "strong drink," therefore, the New International Version correctly translates the drink as "beer."

The Bible mentions garden herbs that the Israelite homemaker raised to season the food on her dinner table—caraway, cummin, mint, dill, and rue (Isaiah 28:25,27; Matthew 23:23; Luke 11:42). There were delicacies produced in Canaan—Genesis 43:11 mentions honey, pistachios, and almonds. But by our standards, meals for an average Israelite were simple and modest.

Grapes

Toward the end of the hot, dry summer, the Israelites harvested their second major crop: the fruit crop—primarily grapes but also figs, dates, olives, pomegranates, and melons. Vine culture is particularly suited to areas in the mountains, on terraced hillsides where tilling the soil with an ox-drawn plow would be difficult, or in the hot, dry Negev to the south where wheat farming cannot be practiced. When the Israelites first approached the Promised Land, Moses sent out 12 spies to explore Palestine and bring back a report. He added, "Bring back some of the fruit of the land" (Numbers 13:20).

Six weeks later the spies returned with a branch bearing a single cluster of grapes from a vineyard near Hebron. The bunch of grapes that they brought back was so large that it took two men to carry it on a pole between them!

Year after year, the grape harvest was a time of joy for all. For one thing, it signaled that the hot summer was just about over. Some of the grapes harvested were eaten fresh; some were spread out to dry in the sun to become raisins. Most of the grape harvest, however, was turned into wine.

Wine was a common beverage in Bible times, served at everyday meals. Milk was not a common beverage for the Israelites as it is for us, because without refrigeration milk soon turned sour in Israel's tropical climate. Water in Palestine was a precious commodity in limited supply, and wine was mixed with it to purify it.

Wine also played a part in Israel's worship service. A quart of wine was poured out on the Lord's altar each day along with each burnt offering (Exodus 29:40). Wine was used also as an article of trade. When Solomon needed lumber to build the temple in Jerusalem, he offered the Phoenicians (Israel's neighbors to the north) wheat, barley, wine, and olive oil as payment for the lumber he needed (2 Chronicles 2:10).

In Psalm 104 the psalmist praises God for the gift of "wine that gladdens the heart" (verse 15). However, every gift of God can be abused. The pages of the Old Testament offer plenty of evidence that God's gift of fermented beverages was in fact abused by many of Abraham's descendants.

The prophet Amos, for example, gives us this unflattering description of the prominent women in the capital city of Samaria, wives of the leaders of the breakaway northern kingdom of Israel: " . . . you women who oppress the poor and crush the needy and say to your husbands, 'Bring us some drinks!'" (Amos 4:1).

At that same time the prophet Micah had this to say to the people of Jerusalem, capital of the southern kingdom of Judah, who had rejected his prophetic message: "If a liar and deceiver comes and says, 'I will prophesy for you plenty of wine and beer,' he would be just the prophet for this people!" (Micah 2:11).

Figs

Several dozen references in the Scripture attest to the fact that the fig tree also provided an important component of Israel's food supply. The fruit of the fig tree could be eaten fresh or dried and pressed into a cake. An abundant fig harvest was considered evidence of the Lord's blessing: "Surely the LORD has done great things. . . . The trees are bearing their fruit; the fig tree and the vine yield their riches. Be glad, O people of Zion, rejoice in the LORD your God" (Joel 2:21-23).

The prophet Jeremiah shows us the exact opposite. The Lord's judgment came down hard on the chosen people for rebelling against him, for stubbornly denying they were accountable to him. God permitted the Babylonian army to invade the Promised Land,

and the results were painful: "They will devour your harvests and food, devour your sons and daughters; they will devour your flocks and herds, devour your vines and fig trees" (Jeremiah 5:17).

The fig was a favorite garden tree because its large, thick leaves offered shade and privacy. Nathanael was sitting under his fig tree before Jesus called him to become one of his disciples (John 1:48). "Sitting under one's vine and fig tree" was a biblical picture of security, of abundance, and of harmony with God and one's neighbor: "During Solomon's lifetime Judah and Israel . . . lived in safety, each man under his own vine and fig tree" (1 Kings 4:25).

It's interesting to note that several of God's Old Testament prophets used this same picture to describe the time when Christ, the promised Messiah, would come to bring his people perfect peace through the forgiveness of their sin. Referring to our New Testament era, the prophet Micah predicted: "Every man will sit under his own vine and under his own fig tree, and no one will make them afraid, for the LORD Almighty has spoken" (Micah 4:4).

Dates

The palm tree referred to in both Old and New Testaments is the date palm, an important source of food in the Middle East (Leviticus 23:40; 2 Samuel 6:19). From the pages of the Bible, we learn, however, that besides providing food for people, the date palm was put to several other interesting uses. Saint John tells us that on the first Palm Sunday, the people who welcomed Jesus into Jerusalem "took palm branches and went out to meet him, shouting, 'Hosanna! . . . Blessed is the King of Israel!'" (John 12:13).

Again, it was the apostle John who, in one of his visions, described the saints in glory as standing in front of the Lamb "holding palm branches in their hands" as they cried out, "Salvation belongs to our God, who sits on the throne, and to the Lamb" (Revelation 7:9,10).

Olives and their oil

Palestine's hill country is ideally suited for growing olive trees. Olive oil was used for cooking and for baking. It was the golden fuel that kept oil lamps burning. For people who lived and worked and played outside, exposed to hot, dry winds and blasting sandstorms, olive oil was used in skin lotions. Just think how good it must have felt to rub clear, fragrant olive oil into your dry, chapped, cracked hands after a day of work! Psalm 23:5 refers to the custom of the host at a banquet anointing the head of an honored guest with oil—an honor that Simon the Pharisee withheld from Jesus (Luke 7:46). The olive harvest in the fall of the year, at the time of the early rains, played an important role in the lives of God's people in Bible times.

Olive oil also played an important role in the worship God designed for his people. Part of the tabernacle's furnishings in the Old Testament was a seven-branched lampstand of pure gold. (Years later, in Solomon's temple, there were ten of these lampstands.) Every day before sunset, one job of the priests was to fill each of the individual lamps on the lampstand with fresh olive oil, to make sure that those lamps would continue to burn throughout the night. This assured God's people that, although the tabernacle or temple was closed from sunset to sunrise and the sacrificing and singing had stopped, their fellowship with God was not interrupted. The communication between a merciful God and his chosen people was continuous. They could go to sleep in peace, knowing Yahweh, the God who had made a covenant with them, would be up all night keeping watch.

Olive oil was one of five ingredients in the holy anointing oil, by which Israel's priests and prophets and kings were inaugurated into their offices (Exodus 30:22-25).

When an Israelite worshiper brought the Lord a grain offering to express thanksgiving, olive oil was poured on it before it went up in smoke (Leviticus 2:1-4).

The hills in which Jerusalem is located are rich in olive groves. These, in turn, created a need for large stone olive presses (*Gath shemanei* in Hebrew). When transliterated this gives us the name Gethsemane—a garden on the Mount of Olives, just east of Jerusalem, across the Kidron Valley.

Meat

Except for the families of the rich, meat was usually reserved for religious festivals. The menu for the Passover meal included a lamb or young goat. Many families kept a few sheep for meat and wool and a goat or two for milk and cheese. Women churned butter in goatskin bags. Fish and fowl provided an additional, though not prominent, component of the Israelites' diet. Several of Christ's disciples had spent time as commercial fishermen on the Sea of Galilee—that beautiful blue gem God set deep in the hills of northern Israel. Each day they would sell their catch—some to be eaten fresh, some to be preserved by drying or salting. You will recall that the boy's lunch that Jesus used to feed the thousands (John 6:9-11) consisted of five barley biscuits and several dried fish. Many families kept a few chickens for meat and eggs. Remember how, in his final word to the Jewish nation, Jesus described as utterly unnatural their stubbornness in rejecting him. What they were doing was as unnatural as a baby chick's refusing to respond to the clucking of the mother hen (Matthew 23:37).

A humble way of life

Once the people of Israel entered the Promised Land and settled down to an ordered existence, they lived in homes that we would call humble. Most families lived in one- or two-room dwellings built of stone and dried mud. These houses had dirt floors and flat roofs. Think of American Indian dwellings in the southwestern United States. The rooms were multipurpose. They served as kitchen, dining room, and living room by day, and at night as bedrooms. An extended family might very well live under one roof, with precious little privacy and few material comforts. There was little furniture. Except for the rich, beds for sleeping were not made of wood but were mats that could be rolled up (Matthew 9:6). Jesus referred to this when he told the story of a man whose friend came to his home at midnight to ask for some bread to serve unexpected guests. The homeowner answered his friend's request: "Don't bother me. The door is already locked, and my children and I are in bed. I can't get up and give you anything" (Luke 11:7 TNIV). In a one-room home, which at midnight was wall-to-wall sleeping people, the man's reluctance is understandable.

A God-centered way of life

In this modest way of life, God's Old Testament children heard the voice of their heavenly Father. Day by day God lovingly reminded them that the world revolved not around them but around him. He built reminders of this into every phase of Israelite culture. God demanded that they dedicate their firstborn sons to him. If that firstborn did not serve God as a priest, he had to be redeemed by the payment of money. Firstborn livestock had to be offered to God on his altar or redeemed with a substitute (Exodus 34:19,20). This thought was the very heart of the day-to-day life of God's people in the years before Christ came.

Clean and unclean foods

When a Hebrew homemaker was planning her family's evening meal, she could never forget that there were certain foods which God had declared *unclean*. Those were foods God had declared unacceptable—either on his altar or on her dinner table. Any seafood she served had to have fins and scales, and she could forget about serving ham or pork chops. *Clean* animals had to meet two qualifications: they had to have a split hoof and they had to chew a cud. The pig met the first qualification but failed the second. (Someone has called the pig the original hypocrite. Its split hoof makes it appear outwardly acceptable, but its digestive system makes it unacceptable.) Some have wondered whether there might have been hygienic reasons for this prohibition.

Without refrigeration, the danger of trichinosis would make eating that meat risky. What we do know is that God taught the Israelites to be concerned not only about the outward appearance of a person or thing but also about its inner nature.

Leviticus chapter 11 specifies which land animals and which creatures living in the waters and which birds were clean and which were not. Of the latter, God simply announced, "You must not eat their meat or touch their carcasses; they are unclean for you" (Leviticus 11:8).

God's blueprint for Israel

Why would God have put these restrictions on his people during the centuries of the Old Testament? He himself explains, "I am the LORD your God, who has *set you apart* from the nations" (Leviticus 20:24). God had erected a wall to separate Israel from its surrounding heathen nations. "You will be for me a kingdom of priests and a *holy nation*" (Exodus 19:6).

Israel was a holy nation not in the sense of being morally spotless, but it was to be *set apart* for God's holy purposes. Day by day in Old Testament times, the laws regulating clean and unclean foods were a daily, and even hourly, discipline by which the nation of Israel was to show that it was different. God had put his claim on the Isrealites. He had special plans for them—plans that determined the ransom and restoration of an entire worldful of sinners. It was never in God's blueprint for Israel to become a superpower in the ancient Middle East. In God's plan, this nation was to be the *custodian of his revealed truth* and the *cradle of the promised Savior.*

Those were big plans. A whole lot was at stake here (including your eternal happiness and mine)! But God's plan would never have been fulfilled if Israel had blended in with the heathen nations that surrounded it and forgotten that God had called it to carry out his holy purpose. God gave his chosen people daily, nonstop reminders that they were special to him. Of all the people on earth, the Lord chose them to be the human ancestors of Christ!

God certainly set a rich table for his chosen people—in Egypt, in the desert, and in their promised homeland. In providing for them, God's goal was not just their physical survival and comfort. God knows there's more to life than making a living and accumulating a bunch of "toys" to pass on to your survivors. He called Israel "my people, my chosen, the people I formed for myself *that they may proclaim my praise*" (Isaiah 43:20,21). "They are . . . the work of my hands, *for the display of my splendor*" (Isaiah 60:21).

Unfortunately, the history of the Israelites shows how Satan messed with their minds. He challenged their faith in the promise God had made in Eden and which he repeated to Abraham. The result was that they failed to appreciate God's loving provision day by day and year after year. Can you sense God's heartache in the words he spoke through the prophet? "I cared for you in the desert, in the land of burning heat. When I fed them, they were satisfied; when they were satisfied, they became proud; then they forgot me" (Hosea 13:5,6).

The reason why God set a table for his chosen people was not just to satisfy the needs of their stomachs, as if they were no more than cattle. His daily gifts of bread and wine and oil were to remind them that he is a merciful God who loved them deeply. He was strong enough to back up his promises with deeds (Psalm 62:11,12). Tragically, the people of ancient Israel failed to recognize God's unbelievable goodness to them. Instead of praising him for the miracles they experienced every day of their lives—most important of which was his forgiving love—they complained about what they did not have. And when you do that, you'll never have enough of anything. Israel ignored the fact that in his covenant God had pledged his love to them. Instead, they rewarded God's kindness with ingratitude and then with contempt for him. The result was that when Jesus Christ arrived, they lost their status as the one chosen people. The good news of free and full forgiveness in Christ went out to the gentile nations (Matthew 2; Acts 13:46).

God's blueprint for us

In a conversation at his dinner table, Martin Luther once made the remark: "If Adam were to return to earth and see the way we live and the food we eat, he would say: 'This is not the world I lived in!'" King Solomon in all his glory never had a chariot like the one parked in your garage. He never knew what a treat frozen orange juice is. Even our brief review of the way God's people lived and ate in ancient Israel must convince us that compared with theirs our standard of living consists of undreamed-of wealth. It's been said that American garbage disposals eat better than most of the world's population.

Satan knows that too. His goal in our lives, as was his goal in the lives of ancient Israelites, is to rob us of our thankfulness for God's good gifts. If it were within Satan's power, he wouldn't let us have a single piece of bread, not a single penny of income, not even a single hour of life. But since that's not in his power, he'll try to rob us of God's blessings by making us ungrateful and unappreciative of them.

As we live our day-to-day lives, how important it is to listen for our Father's voice saying:

"My child, I love you!"

"My child, I will provide you with everything I know you need!"

"My child, nothing in all of creation can separate you from my love in Christ Jesus!"

Like the ancient Israelites, you have a God who has obligated himself by making a covenant with you. That means you have a God you can count on. The ancient Israelites forgot that. Don't you forget that, dear Christian. Today is your day to give God your personal, individual thanks.

The LORD, the LORD, the compassionate and gracious God, slow to anger, abounding in love and faithfulness, . . . forgiving wickedness, rebellion and sin . . . a jealous God, punishing the children for the sin of the fathers to the third and fourth generation of those who hate me.

~ Exodus 34:6,7; 20:5

Consider . . . the kindness and sternness of God.

~ Romans 11:22

Living under Law and Gospel

An interesting story is told about a five-year-old boy sitting at his kitchen table, busy with crayons and construction paper. His mother asked him, "What are you doing, honey?"

"I'm drawing a picture."

"What are you drawing a picture of?"

"I'm drawing a picture of God."

"Why, honey, nobody knows what God looks like," said the mother.

"They will now," the little guy responded.

We smile at the way a child's mind works. In his mind that five-year-old had his own picture of God. Unfortunately, isn't that where many people get their ideas of God? In their minds they've drawn their own pictures of what God is like, and if somebody says something about God that doesn't fit their pictures—well, that somebody must be wrong.

Do you see how dangerous that attitude is? Whether on judgment day we're going to be welcomed with God's family on the right, or sentenced along with God's enemies on the left (Matthew 25:31-33), depends on whether or not we have a correct picture of God—who he is and what he has done for us.

The ancient Hebrews lived in a world with many different ideas about God. *National Geographic* has called the ancient Middle East "the birthplace of civilization." That's where culture as we know it originated. That's where we got our alphabet. The Middle East also gave birth to many pagan religions—vile forms of idolatry, some even involving temple prostitution and human sacrifice. The gods of the heathen were selfish, arbitrary beings; they had to be forced or coaxed to grant their gifts.

A double picture

In the written Scriptures that God gave to his chosen people, he painted a true picture of himself. He shared some of his sacred secrets with them. He actually put down, in writing, what he is really like. On the pages of the Old Testament, wherever we see God dealing with people, we learn that there are two great emotions in the heart of God. We see God's hatred of sin and his absolute unwillingness to compromise with it. He is a holy God, the sworn enemy of anything that destroys his people. We call this the message of God's *law*. But we also see God's burning desire to reach out for sinners, to restore them to peace and fellowship with him. God is a merciful God—the only hope for sinners. We call this the message of God's *gospel*.

This double picture of God is the only true picture of God, and it confronts us on every page of the Old Testament. Philip Yancey, in his book *The Bible Jesus Read,* describes the God who revealed himself to ancient Israel as:

a lion but also a lamb.

an eagle but also a mother hen.

a king but also a servant.

a judge but also a shepherd.

You may recall that when God announced his holy law to the Israelites from Mount Sinai, he introduced it by reminding his people that he is Yahweh, their Savior-God. He had chosen them for himself. He had even entered into a covenant, a solemn contract, with them. Apart from his promises of love in Christ, their lives had no meaning, no purpose. This basic truth stands behind every commandment God announced. "This is what your Father is like. Now live like his child."

Different from pagan law codes

Many biblical commandments have parallels in ancient law codes. Both, for example, announce the standard of justice: "an eye for an eye, a tooth for a tooth." What distinguishes the law God gave to his chosen people of Israel from the dozen pagan collections of law that have come down to us from the ancient Middle East?

Ancient Hittite, Egyptian, and Mesopotamian law codes (the Code of Hammurabi, to name just one) assumed there were many gods—more gods than you could possibly count. In sharp contrast to this, God's chosen people heard him say, "Hear, O Israel: The LORD our God, the LORD is one" (Deuteronomy 6:4). The law God announced at Mount Sinai said simply "no other gods" (Exodus 20:3). "I am the LORD; that is my name! I will not give my glory to another" (Isaiah 42:8).

God's laws governing day-to-day life in ancient Israel were permeated with grace. God's law, for example, shows a *greater respect for human life* than any pagan law code did. Only God's law announced: "Love your neighbor as yourself" (Leviticus 19:18).

The Code of Hammurabi said: "If you kill a slave, you must pay his master." Compare that with what God's law says: "If [a man] knocks out the tooth of a manservant or maidservant, he must let the servant go free to compensate for the tooth" (Exodus 21:27).

Among all law codes from the ancient world, the one God established with Israel is by far the most careful to safeguard human rights and to protect the innocent and the disadvantaged— especially widows and orphans. "One witness is not enough to convict a man accused of any crime. . . . A matter must be established by the testimony of two or three witnesses" (Deuteronomy 19:15). "[The LORD] upholds the cause of the oppressed and gives food to the hungry. . . . The LORD watches over the alien and sustains the fatherless and the widow, but he frustrates the ways of the wicked" (Psalm 146:7-9).

At harvesttime God's law forbade Israelite farmers to cut the grain growing in the corners of their fields. They couldn't go over their fields or vineyards twice to get the last stalk of wheat, every last grape on the vine. Those were to be left for the poor. That was God's poverty program for his people.

The collections of laws that came out of the ancient Middle East tried to control the *behavior* of the people who lived under them. By contrast, the God who announced his law from Mount Sinai was much more interested in the *attitudes* of his people than merely in their actions. God knows that a person's actions are really only symptoms, showing what his attitudes are.

God's Ten Commandments emphasize that God looks for two attitudes in particular: Love God above everything else. Love your neighbor as yourself.

The very first pages of the Bible make it clear that God designed human creatures for himself. The goal of life is to live for God, to proclaim his praise. In the very first commandment announced from Mount Sinai, God made it clear that he will not share his glory with anyone else. In ancient Egypt, where God's people lived for centuries before moving to Canaan, Ra was the sun god, Apis was the sacred bull. "What good is a god you can't see?" the otherwise brilliant Egyptians reasoned.

When God rescued his chosen people from slavery in Egypt, he announced in advance, "I will *bring judgment on all the gods of Egypt*" (Exodus 12:12). The method God used to rescue his people from Egypt was designed to humble the gods of Egypt, to show them up for what they were—creations of the human mind. And one by one the Egyptian gods fell before the plagues unleashed by the God of Abraham, Isaac, and Jacob. The Nile River god, Hapi, who was believed to give life to a country that is 95 percent desert, turned to blood (Exodus 7:20). Egyptians worshiped gods with animal heads, among them the frog-goddess, Heket, and the cow-goddess, Hathor. Frogs and livestock died at God's command (Exodus 8:13; 9:6). The sun god, Ra, was humbled when total darkness covered the land of Egypt for three days (Exodus 10:22). In these awesome actions of judgment, you can hear the voice of Israel's God announcing, "My glory I will not give to another" (Isaiah 42:8 TNIV).

Coarse idolatry

Worshiping an image of a god is a coarse form of idolatry. It's an attack on God. Through the prophet Isaiah God condemned that:

To whom will you compare me or count me equal? To whom will you liken me that we may be compared? Some pour out gold from their bags and weigh out silver on the scales; they hire a goldsmith to make it into a god, and they bow down and worship it. They lift it to their shoulders and carry it; they set it up in its place, and there it stands. From that spot it cannot move. Though one cries out to it, it does not answer; it cannot save him from his troubles. (Isaiah 46:5-7)

God condemns worshiping idols because it's blasphemy, an insult to God. Isaiah points out, furthermore, that worshiping the work of one's own hands is also the height of stupidity:

The carpenter measures with a line and makes an outline with a marker; he roughs it out with chisels and marks it with compasses. He shapes it in the form of man, of man in all his glory, that it may dwell in a shrine. He cut down cedars, or perhaps took a cypress or oak. He let it grow among the trees of the forest, or planted a pine, and the rain made it grow. It is man's fuel for burning; some of it he takes and warms himself, he kindles a fire and bakes bread. But he also fashions a god and worships it; he makes an idol and bows down to it. . . . He prays to it and says, "Save me; you are my god." (Isaiah 44:13-17)

At Mount Sinai, God made it clear he cannot and will not tolerate that: "You shall not make for yourself an idol in the form of anything in heaven above or on the earth beneath or in the waters below. You shall not bow down to them or worship them" (Exodus 20:4,5).

A different form of idolatry

There is, however, another form of idolatry that is not nearly as obvious but is much more dangerous. It's a more refined form of idolatry, which constituted an even greater danger for God's chosen people than worshiping before an image of wood or stone. In the Garden of Eden, our first parents did not kneel down before an image. They did something even worse. They rebelled against living *under* God, in the master-and-servant relationship he had designed for them. Because Satan had gotten inside their heads, they wanted to live *alongside* God as his equals, as though they had the right to disagree with him. They wanted to invent or investigate another word besides God's, one which promised happiness and satisfaction and liberty apart from this Father. The word Satan whispered in Eve's ear was a lie right out of hell: "If you listen to me and do what God has forbidden, *you will be like God.*"

But it was never God's plan for Adam and Eve to be gods. A holy God will never tolerate a rival. He cannot and will not permit people to play God. He designed his human creatures to be his children and his servants, finding their joy in doing what pleases him. God had given Adam and Eve a free will, the inborn freedom to do what pleased God, but they were not free to disobey him. God even gave them an opportunity to put their free will into practice. He placed a tree—some kind of fruit tree—right in the middle of the garden, where they couldn't miss it. Every time they walked past that tree—maybe a dozen times a day—they remembered that God had said: "Other trees you use properly by taking their fruit. This one—trust me on this—you use rightly by *not* taking its fruit."

An opportunity for worship

God has been criticized for placing temptation in front of his children, but that criticism is not fair. He had created those two people holy, and his command offered them an opportunity to exercise their holiness. If they had, they would have advanced from their *created innocence* to a state of *self-chosen holiness*. By refusing to eat, they would have been changed to a new and higher level of holiness. They would have reached a stage like that of the holy angels, for whom it is impossible to sin. Martin Luther called that fruit tree in the middle of the garden "Adam's church, his altar, his pulpit." That's where Adam and his beloved were to worship God with glad obedience, which announced: "God, you come first in our thinking and in our actions!"

The heart of sin: unbelief

Satan, however, seduced them into thinking God could not be trusted. Satan is not the jolly king of hell that cartoons and bad jokes picture him to be. He is a terrorist, the sworn enemy of God. He is the twisted, sick mind behind all the evil in the world. In the Garden of Eden, you can see how he works. He persuaded Adam and Eve to rebel against God's command. Satan got them to believe his two lies:

"*God is not good*. He does not have your best interests at heart. If you listen to me, you will be like God."

"*God cannot be trusted*. You will not surely die."

But their sin did not start with their hands. Adam and Eve first doubted God's love, and then they doubted God's Word. Basically their sin was not the stealing of a piece of fruit. Their sin was unbelief.

Disobedience followed

But unbelief never lives in human hearts all by itself. Martin Luther once remarked: "Faith does not just lie on the heart, like foam on beer." Faith becomes active; it shows itself. So does unbelief. We can see that in Adam and Eve. Because they questioned God's love and doubted his promise, living according to the will of their Creator no longer brought them joy and satisfaction. Instead, they looked upon obeying God as humiliating slavery—being forced to obey somebody when you'd rather not. Isn't that strange? Normally God's creatures are happy to be what God has made them. Robins sing to the glory of God, and moles dig holes because that's what the Creator designed them to do. Dogs are happy with their dogginess, and sheep are satisfied with their sheepishness. It's only God's highest creatures who rebel against the role God has assigned for them. God calls that *sin*.

The Hebrew Bible uses several different terms to describe sin. The most common word means *to become guilty*. Another word means *to rebel*. And still another is a word that means *to miss the mark*. Life works only one way, and that's God's way. When God's first two human creatures refused to accept life on God's terms, they *rebelled* against God's good will for them, they *missed God's target* for them, and as a result, they *became guilty*. When God came to visit Adam and Eve in the garden later that day, he had bad news for them. He announced a frightening judgment on their rebellion.

Thoughts are important

Can you see how God's idea of sin is different from the idea of sin most people have? Most people feel: "Thoughts are free! You can't go to jail for what you're thinking!"

God disagrees. He knows that sin doesn't start with your hands; it starts between your ears. In his Sermon on the Mount, Jesus pointed out that a man who looks at a woman with lustful thoughts has committed adultery. Why does God feel that way? For two reasons:

1. God has designed our bodies to be his temples. To trash God's temple with garbage thoughts is something God cannot and will not tolerate.

2. The apostle James points out that sinful thoughts are only the first step in an ugly and frightening three-step process. Sinful thoughts lead to sinful actions. Both of them lead to eternal damnation. "Each of you is tempted when you are dragged away by your own evil desire and enticed. Then, after *desire* has conceived, it gives birth to *sin*; and sin, when it is full-grown, gives birth to *death*" (James 1:14,15 TNIV).

Bad news

When Adam and Eve broke that bond of perfect trust between themselves and God, God did not say: "Well, I disagree, but you have to do what's right for you." He told two people (still humiliated by their first sin), "Dust you are and to dust you will return" (Genesis 3:19). Their perfect life in their lovely garden home had ended. Now "the wages of sin"—death—was staring them in the face. The same is true of every one of their descendants. "Flesh gives birth to flesh," Jesus said (John 3:6). Someone has remarked: "Down through the years the death rate has remained the same: one per person."

This was the first judgment God pronounced on human sin. Adam and Eve were the first to hear this, but not the last. From the moment we were born, each of us has been stamped "PERISHABLE!" It's not only automobiles that can be recalled by their maker.

You and I inherited more from our first parents than just a *body* that is one day going to die. Much worse, we inherited a sinful *nature* that is hostile to God (Romans 8:7). We were born with our backs to God. When we entered the world, we brought with us a restless evil urge to play God. With our *intellect* we dare to challenge God's claim on us. With our *emotions* we don't stand in awe of God, but we find pleasure in doing things that displease God. With our *will* we rebel against God's will in a thousand ugly ways every day.

God's law announces some frightening news about that sinful nature of ours.

We live in a world that has an easy conscience about sin. We put God "on hold"; we drag our feet when God calls. We have short memories of God's mercy to us, we wonder about his threats, we challenge his wisdom as he guides our lives, and we dare to question his love. Day by day we carry on a proud love affair with ourselves (our achievements, our management skills, our good looks, our athletic skills, our sharp minds). All in all, the record each of us has established is enough to break a Father's heart. Deep down inside, each of us knows that.

Our excuses

And yet we try to excuse ourselves. We defend the ungodly attitudes that have just been described. We argue that these attitudes are common, that we're no different from other people. "Hey, no one's perfect! I'm no worse, and maybe a whole lot better, than a lot of people I could name!" Sound familiar?

How easy, how natural it is to compare ourselves with others and to conclude: "I'm not so bad!" You know, if a pig could talk, I suppose it could say the same thing. It might look at the other critters at the feeding trough and announce: "I'm just as clean as any of the others, and a whole lot cleaner than some of them!" But pigs don't set the standard for what it means to be clean. And the standard for a holy life is not determined at the hog pens of this world but at the throne of God. His standard is "Be holy because I, the LORD your God, am holy" (Leviticus 19:1).

And when his first two children ignored the voice of their God, they heard him pronounce a horrible sentence: "Dust you are and to dust you will return." God had said no to human pride. From then on, everything we touch turns to sand.

Final judgment

God is going to have the last word in history, just as he had the first word at creation. He does not treat people like puppets or robots. He pays people the immense compliment of allowing them to live without him if they choose. But the Scriptures of the Old and New Testaments make it very clear: If people choose to live without God in this life, they must also live without him in the next life.

Listen to several of God's Old Testament messengers speak about the day God will return to judge the rebellion and the unbelief of people he created for himself. Through the prophet Joel, God predicted:

> The day of the LORD is coming. "I will show wonders in the heavens and on the earth, blood and fire and billows of smoke. The sun will be turned to darkness and the moon to blood before the coming of the great and dreadful day of the LORD." (Joel 2:1,30,31)

Through the prophet Zephaniah, God once called out to people who argued with his claim on them and laughed at the idea that they were accountable to him:

> The great day of the LORD is near. . . . That day will be a day of wrath, a day of distress and anguish, a day of trouble and ruin. . . . "Wait for me," declares the LORD, "for the day I will stand up to testify. I have decided to assemble the nations, to gather the kingdoms and to pour out my wrath on them—all my fierce anger. The whole world will be consumed by the fire of my jealous anger." (Zephaniah 1:14,15; 3:8)

God means business with the demands of his holy law. Coupled with his absolute demand is his absolute curse over the person, over every person, who does not give God what his law demands. Someone has described our generation by saying: "Our brains are no longer conditioned for reverence and awe." The average person today is pretty sure that if he works hard, pays his bills, and stays out of jail, he doesn't have to be afraid to meet God—if that ever really happens. Is that really so?

The answer to that question is simple. God is perfectly fair, just, and even-handed. Keep his law perfectly, and you have nothing to be afraid of when you meet him. Break it, and in his sight you are a rebel and a terrorist. Criminals do not mix with a majestic and pure God. God's spokesmen to the ancient people of Israel refused to muffle the thunder of God's law:

"You are not a God who takes pleasure in evil; with you the wicked cannot dwell. The arrogant cannot stand in your presence; *you hate all who do wrong*" (Psalm 5:4,5).

"My inheritance has become to me like a lion in the forest. She roars at me; *therefore I hate her*" (Jeremiah 12:8).

"Because of all [Israel's] wickedness . . . *I hated them* there. Because of their sinful deeds, I will drive them out of my house. *I will no longer love them*" (Hosea 9:15).

When God's law convicts us of having rebelled against him, it's as though a noose is pulled tight around our throats. A bag is placed over our heads, and we can almost hear the trapdoor creak beneath our trembling knees. God's law condemns us, and it offers no hope of escape.

God's good news

Day by day in Old Testament times, the harsh message of God's law was an *important* part of the message he gave to his chosen people of Israel. God never intended his law, however, to be his *final* message to the human race. Martin Luther once wrote, "When the Lord wants to make us *happy,* he first of all makes us *sad;* when he wants to make us *rich,* he first of all makes us *poor;* and when he wants to give us *life,* he lets us *die.*"

The reason why God sent messengers to speak to his people throughout the centuries of the Old Testament was not only to *humble* them but to *help* them, not only to *shame* them but to *save* them.

To bring that about, God made sure that his Old Testament people heard another message besides the message of his holy law. That's the message we know as the gospel. Philip Melanchthon, Luther's coworker, said: "There are two parts to the Scripture: the law and the gospel. The law indicates the sickness, the gospel the remedy." Day by day in Old Testament times, God's chosen people lived under law and gospel.

When God created a perfect world, he did so by making use of his almighty power. "By the word of the LORD were the heavens made. . . . For he spoke, and it came to be" (Psalm 33:6,9). Would God use the same method to rescue the sinful world from the consequences of its rebellion? To save a sinner from the awful doom the prophets described, was it enough for God simply to say: "I'm God Almighty. I can do anything I want. I herewith decree: 'That sinner is saved?'" Was it that simple?

No it wasn't. It couldn't be that simple. Five centuries before Christ was born, God announced through the prophet Ezekiel: "The soul who sins is the one who *will die.* . . . The wickedness of the wicked *will be charged against him*" (Ezekiel 18:20).

God is magnificent, sincere, committed, right, and lovely, but he is the enemy of injustice, lies, and liars. His white-hot holiness cannot and will not overlook rebellion any more than the United States government would overlook an attempt by one of its citizens to overthrow it. Sin is an attack on God, and a God who is truly holy cannot tolerate that and remain a holy God. How could God be faithful to both of his two great emotions?

1. His *holy hatred of sin*, his absolute unwillingness to compromise with it.
2. His *burning desire to reach out for sinners*, to restore their family relationship with him.

The problem that God faced

After God's first two children declared their independence from him, he was faced with a problem. How could he be *holy* and *merciful* at the same time? How could he offer mercy without endorsing sin? Could he lower his standards? Could he relax his demands so that Adam and Eve could remain in his family? God's holiness demanded that he punish sin. God's mercy demanded that he love the sinner. How could God do both?

God found the answer to that question. It did not involve using the principle of God's almighty power. The solution God found was not the barter system so common in the pagan religions we meet on the pages of the Old Testament.

Maybe you remember how the barter system worked. About 800 B.C. the people of Israel were considering giving up the worship of the true God in favor of worshiping Baal, the Canaanite god of fertility. At that time the prophet Elijah challenged the Baal priests to a sacred showdown. They and he would each kill a sacrificial animal, place it on an altar, and ask God (god) to send down fire to consume the sacrifice. When their Baal god failed to answer by fire, his priests slashed themselves with swords till the blood flowed. That's what a bartering system is: *If I do this, God will do that.*

A few years later the armies of Israel were involved in a battle with the Moabites, an enemy east of the Jordan. The heathen king of Moab also knew a thing or two about bartering with his pagan gods: "When the king of Moab saw that the battle had gone against him . . . he took his firstborn son, who was to succeed him as king, and offered him as a sacrifice on the city wall" (2 Kings 3:26,27).

The solution God found

The Bible teaches that you and I have nothing we could bring to the bargaining table. This is what made the Hebrew religion of the Old Testament different from any other religion in the ancient world. The costly solution God worked out to solve the conflict between his holiness and his mercy involved the *principle of substitution*. God would arrange to have a perfect substitute *trade places* with sinners under his condemnation.

Substitution at the time of Abraham

From their earliest history, God taught his people this important principle on which their eternal happiness would depend. On Mount Moriah, God taught this principle to the father of the Israelite nation. Instead of permitting Abraham to take the life of his son, God provided a substitute: "Abraham looked up and there in a thicket he saw a ram caught by its horns. He went over and took the ram and sacrificed it as a burnt offering instead of his son" (Genesis 22:13).

Substitution at the time of the exodus

Five hundred years later, at another critical time in the history of the Israelites, God again provided a substitute to bring blessings to his people. After spending several centuries in Egypt, "the Israelites groaned in their slavery and cried out, and their cry for help . . . went up to God" (Exodus 2:23). To force the Egyptian king to release his Israelite slaves (and also to unmask the impotence of the Egyptian gods), God sent ten plagues, ten terrible tragedies, over the land of Egypt. God let Moses know that the tenth of these plagues would be the worst:

> About midnight I will go throughout Egypt. Every firstborn son in Egypt will die, from the firstborn son of Pharaoh, who sits on the throne, to the firstborn son of the slave girl, who is at her hand mill, and all the firstborn of the cattle as well. There will be loud wailing throughout Egypt—worse than there has ever been or ever will be again." (Exodus 11:4-6)

To guarantee that the angel of death would not enter any Israelite home, God instructed his people to kill a lamb. They were to catch its blood in a basin and to smear the blood on the outer doorframes of their houses. The blood was the saving marker. That same night they were to eat the meat roasted over the fire. They ate that Passover meal fully dressed, with sandals on their feet and staffs in their hands, ready to leave on their nighttime journey at a moment's notice.

That night the God who had made a solemn covenant with Abraham's descendants entered every unmarked home in Egypt on a deadly mission. He *passed over* those homes that were protected by the blood of the sacrificial lamb. On the night that marked Israel's

birth as a nation, an animal substitute died so that God's people could be spared. For 1,500 years each family slaughtered a lamb to commemorate that night of terror and liberty. Then John the Baptist pointed to Jesus of Nazareth and shouted, "Look, the [two-legged] Lamb of God, who takes away the sin of the world!" (John 1:29).

Substitution in Israel's worship and the scapegoat

Israel's worship life offered an excellent opportunity for God to teach his people this important principle of substitution. When God drew up the blueprint for Israel's public worship, he made animal sacrifices an important part of it. These sacrifices were of different kinds—*burnt* offerings, *fellowship* offerings, *sin* offerings, and *guilt* offerings. (The specific emphasis of each of these will be discussed in the next chapter.) Although there were important differences in these offerings, all four were similar in that they were all blood sacrifices.

God taught his people that sin is not something to be taken lightly. Sin is not just an error in judgment, which we could have avoided if we had only taken time to count to 10. At his sanctuary day after day, God impressed upon his people that sin separates the sinner from his God. Day after day the truth was acted out before the eyes of God's people: *Sin costs a life.* A worshiping Israelite, for example, who desired personal assurance of his forgiveness, could bring a lamb or a goat or a bull calf as a sin offering. That animal substitute had to forfeit its life, as a type or symbol of another Lamb, who on a skull-shaped altar many years later would offer his life as our substitute. Century after century, every one of the tens of thousands of animals slain and sacrificed on Jewish altars announced all over again and again, "The life of a creature is in the blood, and I have given it to you to make atonement for yourselves on the altar; it is the blood that makes atonement for one's life" (Leviticus 17:11).

God taught his people the principle of substitution. He wanted them to understand that he forgives sins by transferring the punishment for sin from guilty sinners to an innocent substitute. This explains the statement the apostle made in the epistle to the Hebrews: "Without the shedding of blood there is no forgiveness" (Hebrews 9:22).

For 1,500 years the Hebrew people acted out Jesus' substitutionary death on the cross with their animal sacrifices. The high point of their sacrificial system was reached in the fall of each year on the *Day of Atonement* (*Yom Kippur*, "yome kip-POOR"). Here again a holy God impressed on his people that it was only through the principle of substitution that he could receive rebel sinners back into his family. The elaborate liturgy for the great Day of Atonement is described in Leviticus chapter 16. It is worth your while to read the details there.

In one especially vivid part of that pre-Christ liturgy, a bull was killed and offered as a sin offering for the sin of Aaron, the high priest. Aaron took a bowl of the animal's blood and entered the Most Holy Place—that innermost room of the tabernacle where the ark of the covenant rested. He dipped his hand into the bowl and sprinkled blood seven times on the golden cover of the ark. He sprinkled blood seven more times in front of the ark.

Then Aaron stepped outside and set aside two goats. The first was killed and offered up as a sin offering, this time for the sins of the people. Aaron entered the Most Holy Place again with the goat's blood and sprinkled it, just as he had done with the blood of the bull.

Can you imagine what Aaron's hands looked like when he stepped back outside the tabernacle? He had dipped them into that bowl of blood at least 28 times, and they were red with blood. Then the second goat was brought to him.

"He is to *lay both hands on the head of the live goat* and confess over it all the wickedness and rebellion of the Israelites—all their sins—and put them on the goat's head. He shall send the goat away into the desert in the care of a man appointed for the task. The goat will carry on itself all their sins to a solitary place; and the man shall release it in the desert." (Leviticus 16:21,22)

This was the so-called *scapegoat*. As it was led off into the desert and left there to die, the worshipers could see blood on its head, the blood of the sin offering, symbolizing their blood-red guilt before God. That guilt had now been transferred to a substitute. The scapegoat was a living picture of how, in God's marvelous plan, God would transfer the sin of the world to an innocent substitute, who would carry it and suffer its penalty.

Here is the very heart of the gospel. Day by day in Old Testament times, God's chosen people lived under the law and the gospel. God moved through the pages of Old Testament history in judgment and in mercy as he worked ceaselessly to win people to his way—the Jesus way. He wanted people for his family and for his eternal home. "We have been made holy through the sacrifice of the body of Jesus Christ once for all" (Hebrews 10:10).

The heart of the Old Testament

No Old Testament writer described this more clearly than the prophet Isaiah. And nowhere did Isaiah express these twin truths of law and gospel more beautifully than in chapter 53 of the prophecy that bears his name. Writing seven centuries before the promised Messiah came to earth, Isaiah described Christ's substitutionary work in a way that has never been equaled:

Surely he took up our infirmities and carried our sorrows, yet we considered him stricken by God, smitten by him, and afflicted. But he was pierced for our transgressions, he was crushed for our iniquities; the punishment that brought us peace was upon him, and by his wounds we are healed. We all, like sheep, have gone astray, each of us has turned to his own way; and the LORD has laid on him the iniquity of us all. (Isaiah 53:4-6)

Because in our place our substitute *lived a life of perfect obedience* to the holy law of God, God considers us to be people who have given him the perfect obedience he demands. Because in our place our substitute *died innocently under God's curse*, God considers us to have been punished for our sin.

And the result? Those joined intimately to Jesus Christ in Holy Baptism go from being condemned orphans without hope to being God's adopted children without fear. What he has becomes ours; what we have becomes his. What a God!

Day by day in Old Testament times, God's chosen people lived under the law and the gospel. The sacred secrets that God shared with ancient Israel centered on those two important truths, which seem to contradict each other:

1. The *law* announces: "God *hates* all sin and all sinners."
2. The *gospel* announces: "God forgives all sin and *loves* all sinners."

These two truths are the very heart of what God has to say to people. They are found in both the Old and the New Testaments. It is incorrect to call the Old Testament a *law* book and the New Testament a *gospel* book. Law and gospel are taught in both the Old and the New Testaments. There is no way you can harmonize these two basic truths of the Scripture. God's Old Testament believers didn't try. They simply accepted them both.

"Abraham believed God, and it was credited to him as righteousness." . . . He did not waver through unbelief regarding the promise of God, but was strengthened in his faith and gave glory to God, being fully persuaded that God had power to do what he had promised. This is why "it was credited to him as righteousness." The words "it was credited to him" were written not for him alone, but also for us, to whom God will credit righteousness—for us who believe in him who raised Jesus our Lord from the dead. He was delivered over to death for our sins and was raised to life for our justification. (Romans 4:3,20-25)

The Christian today must learn to live under the constant tension between the message of God's law and the message of his gospel. Martin Luther made the interesting comment about law and gospel: "Where one is missing, the other is wrong."

Siegbert W. Becker, in *The Foolishness of God*, describes it thus:

The purpose of the law is to make us feel guilty, to humiliate us, to kill us, to lead us to hell, and to take everything from us. The purpose of the gospel is to declare us not guilty and to make us possessors of all things. Between the two of them, they manage to kill us to life.

The LORD, who brought you up out of Egypt . . . is the one you must worship. To him you shall bow down and to him offer sacrifices.

~ 2 KINGS 17:36

God's Path of Worship

Worship is an important part of your life, and that's as it should be. You realize what an awesome God the true God is. When the roar of his thunder pounds your eardrums, or when the curse of God's holy law cuts deep into your heart, you tremble before his majesty. When you hold a tiny baby in your arms, you can't help smiling at this miniature human being—a miracle of God's wisdom and of his almighty power. Best of all, you marvel at God's amazing love—a love that, at a frightful cost, reached out to find you. In Jesus Christ, God put his arms around you. The result of all this is that you worship God not because you're *afraid* of what might happen if you don't, not because you hope to *persuade* God to love you, but only *because of who God is*—your Father, who loved you even before he created the world.

Family worship

It's always been that way with God's people. As far as we know, our first parents, Adam and Eve, didn't have formal worship services as we do. Day by day they simply shared all of life with God. It doesn't get any better than that. Genesis chapter 4 names Adam and Eve's children as the first ones who worshiped God by bringing sacrifices to him. Cain, their firstborn, brought his offering from the produce of the field. Abel, his younger brother, brought his offering from the first and best of his flock. Their offerings were like the *grain offering* later prescribed by God at Sinai to give worshipers a way to express their thanks to him for his gifts.

We have no way of knowing whether God had directed Cain and Abel to place offerings on an altar and offer them to him by fire. Martin Luther was inclined to think that God had commanded the family of Adam and Eve to worship him with burnt offerings. Some Bible scholars have suggested that if the manner of worship had been left up to each worshiper, it's unlikely that the two brothers would have happened to choose the same form. What we do know for sure is that God was pleased with Abel and with the offering he brought but God was not pleased with Cain and with his offering.

According to Hebrews 11:4, Abel was a child of God who trusted in the Savior whom God had promised; the offering he brought was a fruit of that faith. Cain, on the other hand, "belonged to the evil one" (1 John 3:12). Since Cain was not a believing child of God, his motivation for worship must have been self-serving. Cain's act of worship was no more than just going through the motions, and God was not pleased with it. Abel's life of humble faith rebuked Cain's self-righteousness and his low opinion of God's grace, and in a fit of anger Cain murdered his brother. To take the place of their two lost sons, God gave Adam and Eve another son, Seth (which means "substitute").

Cainites and Sethites

Genesis chapter 4 gives us a brief description of both the Cainite and the Sethite branches of the family of Adam and Eve. Unfortunately, the descendants of Cain followed their ancestor and turned their backs on the Savior. They imagined they could be happy apart from God. Since they were living independently of God, they tried to find happiness in life by making their day-to-day existence more pleasant. We're told that the Cainites raised livestock, made musical instruments, wrote the first poetry recorded in the Scripture, and were skilled in working with metals. That was cultural progress—sort of. Tragically, however, Cain's descendants did not allow God to play an important part in their lives, and after a few generations they disappeared from the Bible record.

The situation with the Sethites is the exact opposite. Genesis chapter 4 describes the Sethites in just a single verse, but that one verse says a lot: "Seth also had a son, and he named him Enosh. At that time [people] began to *call on the name of the LORD*" (Genesis 4:26). When we today use the expression "to call on the name of the LORD," we're referring to the practice of prayer. This, however, cannot be the meaning of that expression when it's used of Seth's descendants. They did not begin the practice of prayer. Seth had learned that godly habit from his parents. What was it that began in the second generation after Adam and Eve?

The first public worship

A footnote in the New International Version offers an alternate (and better) translation of Genesis 4:26: "At that time [people] began to *proclaim* the name of the LORD." Note the spelling of the name: LORD. Remember that when the divine name is spelled with all capital letters, it indicates a translation of the name Yahweh, God's Old Testament Savior name. At the time of Adam's grandson Enosh, the Sethites no longer worshiped only privately as a family, but they proclaimed the Savior's reputation publicly. They spread the marvelous news of the great good plan God had announced to their first parents in the Garden of Eden. One of Eve's descendants would come and hunt down the serpent Satan and crush his head but not before being struck down dead himself.

Public worship at the time of Noah

Genesis chapter 8 tells us what happened when Noah and the seven members of his family stepped out of the ark that had been their home for more than a year. The first thing Noah did was build an altar. It is the first altar mentioned in the Bible. (Cain and Abel had most likely used the ground as their altars.) Noah led his family in worship by taking one of each of the clean animals (those God had designated as acceptable for food and for sacrifice) and offering them as a *burnt offering*. He offered them to the "LORD," the merciful Savior-God.

What truth was Noah expressing with this act of public worship? He offered a *blood sacrifice*, which cost the life of the animal victim. This indicates that Noah was humbly confessing: "Our fellowship with God rests upon the atoning work of the promised Savior, who alone can make sinful people acceptable to God." He sacrificed the *entire animal*. With this Noah was declaring: "We consecrate ourselves totally to God."

Scripture is silent about whether or not God had specifically commanded the form of worship Noah followed. The same is true of the altars Abraham, Isaac, and Jacob built as places to offer sacrifices and to proclaim the reputation of the God who had made a covenant with them. At a time when the Canaanites still occupied Palestine and the land was cluttered with their heathen altars, Abraham built altars to the true God. He built altars at Shechem, in the center of the land (Genesis 12:6,7); at Bethel, 20 miles farther south (Genesis 12:8); and at Hebron, 30 miles still farther south (Genesis 13:18). Abraham's son Isaac did the same (Genesis 26:23,25), as did Isaac's son Jacob (Genesis 33:20; 35:7).

The situation changed several centuries later after the slavery years in Egypt. As Israel prepared to begin its life in its new homeland, God recognized that the pagan worship surrounding his people on all sides presented a deadly danger for them. At Mount Sinai, therefore, he gave them a detailed blueprint for their worship. These worship forms were carefully designed for a land once belonging to pagan Canaanites.

Pagans worshiped many gods

The worship of one God is a common way people worship today. It wasn't that way in Bible times. Back then it was taken for granted that every country had its own gods. The idolatry that was practiced by the people with whom the ancient Israelites came into contact provided a deadly temptation for the Old Testament people of God. During the centuries they spent in Egypt, for example, the Israelites were exposed to the worship of many different gods. And a couple months after God led his people out of Egypt, Moses' brother Aaron—Israel's high priest, no less—made a golden image of a calf. Worse yet, he gave this idol the credit for delivering the people of Israel from slavery! "These are your gods, O Israel, who brought you up out of Egypt" (Exodus 32:4). And then, with his very next breath, Aaron announced, "Tomorrow there will be a festival *to the* Lord" (verse 5).

Israel's heathen neighbors simply took for granted that different gods controlled different aspects of human life. Day by day the idolatry surrounding the Israelites was a constant temptation for them to abandon their total trust in the coming Savior. If this happened, they would lose their identity as God's chosen people.

Baal worship

When Israel marched across the Jordan River, they entered a land occupied for centuries by pagan Canaanites. Several new dangers now faced the people of God. The Canaanites had built fortified cities on the coastal plain, in the fertile valleys, and in the central highlands. But it was Canaanite religion that presented the greatest threat to God's people—an unholy combination of mysticism, magic, and sex. Canaan annually went without rain for almost half of the year. The Canaanites, therefore, worshiped Baal, a god who they believed sent the rain and who granted fertility to crops, herds, and families. And how did one persuade Baal to send the rain needed to stay alive?

The Canaanites observed that rain fell from the sky and watered the earth so that things grew. They compared human sexuality to what happened between the earth and the sky. They believed that Mother Earth and Father Sky were gods who could be induced to copulate in the realm of nature if only their human worshipers would do the same. Thus sex of every kind was encouraged as worship.*

Baal worship presented a seductive threat to God's people. *Baal* was the storm god; his sister/spouse *Asherah* was the mother-goddess. *Sacred stones* and *Asherah poles* were erotic representations of the human organs of reproduction (male and female, respectively). Canaanite priests and worshipers engaged in ritual sex with "holy" prostitutes (male and female, homosexual as well as heterosexual) in what they called "sacred marriage." Canaanite worship, consisting of religious orgies, acted out the reproduction theme in an attempt to persuade Baal and Asherah to follow their example and make it possible for a woman to bear a child, a cow to calve, and a farmer's field to produce the crops people needed to stay alive.

Misguided Baal worshipers even offered up their children as human sacrifices (2 Chronicles 28:3). Or they would slash their bodies with knives in an attempt to attract Baal's attention and convince him to notice their intense zeal, pity them, and perhaps answer their prayers (1 Kings 18:28).

God's reaction to Baalism: a promise

God is fiercely intolerant of the worship of other gods. Day by day in Old Testament times, he claimed the absolute, undivided loyalty of all people: "I am the LORD; that is my name! I will not give my glory to another or my praise to idols" (Isaiah 42:8).

As God's chosen people entered their new homeland and observed how the previous occupants had permitted their filthy idolatry to determine how they practiced agriculture, God first of all gave his people a promise:

"If you faithfully . . . love the LORD your God and [serve] him with all your heart and with all your soul—then *I will send rain* on your land in its season, both autumn and spring rains, so that you may gather in your grain, new wine and oil. *I will provide grass* in the fields for your cattle, and you will eat and be satisfied. Be careful, or you will be enticed to turn away and worship other gods and bow down to them. Then the LORD's anger will burn against you, and he will shut the heavens so that it will not rain and the ground will yield no produce, and you will soon perish from the good land the LORD is giving you." (Deuteronomy 11:13-17)

With these words the God who had entered into a solemn covenant with Israel promised his people that he alone—not Baal—could and would grant the blessing of fertility to family, to field, and to flock. Life is God's creation and his wonderful gift.

God's reaction to Baalism: a command

God did not allow his people to think: "We're newcomers here in Canaan. If we want to be successful farmers, we'd better learn from the people who have farmed this

*John C. Lawrenz, Judges, Ruth, *The People's Bible commentary series, page 25.*

land for centuries." At Mount Sinai God gave his people a command for what they were to do whenever and wherever they confronted the perverted religion of Baal worship: "*Break down* their altars, *smash* their sacred stones and *cut down* their Asherah poles. Do not worship any other god, for the LORD, whose name is Jealous, is a jealous God" (Exodus 34:13,14).

If a physician examines you and discovers that a cancer has attached itself to one of your body's vital organs, he knows your life is in danger. That cancerous cell has gone berserk and is growing by eating away the organ it's attached to. The doctor knows the deadly tumor has to be cut out. Similarly, God knew that the Canaanite fertility cult was a cancer, which if allowed to remain would attack and destroy the faith of his people. And so God's command was blunt and unmistakably clear: "Break down . . . smash . . . cut down" (Exodus 34:13; Deuteronomy 12:3).

God's intolerance

Before his people entered their new homeland, God made it clear that the truth he had shared with them was not just one of many legitimate ways to approach God. It was the *only* way to approach the only true God. Any other approach to worshiping God was a lie. It could only lead people away from the true faith based on God's promise made in Eden to his fallen children. False worship was to be eliminated. God made his will perfectly clear: "Whoever sacrifices to any god other than the LORD must be destroyed" (Exodus 22:20). People who worshiped a false god showed that they scorned their identity as people of the promise. By so doing, they forfeited their right to live.

God's blueprint for Israel's worship

When Abraham's descendants entered Canaan, the land that would be their new homeland, God did more than simply to forbid them to worship false gods. He designed a path of worship for his chosen people. He specified their place of worship, their worship leaders, their service of worship. Christians living in the New Testament might have a hard time understanding this. We have much more freedom in worshiping God than the Israelites had. We can choose the *place* where we worship and the *times* when we gather to worship God. We can decide what *form* our worship will take. For the descendants of Abraham, God made all of those decisions. He instructed his people exactly where and how he wanted to be worshiped, down to the last detail. Remember what was riding on this: keeping this family of faith intact until Christ would come to trade places with sinners under God's curse.

One place of worship

History tells us that people have always been attracted to high mountain shrines and wooded groves as places of worship. The Canaanite tribes whom the Israelites dispossessed worshiped their gods at many different locations all across the land, "on the high mountains and on the hills and under every spreading tree" (Deuteronomy 12:2).

The centralization of Israel's worship stands in sharp contrast to this. Before God's chosen people ever set foot in their new homeland, God made it clear to them: "You must not worship the LORD your God in their way. But you are to seek the place the LORD your God will choose . . . to put his Name there for his dwelling. To that place you must go; there bring your burnt offerings and sacrifices" (Deuteronomy 12:4-6).

Until King David captured the city of Jerusalem and made it the political and religious center of the nation, the Lord chose various localities as temporary worship sites for the Israelites. The first place God designated was Gilgal, Israel's first campsite after crossing the Jordan River (Joshua 4:19,20). It was at Gilgal that they celebrated their first Passover on the soil of Palestine (5:10). For many years God's house of worship was located at Shiloh, about 20 miles north of Jerusalem (Joshua 18:1; 1 Samuel 1:3). And finally, when King Solomon built the beautiful temple in Jerusalem, that became the permanent center of Israel's worship. In Psalm 122 the poet sang: "I rejoiced with those who said to me, 'Let us go to the house of the LORD.' Our feet are standing in your gates, O Jerusalem. That is where the tribes go up, the tribes of the LORD, to praise the name of the LORD" (verses 1,2,4).

The tabernacle

When Moses climbed up Mount Sinai to receive God's law, God gave him instructions for building the *tabernacle*, Israel's first house of worship. The tabernacle was a large tent, 15 feet by 45 feet, made of sheets of linen cloth embroidered in bright colors of blue, purple, and scarlet. Actually it was *four* tents, one inside the next. Over the linen inner tent was a covering of black goat's hair; over that was a covering of ram skins dyed red; and over that was a covering of the hides of sea cows (Exodus 26:1-14). Surrounding this large tent was a courtyard, 75 feet by 150 feet, enclosed by curtains.

Since only the priests were permitted to enter the tabernacle, it was in this courtyard that the Old Testament people of God gathered to worship the Lord.

In pure mercy God, who is present everywhere and whom the heavens cannot contain, condescended to establish an earthly dwelling place among his people. Two things about the tabernacle should be noted in particular:

1. It was perfectly suited to Israel's desert wandering.
2. Every detail of its design and furnishings taught the Israelites something about the sinner's relationship with the holy God who had made the Savior-promise to Abraham.

A portable sanctuary

During 40 years of wandering in the desert, the Israelites camped in at least 40 different places that we know of (Numbers 33:1-48). When the pillar of cloud and of fire, which guided the Israelites during their desert wandering, would signal: "Stop here!" members of the tribe of Levi would get to work. One group would fit together the tabernacle framework—posts and crossbars made of acacia wood and overlaid with gold—in the very center of the camp. Over this framework a second Levite clan would then set up the tent and its coverings. A third would put the furnishings and equipment in place (Numbers 3:25-37). And then the fiery cloud symbolizing the Lord's presence could be seen entering the tabernacle. With that fiery cloud, which the people knew as "the *glory of the LORD*" (Exodus 16:10), God reassured his people that he was present among them with all his grace and his favor. Because sin separates a person from God, the Israelites could not approach God by themselves. And so God came to his people.

"Have them make a sanctuary for me, and *I will dwell among them*" (Exodus 25:8). The tabernacle was a faint foreshadowing of the time when the Son of God took on a human body in the womb of a Jewish peasant girl and "made his dwelling among us" (John 1:14). It also foreshadowed still another time in the more distant future when, in a new heaven and a new earth, we will hear the wondrous words: "God's dwelling place is now among the people, and *he will dwell with them*. They will be his people, and God himself will be with them and be their God" (Revelation 21:3 TNIV).

Tabernacle furnishings: the altar

When an Old Testament worshiper entered the enclosed courtyard, he saw the *altar of burnt offering* and, off to the right, a big *bronze basin* for the priests' ceremonial washing. That altar was big; it had a surface area of more than 55 square feet for the animal sacrifices. To teach his people what a serious thing sin is, God announced: "Without the shedding of blood there is no forgiveness" (Hebrews 9:22).

Day after day, as part of their worship, the Old Testament people of God brought goats and bulls and lambs as blood sacrifices and offered them up on that altar of burnt offering. When they brought their sacrifices, they did so for one of two reasons:

1. to give expression to the fellowship they enjoyed with God.
2. to restore that fellowship when it had been broken.

The worshiper would kill the animal, and the priest would sprinkle its blood against the altar. The Levites would cut apart the carcass and wash the pieces. Then the priest would offer all or part of the meat by fire to the Lord.

The Holy Place

Day by day when the priest entered the tabernacle to pray to God for the people, he entered a room known as the Holy Place. On the hem of his robe he had little golden bells to enable the worshipers, who were standing outside in the courtyard and couldn't see the priest, to follow his activities. In the Holy Place was the golden *lampstand*, which resembled a stylized tree with seven branches. Each morning the wicks on the seven oil lamps were trimmed and the lamps filled with olive oil. Each evening the lamps were lighted and would burn through the night to symbolize that the Israelites enjoyed uninterrupted fellowship with their God. Even during the hours when the tabernacle was closed down and the people were sleeping, God was awake and alert to their needs.

Opposite the golden lampstand was a table of wood overlaid with gold. Every Sabbath 12 loaves of freshly baked bread (*bread of the Presence*) were placed on this table. This symbolized that the 12 tribes of Israel were constantly in the presence of the Lord. Their needs and their well-being were a matter of constant concern to him.

"Make an altar . . . for burning incense," God had told Moses on Mount Sinai (Exodus 30:1). Against the curtain that formed the far wall of the Holy Place was a small golden *altar of incense*. Every morning the priest would approach this altar and kindle incense on it with fire taken from the altar of burnt offering. All day long priests would approach this incense altar with the prayers and the praises of God's people. God wanted his people to understand that, just as clouds of fragrant smoke rose from the burning incense, so their prayers were pleasing to him, for the sake of Christ, and were heard and answered by him.

The Most Holy Place

The innermost room in the tabernacle was the Most Holy Place, a perfect 15-foot cube. Separating the Holy Place from the Most Holy was a thick *curtain* of blue and purple and scarlet yarn with figures of cherubim embroidered on it. Since the Most Holy was God's earthly dwelling place, that curtain announced: "The sinner's way to God is blocked by sin!" Sin separates God's people from him. God is the sworn enemy of anything that destroys his people. That is not good news for people.

If the Lord had left things as they were, that curtain would have announced: "Sinner, there's distance between you and God!" But the path of worship God designed for his Old Testament people announced another message. Once a year the high priest, carrying the blood of a sin offering, could pass through that curtain. As he stepped into God's earthly presence, God was announcing: "I will accept the death of a substitute!"

This is the curtain that was ripped in two from top to bottom when Jesus died on Calvary (Mark 15:37,38). By living the perfect life we sinners owed and by dying the accursed death we sinners had coming, Jesus brought separated sinners and God together again. By tearing that great curtain, God announced to every sinner on the planet: "Instead of a barrier, there's now accord between you and me!"

There was only one piece of sacred furniture in the Most Holy Place, and that was the *ark of the covenant*. That was a wooden chest overlaid with gold, with a cover of pure gold (remember *Raiders of the Lost Ark*?). This chest—about as big as a wardrobe trunk—contained the two stone tablets inscribed with the Ten Commandments, the staff that confirmed the priesthood of Aaron, and a jar of the manna by which God fed Israel in the desert.

God also told Moses: "Make an *atonement cover* of pure gold . . . and make two *cherubim* out of hammered gold at the ends of the cover" (Exodus 25:17,18). *Atonement* is not an everyday word for most of us. Actually it's a made-up word. Through the death of our great substitute, God brought people who had been separated from him by their sin back *at one* with him. "At–one–ment" becomes *atonement*. It's another way of describing the reconciliation between God and the sinner that resulted from the blood sacrifice on Calvary.

The atonement cover, with the two golden cherubim (angels) welded to it, was to symbolize the earthly throne of the heavenly God. In 1 Samuel 4:4, the Lord is described as "enthroned between the cherubim." This atonement cover is sometimes referred to as God's "throne of grace." Here the high priest, representative of the sinful people, would approach God with the blood of sacrifice to make atonement for the sin of the people.

The temple building project

For more than 450 years, the tabernacle served as the sanctuary of the Israelites, God's earthly dwelling place among his chosen people. During those years, leaders like Joshua led the armies of Israel in breaking Canaanite resistance in the new homeland. Later King David conquered the enemies that surrounded God's people on all sides. He established Jerusalem as his capital and built a beautiful new palace there. Then he had a dream—a dream he shared with the prophet Nathan, who was also his pastor: "Here I am, living in a palace of cedar, while the ark of God remains in a tent" (2 Samuel 7:2).

David wanted to build a permanent house for the Lord. The Lord, however, had other plans. David had been a man of war; his hands had been stained with blood. God therefore announced that David's son Solomon, a man of peace, would build a temple for the Lord. And that's what happened:

> David gave his son Solomon the plans for the portico of the temple, its buildings, its storerooms, its upper parts, its inner rooms and the place of atonement. He gave him the plans of all that the Spirit had put in his mind for the courts of the temple of the LORD and all the surrounding rooms, for the treasuries of the temple of God. . . . He gave him instructions for the divisions of the priests and Levites, and for all the work of serving in the temple of the LORD, as well as for all the articles to be used in its service. (1 Chronicles 28:11-13)

The 40 years of King Solomon's reign favored the temple building project for several reasons:

1. Israel enjoyed prosperity, wealth, and peace such as it had never attained before and would never see again.
2. God saw to it that just at that time the king of Phoenicia, Israel's neighbor to

the north along the Mediterranean seacoast, was a man named Hiram. He had been a friend of King David with whom David had discussed plans for the proposed temple.

Solomon, therefore, contacted King Hiram to order the timber and the stone he would need for the temple building project: "Send me cedar logs as you did for my father David when you sent him cedar to build a palace to live in. Now I am about to build a temple for the Name of the LORD my God" (2 Chronicles 2:3,4).

Since Phoenicia's mountainous country was great for growing forests of tall coniferous trees but ill suited for agriculture, it depended on Palestine for its food supply. Hiram was happy to make a deal with Solomon: "I'll give you all the timber you need, in return for food." According to 1 Kings 5:10,11, Solomon offered an annual payment of 125,000 bushels of wheat and 115,000 gallons of olive oil.

King Hiram eagerly responded: "Let my Lord send . . . the wheat and barley and the olive oil and wine he promised, and we will cut all the logs from Lebanon that you need and will float them in rafts by sea to Joppa. You can then take them up to Jerusalem" (2 Chronicles 2:15,16).

Each month Solomon sent shifts of ten thousand Israelites to help the Phoenicians cut and dress the timber, which was then floated down the Mediterranean coast to Joppa (40 miles west of Jerusalem). In addition, Solomon also sent 150,000 resident aliens as slave laborers to Phoenicia to work as stonecutters and carriers (1 Kings 5:13-18; 2 Chronicles 2:17,18).

Solomon's temple

We read that "Solomon began to build the temple of the LORD in Jerusalem on Mount Moriah" (2 Chronicles 3:1). It was the same mountain on which the Lord, ten centuries earlier, had asked Abraham to offer up his son Isaac.

> In the four hundred and eightieth year after the Israelites had come out of Egypt, in the fourth year of Solomon's reign over Israel, . . . he began to build the temple of the LORD. In building the temple, only blocks dressed at the quarry were used, and no hammer, chisel or any other iron tool was heard at the temple site while it was being built." (1 Kings 6:1,7)

Because of all the preparations David had made, the huge building project was completed in seven years (1 Kings 6:38).

Unlike the tabernacle, a tent made of sheets of linen and covered with animal skins, *Solomon's temple* was an impressive structure of stone and wood and precious metals. But both shared the same basic design and the same furnishings. The temple had the same two rooms as the tabernacle—the *Holy Place* and the *Most Holy Place*—except that they were twice as large as in the tabernacle and lavishly decorated. The ceilings, walls, and floor of the Most Holy Place, for example, were made of cedar that was overlaid with gold. Twenty-three tons of gold were used just for the Most Holy Place, a 30-foot cube (2 Chronicles 3:8)!

Built out from the side walls of the temple were three stories of meeting rooms, apartments for the priests, and storage rooms for the sacred vessels. In the surrounding courtyard stood the huge *altar of burnt offering* (30' x 30'), facing the entrance to the temple. Instead of a portable basin holding water for the priests' and Levites' ceremonial washing, the temple courtyard had an immense *Sea of bronze*, holding 11,500 gallons. Ten movable bronze carts, each with a capacity of 230 gallons, held water for washing the pieces of sacrificial meat before they were placed on the altar (1 Kings 7:27,38).

The temple building project took seven years to complete. At its dedication, the Israelites might have been tempted to be proud of this new, impressive national monument. God therefore reminded Solomon what the true purpose of the temple was: "As for this temple you are building, if you . . . keep all my commands and obey them, I will fulfill through you the promise I gave to David your father. And *I will live among the Israelites* and will not abandon my people Israel" (1 Kings 6:12,13).

The temple was important because it served as God's earthly dwelling place. Here he would meet regularly with his people. Through sacrifice and proclamation and song he would explain his great plan for reconciling a world a world of sinners to himself.

Destruction of Solomon's temple

The temple of Solomon stood for about four hundred years. And then in 587 B.C. God permitted the armies of Babylon, superpower of that day, to invade Palestine, surround Jerusalem, and destroy the temple. The prophet Jeremiah lived in Jerusalem at that time. Listen to him choke back the sobs as he described what happened:

> How deserted lies the city, once so full of people! How like a widow is she, who once was great among the nations! . . . Her foes have become her masters. . . . The LORD has brought her grief because of her many sins. Her children have gone into

exile, captive before the foe. . . . Jerusalem has sinned greatly and so has become unclean. . . . The enemy laid hands on all her treasures; she saw pagan nations enter her sanctuary. . . . How the Lord has covered the Daughter of Zion with the cloud of his anger! He has hurled down the splendor of Israel from heaven to earth; he has not remembered his footstool in the day of his anger. . . . He has laid waste his dwelling like a garden; he has destroyed his place of meeting. . . . The LORD has rejected his altar and abandoned his sanctuary. (Lamentations 1,2)

Somebody has said: "You can't break the Ten Commandments. You can only break yourself against them." In pure love God had made a covenant—a solemn contract with Abraham and his descendants: he would be their God, and they would be his special people. The Savior would come from their bodies. But the reverse side of God's love is his hatred of evil. Israel's kings and its citizens made it clear to God that they really weren't interested in being his people. When they refused to live under his will and insisted on living independently of him, the holy God responded. He permitted the Babylonian army to break down the city walls of ancient Jerusalem, to steal anything that was loose on both ends, and then to torch the city. Listen to a Hebrew poet pour out his heart to the Lord about what he witnessed:

Your foes roared in the place where you met with us; they set up their standards as signs. They behaved like men wielding axes to cut through a thicket of trees. They smashed all the carved paneling with their axes and hatchets. They burned your sanctuary to the ground; they defiled the dwelling place of your Name. (Psalm 74:4-7)

After the Babylonians were finished, the top of Mount Moriah, where Solomon's magnificent temple had stood, looked like a big barbecue pit. And it remained like that during the years of the exile, when what was left of the people of Jerusalem and Judah had been shipped in chains to Babylon, a thousand miles away from home.

The second temple

Usually when an ancient nation was defeated in battle and led off into captivity, that was the end of that nation. That was, however, not God's plan for Israel. Remember the promise of the Savior! Through the prophet Isaiah, God had promised that his people would return from Babylon; and they did. In 539 B.C., about 50 years after Babylon's armies had destroyed Jerusalem, the Persian Empire replaced Babylon as the superpower in the Middle East. Persia's King Cyrus, an enlightened ruler, authorized the Jewish exiles to return to their homeland. He even directed that the temple in Jerusalem be rebuilt with funds from the royal treasury. Can you guess what the first thing was that the little remnant of returning exiles did when they got back to Jerusalem? They laid the foundation for a new temple!

Construction delays

But then several problems arose that brought the building project to a standstill. The *Samaritans* were in the land. These "new" neighbors, of mixed ancestry and religion, became angry when the Jews refused their offer of help in building the temple. They wrote a letter to the Persian authorities accusing the Jews of planning revolt, and they managed to shut down the building project for 16 years.

An even worse problem arose among the returned exiles. Life was hard for them, and they began to give their personal needs priority over building the Lord's house. Now there are many things the Lord will put up with in the human heart, but second place is not one of them. Through the prophet Haggai, the Lord called his people to repent:

> This is what the LORD Almighty says: "These people say, 'The time has not yet come for the LORD's house to be built.' . . . Is it a time for you yourselves to be living in your paneled houses, while this house remains a ruin? . . . Give careful thought to your ways. You have planted much, but have harvested little. You eat, but never have enough. You drink, but never have your fill. . . . You earn wages, only to put them in a purse with holes in it. . . . Why? . . . Because of my house, which remains a ruin, while each of you is busy with his own house." (Haggai 1:2-9)

The Lord first of all pointed out their wrong priorities: building comfortable homes for themselves before building the Lord's house. And then, to encourage the builders, the Lord gave them a promise: "'Be strong, all you people of the land . . . and work. For I am with you,' declares the LORD Almighty. . . .'And my Spirit remains among you. Do not fear'" (Haggai 2:4,5).

What was the result? Under the leadership of Zerubbabel the governor, and with the spiritual encouragement of the prophets Haggai and Zechariah, the second temple was completed about 20 years after the exiles returned home. (Many years later, King Herod enlarged and remodeled that temple. That was the building to which Jesus was brought as a baby, and where he later taught.) Compared to Solomon's magnificent temple, however, the temple built by the returning exiles wasn't very impressive. "Many of the older priests . . . and family heads, who had seen the former temple, wept aloud when they saw the foundation of this temple being laid" (Ezra 3:12).

But although the second temple—usually called Zerubbabel's temple—couldn't compare with its predecessor in splendor, it was very important for the people who carried the promise. Remember, God wanted every feature of his temple to illustrate the relationship between the sinner and his God:

> The *building* itself represented God's earthly dwelling place among his people.
> The *worship leaders* emphasized that all sinners need the mediation of a priest before they can ever approach God.
> The *service of worship* in that temple illustrated that sinners are reconciled to God only through blood atonement.

Worship leaders

When God designed a path of worship for his chosen people, he specified not only where they were to worship him. He also gave them specific instructions about who was to lead them in worship. God set *the entire tribe of Levi* apart for public ministry, to serve him by assisting with the worship services of his chosen people. From all the clans of Levi, God set apart *the family of Aaron* to serve him as priests.

Priests

During the year Israel spent at Mount Sinai, God spelled out the division of labor between the *priests* (Aaron's descendants) and the rest of the *Levites*. The Lord told Aaron: "Only *you and your sons may serve as priests* in connection with everything at the altar and inside the curtain. I am giving you the service of the priesthood as a gift. Anyone else who comes near the sanctuary must be put to death" (Numbers 18:7).

By instituting this priesthood, God announced to his chosen people: Don't think you can simply come barging into God's throne room whenever you feel like it and say whatever is on your mind. Don't ever forget, "Your iniquities have separated you from your God" (Isaiah 59:2).

For God's people during the centuries of the Old Testament, the priest was the go-between—the middleman—between sinful people and a holy God. God was teaching them about the one-of-a-kind role that Christ plays between guilty sinners and a holy God. Israel's priests were the mediators between the people and God. For Old Testament believers, this was the rule. The only way to God is through the priest.

Silver trumpets announced the beginning of each new day in Jerusalem. Huge temple gates swung open and, day by day, God's chosen people again walked the path of worship God had designed for them. A priest approached the great altar of burnt offering and stirred into flame the embers that had been smoldering all night under the sacrifices. Now the first offering of the day, a burnt offering on behalf of the nation, could be offered to God. In God's design, the Levites could assist with preparing the animals for sacrifice, but the priests were the only ones who could approach the altar and actually offer the sacrifice. In this way they were living symbols of Christ, our great Priest. By offering himself on the altar of the cross as our substitute, he opened up our path to God. In each generation, one man from Aaron's family was chosen as the high priest. He was the one, the only one, who once a year, on the great Day of Atonement, could enter the Most Holy Place with the blood of a sin offering.

Serving as a priest was a high privilege, restricted to only a select few in Israel. (Priests had to be able to trace their family tree all the way back to the tribe of Levi and to the family of Aaron.) That's why it must have come as a distinct surprise when the apostle Peter wrote to the scattered Jewish Christians in the years after Easter and Pentecost: "You are a chosen people, *a royal priesthood*, a holy nation, God's special possession, that you may declare the praises of him who called you out of darkness into his wonderful light" (1 Peter 2:9 TNIV). When they first read that statement, Peter's original readers may have done a double take. Their immediate reaction may very well have been: "Who, me—a priest?"

Centuries later, when the Roman church taught that the priesthood is a privilege the church confers only on certain selected leaders, you can imagine what a bombshell Martin Luther exploded when he taught from Scripture the *universal priesthood of all believers*—in other words, that *every Christian is a priest of God!* Through Christ's perfect life as your substitute and through his innocent death as your substitute, *you have the right of direct access to God*. Through your baptism *God has called you and equipped you to represent him* in that particular slice of life where he has placed you.

Priests—whether in the Old Testament or in the New Testament—bring the needs of hurting people before the throne of God. Priests also transmit God's message of judgment and of mercy to sinners who need to hear it.

Levites

Toward the end of his life, King David took a census of all the men descended from the tribe of Levi. There were 38,000 of them. David announced: "Of these, twenty-four thousand are to supervise the work of the temple of the LORD and six thousand are to be officials and judges. Four thousand are to be gatekeepers and four thousand are to praise the LORD with musical instruments" (1 Chronicles 23:4,5).

The largest group of Levites served right in the temple, assisting the priests in the work of offering sacrifices. They skinned and gutted and dismembered the sacrificial animals and washed the pieces before the priests placed them on the altar.

They were *in charge of the bread set out on the table*, the flour for the grain offerings, the unleavened wafers, the baking and the mixing, and all measurements of quantity and size. They were also to stand every morning to *thank and praise the LORD*. They were to do the same in the evening and whenever burnt offerings were presented to the LORD on Sabbaths and at New Moon festivals and at appointed feasts. (1 Chronicles 23:29-31)

King David set apart some of the Levites "to sing joyful songs, accompanied by musical instruments: lyres, harps and cymbals" (1 Chronicles 15:16) and to conduct *"the ministry of prophesying"* (1 Chronicles 25:1). God worked through these singers to prophesy, to proclaim messages inspired by God. Other Levites were to *take care of the sacred furnishings* of the temple, making sure that the hundreds of gold and silver dishes and pans and bowls used in each day's worship were returned at day's end. Some *baked the offering bread* and *provided oil* for the lamps, the *wine* used in offerings, and the *incense* that symbolized prayers offered up to God. Some were *"in charge of the treasuries of the house of God"* (1 Chronicles 26:20). Others were designated to be gatekeepers, *"guarding the gates of the house of the LORD"* (1 Chronicles 9:23). They would spend the night stationed around the house of God, and they had the key to open it each morning. One final group of Levites was "assigned duties away from the temple, as officials and judges over Israel" (1 Chronicles 26:29).

When God designed a path of worship for his chosen people of Israel, he left nothing to chance or to guesswork. He specified, in great detail, the place where his people would worship him, as well as the designated persons who would lead them in worshiping God.

The worship service

When Christians today worship their Lord, their activity consists primarily of *hearing* God speak and then *responding*—in prayer and praise.

The worship experience of the Old Testament child of God was quite different. In one sense, the Old Testament worshiper participated less actively in the worship service than we do in our worship services today. At first it might seem to us that an Old Testament worshiper was more of a spectator than a participant, just watching what the priests and Levites were doing.

In another sense, however, the Old Testament child of God participated more fully in the worship services God designed for Israel than Christians do in their worship today. The ears and mouths of Israelite worshipers were active, and so was their sense of smell. Worshipers in that temple court could smell the fragrance of incense, which accompanied the offering of prayer. The huge altar standing outside the temple had a surface area of 900 square feet, over fires that never went out. Day after day hundreds and hundreds of pieces of sacrificial animals were placed on that altar. The smell of roasting meat must surely have attracted the attention of the worshipers' noses, as well as their taste buds.

And how about their eyes? Think of all there was for Israelite children to see when they accompanied their parents to the temple on the Sabbath. They saw their father lead a lamb by a rope—a lamb born on their little farm the past spring. He handed the rope to the Levites who assisted the priests and heard him declare the particular kind of offering he was bringing. Perhaps it was a *sin* offering, perhaps a *fellowship* offering. The children watched as a priest inspected the animal for any imperfection. After he approved the animal for sacrifice, they watched as the priest laid his hand on the head of the lamb. That showed the lamb was about to become the vehicle of the particular offering that family was bringing. And then came the moment that was hardest for them to watch. With a knife given to him by the priest, their father stabbed the lamb. Then the priest sprinkled the lamb's blood against the sides of the altar. Finally, the animal was skinned and cut apart and the body pieces placed on the altar. How distressing to be reminded that sin caused the death of an innocent victim!

The heart of Israel's worship

In directing his Old Testament people to bring blood sacrifices, God taught them an important truth. Sin cannot be forgotten. Sin costs a life. The justice of a holy God demands the ultimate thing of value—one's *soul* for one's *sin*. God doesn't condone our sin, nor does he compromise his standards. He doesn't ignore our rebellion, nor does he relax his demands. But by becoming a human being, the eternal God became our *substitute*, took our sin on himself and—incredibly—sentenced himself to death! God is still holy, sin is still sin, and a world of sinners was redeemed. For 1,500 years the Jewish people acted out Jesus' substitutionary death on the cross with the drama of their God-scripted sacrifices. The animals chosen for sacrifice had to be *perfect, without any blemish.* Only perfect animals could point forward to Christ, "a lamb without blemish or defect" (1 Peter 1:19). The blood sacrifices were commanded by God to announce the basic Bible truth: *God will accept a substitute.*

The four blood sacrifices

When God designed a path of worship for his chosen people, he instructed them to worship him with various kinds of blood sacrifices—four in all. The first seven chapters of Leviticus describe *burnt* offerings, *fellowship* offerings, *sin* offerings, and *guilt* offerings. It's important that we see the similarities between the four, but also to recognize the distinctive differences among each of them.

All four were *similar* in that the animal victim had to be a perfect specimen. All four were similar in that the life of the animal was taken. With all four God made the announcement, I have made atonement for your sin! "The life of a creature is in the blood, and I have given it to you to make atonement for yourselves on the altar; it is the blood that makes atonement for one's life" (Leviticus 17:11). "Without the shedding of blood there is no forgiveness" (Hebrews 9:22).

Each of the four sacrifices, however, was *different*, because each had a specific emphasis. To see the differences among the four blood sacrifices, think of them as falling into two groups:

1. Burnt offerings and fellowship offerings *gave expression* to the worshiper's covenant relationship with God and his joy at being in fellowship with God.
2. Sin offerings and guilt offerings *repaired* that covenant relationship when it had been broken by sin and *restored* fellowship with God.

The burnt offering (Leviticus 1)

The *burnt offering* was by far the most common of all the blood sacrifices. It was the first offering to be made every morning and the last one to be made before the temple gates closed at sunset. The burnt offering was the only one of the four blood sacrifices in which the entire sacrificial victim went up in smoke. This fact gives us a clue as to the specific purpose of the burnt offering. By offering the entire animal on God's altar, Israelite worshipers expressed complete dedication to the God who had made a covenant of mercy with them.

The two burnt offerings that began and ended each day's worship at the temple were sacrificed on behalf of the entire nation. With these offerings the people of Israel declared: "Our covenant God, we dedicate ourselves totally to you!" Individuals or families could also bring personal burnt offerings to express their total consecration to the God who had made a covenant of mercy with Abraham and with them.

You can hear a New Testament echo of the burnt offering in the statement Saint Paul wrote to the Christians in Rome: "I urge you, brothers and sisters, in view of God's mercy, to *offer your bodies* as living sacrifices, holy and pleasing to God—this is your proper worship as rational beings" (Romans 12:1 TNIV).

The fellowship offering (Leviticus 3:1-17; 7:11-34)

The *fellowship offering* was the second blood sacrifice that expressed the loving relationship between God's Old Testament people and the God who had made a solemn contract with them. When an Israelite brought a fellowship offering, only a small portion of the animal victim went up in smoke. Part of the animal was given to the officiating priest (Leviticus 7:31-34). The priest's only income came from the offerings God's people brought. The rest of the animal was roasted and eaten at a fellowship meal with the priest as God's representative and the worshipers as God's guests. God, the gracious Host, actually fed the worshipers with some of the meat that had been offered up to him. What an unusual blessing and privilege—to hear God say: "Be my guests! I want to be close to you!"

The sin offering (Leviticus 4:1–5:13; 6:24-30)

The two blood sacrifices that have just been described *expressed the covenant relationship* the Old Testament believer had with God. God designed two other blood sacrifices as part of his people's worship, however, that had a different purpose. These were intended to *restore the covenant relationship* with God, which had been interrupted by sin.

The first of these was the *sin offering*. Leviticus chapter 4 sketches four different scenarios, each of which called for bringing a sin offering—a sinful act on the part of the priest, or of the entire community, or of a leader, or of any member of the community. The purpose of the sin offering was to offer guilty sinners an opportunity to *confess the sin* that had interrupted their fellowship with God and to *receive God's assurance of forgiveness.*

The ceremonial spilling of blood was especially prominent in the sin offering. After killing the sacrificial animal, the priest would put some of its blood on the altar of burnt offering (and sometimes even on the altar of incense inside the sanctuary). He would then pour out the rest of the blood at the base of the altar. "What the law was powerless to do . . ., God did by sending his own Son . . . to be a sin offering" (Romans 8:3).

The most elaborate form of the Old Testament sin offering occurred on the great *Day of Atonement,* sometimes called "the Good Friday of the Old Testament." The central feature of this special day's events was the sin offering, which the high priest would make for the people of Israel. But before he could offer a sacrifice to atone for the sin of others, he first of all had to make a sacrifice of atonement for his own sin. The high priest, therefore, first sacrificed a bull as a sin offering for himself. He took the blood of that sin offering, entered the Most Holy Place, stepped in front of the ark of the covenant, and sprinkled blood. The blood of animals could not, of course, take away sin; only the precious blood of Christ can do that. But the sacrifice of the bull pointed forward to Christ's sacrifice, which atoned also for the sin of the high priest.

After making atonement for his own sin, the high priest again stepped before the altar of burnt offering and offered a goat as the sin offering for the people. Their sin had separated them from their God, and the high priest was a mediator between them and God. Once again the high priest entered the Most Holy Place and stepped before the ark of the covenant. He sprinkled blood again, this time with the prayer: "Lord, forgive the sins of your people!"

What took place inside the Most Holy Place each year on the Day of Atonement gives us a beautiful picture of exactly how God forgives sin. The high priest sprinkled blood on the atonement cover of the ark. Remember that the cloud over the ark symbolized the very presence of God on earth among human beings. Remember too that inside that ark were the two stone tablets of God's law, which accused and convicted the Israelites of sin and threatened them with God's punishment.

Do you see the picture God was drawing for his people? As the holy God looked down from the cloud above the ark, he saw his Ten Commandments and heard them condemn his people. But after the high priest sprinkled blood on the atonement cover, what did God see when he looked down? He saw blood that covered the sins of his people. He saw splashes of blood that—in God's eye—blended into the blood shed on Calvary centuries later. Jesus' blood atoned for their sin. It's interesting to note that the Hebrew word for "to atone" is a verb meaning "to cover."

Year after year, what took place *inside the Most Holy Place* on the Day of Atonement gave God's people a picture of how he forgives sin. The blood of Christ covers our sin so that "there is now no condemnation for those who are in Christ Jesus" (Romans 8:1).

But the worship service on the Day of Atonement included another significant action of the high priest. This event took place *outside the temple* for all the people to see. When the high priest had finished making the two sin offerings and praying to the Lord for forgiveness for himself and for the people, he stepped outside. His hands were dripping with blood, which he had sprinkled seven times on the atonement cover and seven times in front of it both times he entered the Most Holy Place. Now a second animal, a goat, was brought forward. In plain sight of all the people, the high priest was to "lay both hands on the head of the live goat and confess over it all the wickedness and rebellion of the Israelites—all their sins—and put them on the goat's head. He shall send the goat away into the desert in the care of a man appointed for the task. The goat will carry on itself all their sins to a solitary place; and the man shall release it in the desert" (Leviticus 16:21,22).

The *scapegoat* was led far away into the desert. Everyone knew it would never return. This was God's way of assuring his Old Testament people that "as far as the east is from the west, so far has he removed our transgressions from us" (Psalm 103:12).

Forgiveness was real, but it came at the price of a life.

The guilt offering (Leviticus 5:14–6:7; 7:1–7)

The path of worship God designed for his Old Testament people included a second blood sacrifice that repaired the covenant relationship which had been broken and restored fellowship with God.

When an Israelite trespassed on the rights of others, putting himself in debt to another person, he had to bring a guilt offering. In contrast to the sin offering, which emphasized confessing sin and receiving God's assurance of forgiveness, the guilt offering emphasized making *restitution*—to God and to the person offended. Like the other three, this was a blood sacrifice. The sinner who brought a guilt offering still needed atonement, which could be supplied only through the means God graciously provided in the spilled blood of the two-legged Lamb of God.

To appreciate the unique emphasis of each of the four blood sacrifices in the lives of God's people, it may be helpful to review a few examples of when each of the four sacrifices was offered.

When Aaron and his sons were anointed as Israel's first priests, they offered *sin offerings* (an opportunity for them to confess their sins and to receive God's assurance of pardon) and *burnt offerings* (dedicating themselves totally to God as they began their new work of being mediators for a sinful people).

When Saul was crowned as Israel's first king, the prophet Samuel assembled the nation at Gilgal (where the ark of God was) for the ceremony. "There they sacrificed *fellowship offerings* before the LORD, and Saul and all the Israelites held a great celebration" (1 Samuel 11:15). The Lord invited his new king and his people to a joyful meal to celebrate their fellowship with him.

When Jesus healed the man with leprosy, he told him: "Go, show yourself to the priest and offer the sacrifices that Moses commanded" (Mark 1:44). Which blood sacrifices had Moses commanded when a person with leprosy was healed? According to Leviticus chapter 14, that person brought all except the fellowship offering. In addition to the three blood sacrifices (the sin offering, the guilt offering, and the burnt offering), the person cleansed from leprosy also brought a grain offering as an expression of thankfulness to the giver of all good gifts.

It should be emphasized once again that all four of the Old Testament blood sacrifices rested on the atonement Christ would make for our sin, when as our substitute he traded places with us.

Israel's sacred calendar

As the people of Israel moved toward their new homeland, God recognized that they were spiritually immature. He recognized also that they were constantly tempted by the idolatry that surrounded them on all sides. (Archeologists find idolatrous figurines at every level of Israelite occupation.) God therefore designed an elaborate path of worship for his people, and he announced this path to them at Mount Sinai. Every seventh day was set aside as the Sabbath (Leviticus 23:3). The worship calendar included a number of annual festivals, which served a double purpose for a spiritually immature people:

1. to help them build their worship life around the true God.
2. to help them to see and to look forward to Jesus Christ, who would complete God's plan to rescue his people.

Three of these annual festivals are referred to as pilgrim festivals because they required heads of families (often accompanied by the entire family) to travel to the central sanctuary. From the time of David on, that was in Jerusalem. God had told his people: "Three times a year all your men must appear before the LORD your God at the place he will choose: at the Feast of Unleavened Bread [Passover], the Feast of Weeks and the Feast of Tabernacles" (Deuteronomy 16:16).

The feasts of Passover and Unleavened Bread

As God prepared to deliver his chosen people from slavery in Egypt, an event that marked their birthday as an independent nation, he gave them a new calendar. At the time he did this, they were in the seventh month of their older civil calendar. God introduced the new calendar by saying:

> This month is to be for you the *first* month, the *first* month of your year. . . . Each man is to take a lamb for his family, one for each household. . . . [On] the fourteenth day of the month, . . . all the people. . . must slaughter them at twilight. Then they are to take some of the blood and put it on the sides and tops of the doorframes of the houses where they eat the lambs. That same night they are to eat the meat roasted over the fire, along with bitter herbs, and bread made without yeast. . . . Eat it in haste; it is the LORD's Passover. This is a day you are to commemorate; for the generations to come you shall celebrate it as a festival to the LORD. (Exodus 12:2,3,6-8,11,14)

After the night the Israelites were liberated from slavery, God told them to start counting time from that day. They were now his free people. What had been the *seventh* month of their older civil calendar (the month of Abib—March/April on our calendars) now became the *first* month of Israel's new sacred calendar. On the 14th day of this month, for the rest of their history, the nation was to celebrate the *Feast of the Passover*. This was their Independence Day. That night every Israelite family ate the meat of a lamb or goat. The menu also included bread made without yeast (because yeast symbolized sin), bitter herbs (symbolic of their bitter slavery), and wine. The first Passover celebration was held the night the Israelites left Egypt. The last Passover of all time for believers was recorded in the Bible as the one Jesus celebrated with his disciples the night before he died. It was then that he replaced the Passover with the Lord's Supper. This was the night on which Jesus earned his reputation as the rescuer whom Israel was to reflect on each Passover. For seven days after the Passover, the Israelites were to eat bread made without yeast.

As the families of Israel celebrated the Passover year after year, there was a double focus to their celebration. They first looked back in time to the night when lamb's blood was spattered over the doorposts of their homes in Egypt. But each year, as they celebrated the Passover, God's people also remembered that God had promised to deliver them from a plague much worse than slavery, much worse even than being put to death. God had promised our first parents that he would send a Champion to crush the power of Satan and to free his people forever from Satan's control. As they celebrated the anniversary of their national deliverance each year, God's Old Testament people looked forward to the greater deliverance God had promised. The New Testament helps us to see that Jesus is the true Passover Lamb. "Christ, our Passover lamb, has been sacrificed," Saint Paul wrote to the Corinthians (1 Corinthians 5:7).

In the People's Bible commentary *Deuteronomy,* author Mark Braun explains:

When Pontius Pilate sent soldiers to break the legs of the men crucified with Jesus, they didn't break any of Jesus' bones because he was already dead; the apostle John cited this as the fulfillment of Exodus 12:46, "Not one of his bones will be broken" (John 19:36). That verse was originally a command regarding the preparation of the Passover lamb. John saw Jesus as the fulfillment of the Passover, the ultimate Passover Lamb.

The Feast of Weeks (Pentecost)

Fifty days after the Passover, the Israelites celebrated the second of their three great pilgrim festivals. The field crops (barley and wheat) had ripened, and this was the time of the grain harvest. On the sixth day of the third month (our May/June), God commanded his people to celebrate the *Feast of Weeks*, also called *Pentecost* or the *Feast of Harvest*. "On the day of firstfruits . . . present to the LORD an offering of new grain during the Feast of Weeks" (Numbers 28:26).

This spring harvest festival was a time when the Israelites brought the firstfruits of their crop to the Lord in gratitude for providing them with all they needed for body and life. It was at the celebration of this harvest festival, 50 days after Christ rose from the dead, that God poured out his Holy Spirit on the gathering of Christians and the apostles began to harvest—not wheat but souls.

The Feast of Tabernacles

At the end of the sunny, rainless summer, when the grapes and figs and olives were ripe for harvest, Israel celebrated the third of its three great pilgrim festivals.

"On the fifteenth day of the seventh month the LORD's *Feast of Tabernacles* begins, and it lasts for seven days. The first day is a sacred assembly; do no regular work. For seven days present offerings made to the LORD by fire, and on the eighth day hold a sacred assembly." (Leviticus 23:33-36)

"On the first day you are to take choice fruit from the trees, and palm fronds, leafy branches and poplars, and rejoice before the LORD your God for seven days. . . . All native-born Israelites are to *live in booths [for seven days]* so your descendants will know that I had the Israelites live in booths when I brought them out of Egypt." (Leviticus 23:40-43)

Five days earlier, the Israelites had celebrated the Day of Atonement. That solemn festival reminded the Israelites of their sin and of the costly solution God had provided for that serious problem. A few days later came the joyous celebration of the Feast of Tabernacles. Here for seven days God's people, who had traveled to Jerusalem for the festival, thanked God, first of all, for giving them another harvest of grapes, olives, figs, and dates. But God wanted them also to recall his mercy in protecting his people during the 40 years they had spent in the desert. He therefore commanded them to build shelters on the streets and rooftops. These were temporary structures of tree branches and vines in which the worshiping Israelites lived for the entire seven-day feast.

What a memory this must have been for Hebrew girls and boys, men and women! The preparation, the trip to Jerusalem, the relatives and friends, the sight of the great walls of the city of God coming into view, the construction of a leafy lean-to and living in it for seven days! They must have thought: What a great God we have! And what a precious identity we have as the nation from which the Savior will be born! What beautiful and meaningful worship God has designed for us!

Joyless rule keeping or joyful celebration?

The person who takes a quick, casual look at the path of worship God designed for his chosen people might be tempted to conclude: What a ton of rules and regulations those poor Israelite worshipers had to remember! How could they ever keep them all straight? Their worship must have been tedious—just following regulations!

God's Old Testament people did not look upon the path of worship God had designed for them as a list of rules that confused and intimidated them. Let several of them tell you what was on their minds as they prepared to worship God.

The poet who wrote Psalm 42 tells what was on his mind as he traveled to Jerusalem with a group of pilgrims to worship the Savior at one of the festivals. Listen to his words. You won't hear a syllable about how boring Israel's service of worship was or how repetitious or how hard it was for worshipers to remember all the things they had to do. Instead, he writes of going "with the multitude, leading the procession to the house of God, with shouts of joy and thanksgiving among the festive throng" (Psalm 42:4).

Listen to David express his attitude toward worship in Psalm 122: "I rejoiced with those who said to me, 'Let us go to the house of the LORD.' Our feet are standing in your gates, O Jerusalem. . . . That is where the tribes go up, the tribes of the LORD, to praise the name of the LORD according to the statute given to Israel" (verses 1-4).

In Old Testament times, God-fearing Israelites expressed joy at the privilege of attending services in God's house. Here was the place where God had chosen to share his sacred secrets with his people. Here is where he met with them, to assure them of his Savior love.

Unacceptable worship

Martin Luther once made the statement: "Where God builds his church, there the devil builds a chapel next door." God designed a path of worship for his people so that he could take up his dwelling among them. When God did that, Satan realized that he had work to do. He wants to be worshiped instead of Jesus Christ. He made it his business to accompany worshipers to the tabernacle and, years later, to the temple in Jerusalem to disrupt their worship.

Day by day in Old Testament times, God trained his people to trust him and his promise, even though they *couldn't see* him. The apostle Paul wrote: "We live by faith, not by sight" (2 Corinthians 5:7). At Mount Sinai, while Moses was receiving the law from God, Satan got inside the heads of the Israelites and actually convinced them it would be a whole lot easier to worship a god they *could see*. They had been exposed to the outward splendor of Egyptian idolatry. Now Satan created in them an appetite that was not satisfied with the spiritual worship into which God had led them. The result was that they asked Aaron the priest to make them a god they could see—a golden calf. When they worshiped that golden calf and thousands of them died under the judgment of God, Satan smiled.

Through the years of the Old Testament, Satan managed to convince many Israelites that as long as they *went through the motions* of worship, God would be satisfied. The prophet Isaiah showed what God thinks of such meaningless worship:

> "The multitude of your sacrifices—what are they to me?" says the LORD. "I have more than enough of burnt offerings, of rams and the fat of fattened animals; I have no pleasure in the blood of bulls and lambs and goats. . . . Stop bringing meaningless offerings! . . . They have become a burden to me; I am weary of bearing them. When you spread out your hands in prayer, I will hide my eyes from you; even if you offer many prayers, I will not listen." (Isaiah 1:11-15)

The path of worship God designed for his people trained them how to bring their offerings to God. God asked for the first and best share—for gifts that acknowledged him as the *giver of all*. Satan persuaded the people to look instead upon God as the *eater of our leftovers*. Instead of bringing the choice animals from their flocks for sacrifice, they brought defective animals. Through the prophet Malachi, God responded to this evidence of their unbelief:

> "When you bring blind animals for sacrifice, is that not wrong? When you sacrifice crippled or diseased animals, is that not wrong? Try offering them to your governor! Would he be pleased with you? . . . Oh, that one of you would shut the temple doors, so that you would not light useless fires on my altar! I am not pleased with you," says the LORD Almighty, "and I will accept no offering from your hands. . . . For I am a great king," says the LORD Almighty, "and my name is to be feared among the nations." (Malachi 1:8,10,14)

To this day Satan will do his dirty devilish best to make sure that your worship is mindless, joyless, Scriptureless, and Christless.

God's faithful worshipers

When we read the Old Testament, it's saddening to see how the majority of Israelites drifted away from God's true worship into false worship. But it gladdens our hearts to see how God always had a faithful "remnant," like a shred of fabric torn from a larger piece. At every period of Old Testament history, God had loyal sons and daughters. They recognized that they were beggars who had nothing and needed everything, but also, by grace, princes and princesses in God's royal family. Throughout the centuries of the Old Testament, God saw to it that there were fathers and mothers in every generation who taught their children the way of the Lord. Day by day they passed on the written Word of God—from generation to generation. This is why, at the time of Christ, there were the Zechariahs and the Elizabeths, the Josephs and the Marys, the Simeons and the Annas whom we get to meet on the pages of the New Testament.

Similarities and differences in worship

As we review the path of worship God designed for his Old Testament people, we see that in one sense it is the same as our worship today, in this period of the New Testament. The Old Testament child of God heard God say:

"My child, you're special to me. I want to be close to you!"

"My child, I have made atonement for your sin!"

Those two truths were the basis for Israel's worship. They are the basis for our worship. They will always be the basis for all true worship of the one Savior-God.

Some of the worship forms God designed for his Old Testament people show that God treated them as spiritually immature. Just as parents today make a lot of decisions for a child who has not yet reached the age of responsibility, so God made decisions for his Israelite people about what special days and festivals they were to observe in their worship, what foods were acceptable on his altar and on their dinner tables, who was authorized to lead them in worship, and how blood had to be shed to make atonement for sin. Always on the horizon was the cross of Christ.

How is the New Testament Christian to know which of these Old Testament worship regulations are still binding on us today and which are not? The question might seem to be a difficult one. There still are churches that teach, for example, the seventh day of the week is the one God set aside for worship, certain foods must not be eaten, and specially called priests must continue to offer sacrifices to take away sin.

But the answer to that question is not difficult. You and I no longer live before Jesus Christ lived, died, and rose from his grave. God no longer looks upon us as immature, minor children. All the Old Testament pictures have been fulfilled. God permits us the freedom to make many decisions about our worship. The worship regulations that are binding on us are the ones *found on the pages of the New Testament*. For example:

"God is spirit, and his worshipers must worship in the Spirit and in truth" (John 4:24 TNIV).

"Do *not let anyone judge you* by what you eat or drink, or with regard to a religious festival, . . . or a Sabbath day. These are a shadow of the things that were to come; the reality, however, is found in Christ" (Colossians 2:16,17).

"Where [sins] have been forgiven, *sacrifice for sin is no longer necessary*" (Hebrews 10:18 TNIV).

In Old Testament times, God designed a path of worship for his people. Day by day, believers listened with their ears and their hearts to God's promises of the rescuer he would send from their own bloodline, and day by day, believers responded with their lips, their hands, and their lives.

Today Christian worship is not just spiritual entertainment; it's not just "playing church." Worship is not just doing religious things like singing and praying. Worship is a meeting with God. *We* don't arrange this meeting; *God* does. When God invites us into his presence, how else can we respond than to tell him: "We are honored, Lord! Come to us now and teach us! Tell us again what you have done for us. What a great gift it is that you come to us this way!" In our worship we listen with our ears and our hearts to God's amazing acts of mercy in Jesus Christ on our behalf. In our worship we respond with our lips, our hands, and our lives.

"I will place shepherds over them who will tend them, and they will no longer be afraid or terrified, nor will any be missing," declares the LORD.

~ JEREMIAH 23:4

Leaders Appointed by God

Parents of young children realize that their children can easily be harmed in many different ways. Two minutes of swimming at a pool without a lifeguard on duty could cost a child's life. A child's immaturity might lead to accepting a ride from a stranger, and the parents might never see their child again. Hundreds of hours spent in a classroom with a teacher who denies God his role in our lives can have a tragic long-term effect on a child's thinking. So parents do what they can to safeguard their children—in body *and soul*.

God is a Father who understands that kind of thinking. Day by day in Old Testament times, God showed how deeply concerned he was about the men, women, and children who were descendants of Abraham. Out of pure love he wrapped his arms around them and adopted them as his special people. He even made a covenant with them that pointed to Jesus Christ, their great rescuer. He told them: "I am your God, and you belong to me. The chief purpose of your lives is to live close to me now and, through faith in the promised Savior, to get ready to live at my side forever." God bound himself by this solemn contract; he even sealed it with an oath.

But down through the centuries, God saw dangers threatening his people. North and south, east and west of their home in Palestine lived neighbors—some of them even shirttail relatives of the Israelites—who hated them and tried repeatedly to wipe them out. Within their own country were rich and powerful people who tried to take advantage of the weak and powerless, the widow and the orphan. Worst of all was the Israelites' own sinful nature, which they brought with them into the world and which threatened constantly to drive a wedge between them and the God who loved them.

Like a concerned parent, God took action to keep his people safe from the dangers that threatened them day by day. One special way he protected them was to appoint representatives to guide his people. Here we will note especially three, one of whom we have already met in the previous chapter. God appointed *priests,* who would speak to God for the people; *prophets,* who would speak to the people for God; and *kings,* who would protect God's people.

When God created our first parents, they didn't need anybody to talk to God for them. Adam and Eve didn't need anybody to teach them how to talk to God. They didn't need to be reconciled to God. They loved God, they believed him when he spoke to them, and they were content to live under him as happy children of a loving Father.

All that changed when Satan got inside their heads and whispered: "Adam and Eve, you could be a whole lot happier if you were independent of God." They listened to another word in place of God's Word. The saddest day in the history of the world was when those two brainwashed ancestors of ours ran away from their Father's house. Just as a bucking bronco tries to throw its rider, Adam and Eve tried to throw off God's Word and will for their lives and, instead, to live for themselves. It was never God's plan to be separated from people, but that's what sin did to God's family.

The tribe of Levi

Since Adam's and Eve's descendants were helpless to bridge the huge gap sin had carved between them and God, he lovingly took the initiative. He picked out one tribe from among those that made up the nation of Israel—the tribe of Levi. Members of that tribe (in the Bible they're called Levites) were not farmers, shepherds, or fishermen like other Israelites. Their full-time job was first to restore and then to maintain the fellowship between sinful people and the holy God. The Levites were to keep alive among the people of Israel the knowledge and worship of the true God. They supervised the religious teaching offered in all of Palestine. God laid this out in painstaking detail in the books of Exodus, Leviticus, and Numbers.

Since God wanted to protect the rights of his people, he chose Levites to supervise the nation's courts of law.

Unlike the people of the other 11 tribes, Levite families did not live together in one single tribal territory. Forty-eight cities throughout the lands of the 12 tribes were *Levitical cities,* in which Levites were given as many homes as needed. These Levitical cities became centers of biblical learning. Thirteen of the 48 were near Jerusalem and were assigned to the priests, the descendants of Aaron, so that they could live close to the temple.

Since the Levites devoted their lives to sacred duties, they couldn't hold outside jobs. Their income was provided by the various freewill offerings of God's people:

1. those portions of the animals brought as sacrifices to the temple but not offered up by fire.
2. the firstfruits of the harvest—"You are to give them the firstfruits of your grain, new wine and oil, and the first wool from the shearing of your sheep, for the LORD your God has chosen them and their descendants . . . to stand and minister in the LORD's name" (Deuteronomy 18:4).
3. the firstborn—God told the Levites: "The first offspring of every womb, both man and animal, that is offered to the LORD is yours" (Numbers 18:15). The firstborn son in every Israelite family had to be redeemed for five silver shekels, and that payment was given to the Levites.
4. the tithes the Israelites brought of all their income—"I give to the Levites all the tithes in Israel as their inheritance in return for the work they do" (Numbers 18:21).

Unfortunately, over the centuries these religious professionals added many commandments to the law God had given. When Jesus of Nazareth began to teach, they actually opposed him. They abused their privilege and misused their authority. The religious establishment at Jesus' time decided that before you sat down for a meal you were supposed to wash your hands seven times. When Jesus' disciples didn't follow this tradition, the religious leaders from Jerusalem asked Jesus: "Why don't your disciples live according to the tradition of the elders instead of eating their food with defiled hands?" (Mark 7:5 TNIV).

Jesus would not accept criticism on the basis of another's word apart from his Father's. Although his critics saw themselves as God's custodians of all religious teaching in the holy land, they actually accused Jesus of being evil and of working in cooperation with the devil (Mark 3:22).

On another occasion "an expert in the law stood up to test Jesus" (Luke 10:25), trying to embarrass Jesus publicly. Jesus responded by telling the parable of the good Samaritan. A traveler was attacked by highway robbers who beat him and left him lying half dead. Three other travelers came along that road and saw the man lying in a pool of his own blood. Two of them passed by without helping the poor man. And can you guess who they were? They were a *priest* and a *Levite*—men whom God had appointed as his representatives to help his people. They should have known better.

The priests

From the tribe of Levi, God chose one clan (the family of Aaron) for a very special assignment—to serve as priests. The priests had a double job as God's agents on earth:

    1. to offer blood sacrifices on behalf of sinful people.

    2. to pray to God to forgive his sinful people.

The priests were one group of representatives God appointed to guide his chosen people during the centuries before the promised Savior came. They were God's official mediators to bring sinful people and a holy God back together again. Since through them God was giving his people a picture of Jesus Christ, our great Priest, the priests had to meet the rigid standards God established for them. An Old Testament priest had to be a perfect physical specimen. He had to maintain a spotless marriage. He could not allow himself to become ceremonially unclean by contact with a dead body. He was required to wear crisp, clean, beautiful robes that were rich with symbolic meaning.

The people of Israel enjoyed great blessings through the ministry of the priests whom God appointed. The New Testament helps us to appreciate, however, the much greater blessings we Christians enjoy through Christ, our great Priest.

- The Old Testament priests were sinners who had to offer sin offerings for their own sins before they could bring offerings for the sins of others. Our great Priest, Jesus Christ, was and is without sin.
- The Old Testament priests could shed the blood of animals, but that couldn't wash away sin. There is a stain on every human soul that only the blood of one who is completely pure can remove. Christ offered himself in payment for our sin. "It is impossible for the blood of bulls and goats to take away sins" (Hebrews 10:4). "The blood of Jesus, [God's] Son, purifies us from all sin" (1 John 1:7).
- The Old Testament priests had to repeat their sacrifices day after day, year after year. Jesus Christ offered his sacrifice once and then announced: "It is finished" (John 19:30). "He sacrificed for their sins *once for all* when he offered himself" (Hebrews 7:27). "Where [sins] have been forgiven, *sacrifice for sin is no longer necessary*" (Hebrews 10:18 TNIV).
- The Old Testament priests could step into an *earthly temple* to ask God to forgive his people, but they could not step into the *very presence of God*. "Christ did not enter a sanctuary made with human hands. . . . He *entered heaven itself*, now to appear for us in God's presence" (Hebrews 9:24 TNIV). "Christ Jesus, who died—more than that, who was raised to life—is *at the right hand of God* and is also interceding for us" (Romans 8:34).

The prophets

If we are to live with real meaning and to die with real peace, we need a God who not only exists; we need a God who has spoken. The problem that immediately confronts us, however, is that God is a hidden God, "who lives in unapproachable light" (1 Timothy 6:16). If we are ever to gain reliable information about who God is and who we are, what God's plan is for our lives and what we've done to mess up that plan, and what God has done to repair and renew his great good plan, we need outside help. We need for God to *reveal* himself.

That word *reveal* is not one we use very often, but it's a mighty important word for a Christian. *Reveal* comes from a pair of Latin words *(re + velare)*, which mean *to pull back the veil*. That's what God did to show us things we need to know but which we could never in a lifetime find out by ourselves. "The secret things belong to the LORD our God, but the things revealed belong to us and to our children forever" (Deuteronomy 29:29).

All true religion is based on special revelation from God. All man-made religions originate in the human mind. They are therefore limited and unable to deal with sin and Satan and death. The brains God gave us are simply not adequate instruments for measuring God. Saint Paul makes this very clear: "The person without the Spirit does not accept the things that come from the Spirit of God but considers them *foolishness,* and *cannot understand them* because they are discerned only through the Spirit" (1 Corinthians 2:14 TNIV).

Unless the Spirit of God breaks the silence and turns on the lights for us through the miracle we call conversion, you and I lack the yardstick we need to measure religious truth. There's no way that we by ourselves can distinguish between what's true and what's false, between what's treasure and what's trash. We can't know the depth of our sin, and we can't know the beauty and power of our Savior Jesus. We lack true fear of God and true faith in God.

God did not choose to reveal all of his sacred secrets to the people of Israel at one time. Instead, he saw fit to share his plans for them when they needed to know them and in ways they could understand. He did this through chosen representatives known as prophets.

Unlike the arrangement God decided on when he instituted the office of king in Israel, there was no dynasty, no royal succession of prophets. God simply chose this or that human being here and there and spoke through him until the time when the Son of God came to announce God's final word to the human race. The Bible says: "In the past God spoke to our forefathers *through the prophets* at many times and in various ways, but in these last days he has spoken to us *by his Son*" (Hebrews 1:1,2).

This is what the Bible teaches about the message of the prophets: it was a miracle God performed among the Israelites to give his people information he wanted them to have. This biblical view of prophecy is not shared by everybody. Some Bible teachers look upon the Old Testament not as God's voice channeled to us through his chosen servants but simply as Jewish national literature. They believe and teach that it is impossible for anyone, including the Old Testament prophets, to predict future events accurately. We would agree that normally such a thing would be impossible, but not when God pulls back the veil. The first line of the Apostles' Creed calls God *almighty*, and that includes the power to accurately and precisely predict the future.

Moses

There is one prophet who stands out head and shoulders above the rest—Moses. What made Moses' prophetic work so special? God himself answered the question: "When a prophet of the LORD is among you, I reveal myself to him *in visions*, I speak to him in *dreams*. But this is not true of my servant Moses. . . . With him I speak *face to face*" (Numbers 12:6-8).

"The law was given through Moses," Saint John tells us in his gospel (1:14). Moses was the man through whom God gave the nation of Israel its sacred constitution. Moses was the mediator of the Sinai covenant. That was the awesome body of legislation God designed to discipline the ancient Israelites, to shape and mold an immature and rebellious people into his kind of people—people who would be obedient children in his family, custodians of his written revelation, and the cradle of the Savior whom God had promised to send.

The Bible says: "No prophet has risen in Israel like Moses" (Deuteronomy 34:10). Nowhere was this more apparent than at Mount Sinai, where the people of Israel spent about a year. During that time, God called Moses up on the mountain half a dozen times to give him the truths that he wanted him to transmit to his people. And what did God have to tell Moses? It cannot be overemphasized that the revelation God shared with Moses, which Moses shared with Israel during 40 years in the desert, was a twofold one: the message of the law and the message of the gospel.

The prophets' message: law and gospel

When the Israelites arrived at the Sinai desert, God told Moses, "Tell the people of Israel: . . . '*If you obey me* fully and keep my covenant, then out of all nations you will be my treasured possession'" (Exodus 19:3,5). Notice that sentence has an *if* in it. That's the message of God's law, and the minute the Israelites heard that they knew: "We can never meet those demands." Yet Moses faithfully transmitted the message of God's law to Abraham's descendants, people whom the apostle Paul later characterized as immature and irresponsible minor children.

Moses knew that the message of God's law is not God's final word to the human race. He had more to say. Before saying good-bye to the people of Israel, Moses told them: "I call heaven and earth as witnesses against you that I have set before you life and death, blessings and curses. Now *choose life*, so that you and your children may live" (Deuteronomy 30:19).

Israel's greatest prophet knew that the only way the people of Israel could "choose life" was through faith in the great Messiah whom God would send. Moses pointed people forward to the Savior, who would trade places with every sinner.

Saint John recorded one of the unpleasant confrontations Jesus had with the religious leaders who opposed him. At the pool of Bethesda in Jerusalem, Jesus had miraculously healed a man who had been crippled for 38 years. The Jewish leaders wanted to kill Jesus. For one, they claimed he had broken the Sabbath by performing a miracle on the Sabbath. What bothered them even more, however, was that he made himself equal with God. Jesus told his opponents, "If you believed Moses, you would believe me, for *he wrote about me*" (John 5:46).

A succession of prophets

Moses was God's chosen representative to guide God's chosen people. But the time came when God told Moses to prepare for his own death. He was not going to accompany the nation of Israel when it crossed the Jordan River and entered Canaan. That new homeland was crowded with false prophets who practiced secret arts that God had forbidden. They dabbled in the occult and even claimed to be able to contact the dead. With Moses no longer around, where could the Israelites find reliable information for their lives? God didn't want his people to copy their Canaanite neighbors and rely on superstition, to consult the dead to find out what God's will was, to try to tap into Satan's powers. But if God's people were not to use the sources of information the Canaanites regularly consulted, how were they to learn what they needed to know? How could they find out what God wanted them to know for their future lives in their new homeland? How could they learn what they needed to know for their long-term future on the other side of the grave?

In his farewell address to the people of Israel, Moses described three offices that God would institute, three groups of representatives, or agents, whom God would appoint to channel his love and power to sinful humans:

1. Deuteronomy 17:14-20 speaks about the *kings*, whose job it would be to protect and provide for God's people.
2. Deuteronomy 18:1-13 speaks about the *priests*, the mediators or middlemen, who would stand between a holy God and rebellious descendants of Adam and Eve.
3. Deuteronomy 18:15-22 speaks about the *prophets*, who would transmit God's Word and his will to Israel day by day.

Proclaiming God's truth

During the centuries of the Old Testament, God promised to create a line of prophets that would find its highest expression in one great Prophet. The New Testament identifies this Prophet as Jesus Christ (John 5:46; Acts 3:22-26). Israel's prophets were not just religious geniuses, each of whom decided for himself that preaching would be a good way to make a living. Saint Peter tells us in his second epistle, "Prophecy never had its origin in the will of man, but men spoke from God as they were carried along by the Holy Spirit" (2 Peter 1:21).

We know the names of a couple dozen prophets whom God appointed to speak to his people and guide them. Samuel, for example, led several schools at which an entire generation of prophets were trained.

Some of the prophets we call *literary prophets*; God used these men to write books that became part of the Old Testament. The primary job of the Old Testament prophets was to proclaim God's truth of law and gospel, sin and grace, death and life.

The prophet with the richest message of human sin and God's mercy was Isaiah. At Isaiah's time (740–700 B.C.), Assyria was the political superpower in the Middle East. Isaiah predicted that an empire called Babylon would topple Assyria and lead God's people into exile because of their persistent unbelief. After that, the nation of Persia would come from the east and crush Babylon. Isaiah even named the Persian king who would authorize the Jewish exiles to return home (Isaiah 45:13).

Isaiah's ministry, however, was bittersweet. The people of Jerusalem generally rejected his message, so he also had to predict God's judgment on their unbelief.

Jeremiah, who lived about a century after Isaiah, had the difficult assignment of being God's spokesman at a time when God's fierce judgment finally struck. Jerusalem's walls were battered down, her temple was stripped and then torched, and most of the Jews who survived were deported as captives of war.

Ezekiel and Daniel accompanied the exiles to far-off Babylon. Even in the land of their captivity, God wanted his people to hear what he had to say to them—the bad news and the good news. That is why they introduced their messages with the words "This is what the LORD says" (Isaiah 22:15; Jeremiah 2:5; Ezekiel 6:11).

What set God's Old Testament prophets apart from false prophets was that the Word *of the Lord* was on their lips. When they spoke, their primary job was to proclaim God's truth. In sharpest contrast, the Lord condemned the false prophets who twisted his Word, who put words into his mouth that he had not spoken:

> Do not listen to what the prophets are prophesying to you. . . . They speak visions from their own minds, not from the mouth of the LORD. I did not send these prophets, yet they have run with their message; I did not speak to them, yet they have prophesied. . . . I am against the prophets who wag their own tongues and yet declare, "The LORD declares." (Jeremiah 23:16,21,31)

Predicting the future

God gave his Old Testament prophets another assignment. He often enabled them to look into the future and to predict future events. A century and a half before it actually happened, Isaiah predicted that Assyria would fall to the Babylonians. Isaiah's best-known and most dearly loved prophecies, however, are his beautiful descriptions of the Savior's virgin birth and of his victorious suffering and death as our substitute (Isaiah 7:14; 9:6-8; 53:3-12).

The prophet Micah even named the little town, six miles south of Jerusalem, where the promised Savior would be born (Micah 5:2).

Jeremiah predicted that the Messiah would be a King, a descendant of David, who would rule wisely and who would *make* his people *right* with God, even better, who would actually *be* their righteousness as demanded by the holy God.

Zechariah foretold the Messiah's entry into Jerusalem on a donkey, his betrayal for 30 pieces of silver, and his rejection by his own people.

The prophet Joel predicted the outpouring of the Holy Spirit on Pentecost and described what Christ will do when he returns on judgment day.

Preaching to unbelieving neighbors

God sent his prophets primarily to speak to Abraham's descendants—to warn them against sin and to encourage them to remain faithful to their Savior-God. But God sometimes used his prophets to direct a message also to Israel's unbelieving neighbors.

For example, about 800 B.C. God sent Jonah (over the prophet's protest) to deliver a call to repentance to the people of Nineveh, capital of the heathen Assyrian empire. We have Jesus' word for it that Jonah's mission was successful: "[The Ninevites] repented at the preaching of Jonah" (Matthew 12:41).

Unfortunately, their repentance was only temporary. Later on they turned their backs on the true God and fell back into their heathen worship. Through another of his prophets, God predicted what the result would be. The prophet Nahum announced this solemn and sobering warning: proud, ruthless Assyria (then at the peak of its power) would be crushed, never to rise again.

God's spokesmen

Israel's prophets were God's chosen representatives, whom God appointed to guide his people. Throughout the centuries of the Old Testament, God never left his people without guidance. He continued to appoint representatives to guide his chosen people.

Malachi, the last Old Testament prophet, spoke to God's people four hundred years before Christ was born. He foretold the coming of John the Baptist, Jesus' immediate predecessor. He described the last day of world history as a fearful day of *judgment* for God's enemies (Malachi 4:1) but also as a joyful day of *deliverance* for God's people (Malachi 4:2).

Between the Testaments

Four centuries intervened between the Old Testament and the New, between Malachi and Matthew. During those centuries God no longer sent his representatives to walk the streets and markets and temple campus of Jerusalem day after day to preach to its inhabitants. That was no longer necessary. God had given his people the messages of the earlier prophets *in writing*. Tragically, the majority in Israel ignored the prophets' appeals to return to God and to accept the forgiveness the promised Messiah would earn for them. Throughout those four centuries, however, God always had among his people faithful fathers and mothers who believed the message of the prophets and passed this on to their children. Their descendants formed the believing Jewish community into which, at just the right time, the Lord Jesus was born.

God's representatives governed Israel

Living in a free country, we're convinced that democracy is the best form of government that human beings ever developed. In a democracy the power lies with the people (*demos* is the Greek word for "people"; *cracy* comes from the Greek word for "to rule"). Government is "*of* the people, *by* the people, and *for* the people."

Ancient Israel was not a democracy. Instead, we speak of ancient Israel as a *theocracy* (*theos* is the Greek word for "God"). God ruled over Israel. But he did not rule over them directly. He appointed representatives of three different kinds—priests, prophets, and kings. We've been introduced to the first two; now we want to meet the third. While the

Israelites were still at Mount Sinai, the first two of God's special representatives were active, bringing special blessings to his people. Aaron, the *priest*, was God's *mediator*, the middleman, reconciling a sinful people to their holy God. Moses, the *prophet*, was God's *spokesman*, bringing them messages from God.

The kings

At the time the nation of Israel entered the Promised Land, it had no king. For hundreds of years God simply provided a series of strong and faithful leaders to guide his people. After Moses died, God appointed Joshua to lead Israel across the Jordan River. He led the armies of Israel in a seven-year campaign that broke the Canaanite military resistance. For several hundred years after Joshua died, leadership passed to a group of leaders known as *judges*—people like Deborah and Gideon and Jephthah and Samson. The last of the judges was Samuel. He was a faithful servant of the Lord, through whom God gave Israel some smashing victories over their enemies, especially the Philistines. Operating from their coastal home base only 35 miles southwest of Jerusalem, the Philistines made life miserable for generations of Hebrews.

As Samuel grew older, however, the people of Israel became dissatisfied. Philistine armies had once again invaded Israel's heartland, and it seemed like the coalition of 12 loosely knit tribes was heading for trouble. Public opinion in Israel began to favor a strong central government—the kind that all the surrounding nations had. The elders of Israel, therefore, came to Samuel and asked, "Appoint a king to lead us, such as all the other nations have" (1 Samuel 8:5).

Can you hear what they were really saying? "God can't be relied on to know what's best for us. Our only hope for survival is a new form of government. The government we have now isn't getting the job done." Those elders, however, were ignoring the fact that Israel's problems were not primarily political but spiritual.

When the Israelites invaded the land, the Lord had commanded them to annihilate the Canaanite occupants. The threat of their fertility-sex worship was that perilous. Satan repeatedly used the local inhabitants to try to overthrow God's plan to send the Savior. If Israel had obeyed God's command, the Philistines wouldn't have been around to cause trouble.

God had also promised his people: "If you fully obey the LORD your God . . . the enemies who rise up against you will be defeated before you. They will come at you from one direction but flee from you in seven" (Deuteronomy 28:1,7). The Israelites had *disobeyed* the Lord's command, and they had *doubted* the Lord's promise. Now they were paying the bitter price for their unbelief and unfaithfulness.

Samuel knew that the big problem facing the people of Israel was not how big and strong the enemy armies were but how puny their own faith was and how weak their loyalty to God was. He was disappointed that the Israelite elders asked for a king. They weren't facing up to their real problem, and Samuel tried to get them to change their minds.

But the people refused to listen to Samuel. "No!" they said. "We want a king over us. Then we will be like all the other nations, with a king to lead us and to go out before us and fight our battles." When Samuel heard all that the people said, he repeated it before the LORD. The LORD answered, "Listen to them and give them a king." (1 Samuel 8:19-22)

Qualifications for the king

The Lord had anticipated this request from his immature and rebellious people. He knew that the time would come when the theocracy *(God rule)* would be replaced by a monarchy *(king rule)*, and he made plans for it. Although Israel's form of government was about to change and they would get the king they wanted, God would still be their ruler, just as he had been during the period of the judges. Years in advance, God had even announced a set of qualifications for the king who would one day sit on the throne of Israel. God had told his people, "[When you choose your king], be sure to appoint over you the king the LORD your God chooses" (Deuteronomy 17:15).

Israel's new form of government was not an *absolute monarchy,* since it was God who determined the qualifications new kings would have to meet. Israel's kings did not have supreme authority, but they ruled according to the religious constitution God had given at Mount Sinai. In the years before Christ came, there was no separation between church and state. Israel's king was to carry out the directions of the Lord, who had the final authority. We're used to thinking of the position of king as the top job in the government. God didn't see it that way. Israel's king was one of God's chosen representatives to guide and protect his people. In Deuteronomy chapter 17, God announced his qualifications for a king:

1. He had to be an Israelite, not a foreigner.
2. He was to rule not with military muscle but in loyalty to God.
3. He was to be an enthusiastic role model for his people by leading a godly life.
4. He was to have his own copy of the Bible (at that time, the five books of Moses), to read it day by day, and to follow it carefully.

The king's most important job

Can you see what God considered to be the king's most important job? Unfortunately, some of Israel's kings thought their big job was to pass laws and collect taxes and control people. But that was never God's idea of a king. God made it clear that Israel's king was to be a shepherd—*to protect God's people*, to keep them safe in body and soul. God knows there's more to a person than body and bone and blood. The worst enemies that threatened God's people were not the warlike Philistines, who had invaded Israel's territory, terrorized its people, killed their sons, and stolen their livestock. God therefore reminded his representative on the throne: The nation's worst enemy is the evil one who is trying to make sure my people never reach their eternal homeland. And so, king, *take care of my people the way I would*! In the Old Testament, God evaluated a king of Israel not on the basis of whether his reign brought prosperity to the country. Israel's king was measured by what he did to keep God's people safe from their enemies and loyal to their Lord.

Good kings

David is an example of a good king. He was a shepherd whom God chose to become king. Shortly after being anointed into his new position, David killed Goliath, a huge Philistine warrior who had been intimidating the army of Israel. Worse yet, this giant of a man had been insulting the God of Israel. While David was king, he captured one Canaanite city after another, until at last the entire land that God had promised to Abraham's descendants belonged to them. The whole country was now united under one leader.

Since the danger of enemy attacks was now past, God's people could move out from behind their fortified settlements and build new communities in the countryside. David's gifts as soldier, statesman, and poet brought great blessing to God's people. Almost half of the 150 psalms in our Bible were written by this man of God.

Abraham	Moses	David		Jesus
2000 B.C.	1500 B.C.	1000 B.C.		B.C./A.D.

David realized that as king he was God's representative, appointed by God to keep his people safe in body and soul. Perhaps David's most enduring act of serving God's church of all time is that he taught us what true repentance is. An outstanding example of this is Psalm 51, in which David teaches us that repentance consists of recognizing our sin and God's grace.

Another king who remembered why God had placed him on the throne was Hezekiah. Three hundred years after the time of David, idolatry threatened to choke the faith of God's people. Hezekiah's father and predecessor, a wicked king named Ahaz, was an idol worshiper. He had actually shut down the temple of the Lord. Although Hezekiah was only 25 years old when he became king, "he did what was right in the eyes of the LORD. In the first month of the first year of his reign, he opened the doors of the temple of the LORD and repaired them. . . . King Hezekiah gathered the city officials together and went up to the temple of the LORD" (2 Chronicles 29:2,3,20).

In a joyful service the temple was rededicated, and the path of worship the Lord had designed for his people was reestablished. Hezekiah and his top leaders, first of all, brought dozens of animals as sin offerings. King and people alike confessed their sinfulness. They also confessed their faith in the great Messiah God had promised to send to pay for their sins and to reconcile them to God. Hezekiah realized his primary task as king was to take the lead in keeping God's people close to their Savior-God:

> Hezekiah gave the order to sacrifice the *burnt offering* on the altar. As the offering began, singing to the LORD began also, accompanied by trumpets and the instruments of David. . . . The whole assembly bowed in worship, while the singers sang and the trumpeters played. . . . The number of burnt offerings the assembly brought was seventy bulls, a hundred rams and two hundred male lambs—all of them for burnt offerings to the LORD. (2 Chronicles 29:27,28,32)

Remember that the burnt offering was Israel's only blood sacrifice in which the entire carcass of the sacrificial animal was offered up by fire. By bringing these offerings, Hezekiah and all the worshipers were declaring: God, we dedicate ourselves totally to you. As king, Hezekiah served as a role model for God's people. He acknowledged publicly that we exist only to serve God and to seek his glory in everything.

That special rededication service closed with the bringing of fellowship offerings. King and congregation praised God for the happy privilege of being members of his family. Perhaps you remember that an important part of that offering was a fellowship banquet. As host, God graciously served a portion of the sacrificial animals to his guests. You can understand that when this rededication celebration (which lasted two weeks!) was over, "There was great joy in Jerusalem, for since the days of Solomon son of David king of Israel there had been nothing like this in Jerusalem" (2 Chronicles 30:26).

Actually it's not quite correct to say that the celebration was over. Good King Hezekiah realized that, as God's chosen agent, there was one more piece of unfinished business he had to attend to: "The Israelites who were there went out to the towns of Judah, smashed the sacred stones and cut down the Asherah poles. They destroyed the high places and the altars throughout Judah" (2 Chronicles 31:1).

Hezekiah was faithful to his God-given assignment: to protect God's people from being infected and contaminated by Canaanite religion. The filthy fertility cult worship that had been present when Israel entered the land had been reintroduced. Hezekiah, therefore, sent out crews with axes and sledgehammers to destroy the vile, sexually explicit worship paraphernalia, which was polluting the country. The king's job was to protect God's people. Hezekiah took his job seriously, and there was a reformation in his generation.

Unfaithful leaders

On the other hand, how disappointing it is to read that so many of the leaders that God had appointed to serve his people—priests, prophets, kings—were often unfaithful to their call from God. *Priests* were often more interested in what they got out of the people's obedience and offerings than in bringing sinful people back into fellowship with God. False *prophets* told people what they wanted to hear, instead of sharing God's message of law and gospel with them. *Kings* often left a grim record of idolatry and disobedience. Many took advantage of God's people, instead of protecting them. To support his lavish building projects, for example, Solomon taxed the people of Israel heavily and subjected them to forced labor. Some of Israel's kings *lived off* God's flock like butchers, instead of *serving* it like shepherds. The prophet Micah complained bitterly about the behavior of the representatives whom God had appointed to bless the people of Israel: "Her *leaders* [kings] judge for a bribe, her *priests* teach for a price, and her *prophets* tell fortunes for money" (Micah 3:11).

Old Testament pictures of Christ

When God instituted the offices of priest, prophet, and king, he was concerned not only about the day-to-day well-being of his Israelite people. He was looking much further into the future. In God's plan, the *priests* who offered sacrifices, the *prophets* who spoke for God, and the *kings* who protected God's people were Old Testament pictures of Jesus Christ:

- "You [Christ] are a *priest* forever" (Psalm 110:4).
- "The LORD your God will raise up for you a *prophet* . . . from among your own brothers. You must listen to him" (Deuteronomy 18:15).
- "The days are coming," declares the LORD, "when I will raise up to David a righteous Branch, a *King* who will reign wisely and do what is just and right in the land. In his days Judah will be saved and Israel will live in safety. This is the name by which he will be called: The LORD Our Righteousness" (Jeremiah 23:5,6).

Scripture portrays the saving work of Jesus as the fulfillment of the three Old Testament offices of priest, prophet, and king:

- Christ is our great *Priest*, the only mediator God has sent to make our peace with God. He alone stands between God's holiness and our degrading sin.
- Christ is our great *Prophet*. Through him God has said all that he had to say,

all that he could say, all that there was to say to a world of sinners: "Forgiveness, free and full, is found in my Christ!"

- Christ is our great *King*. His highest goal is not to make us rich or successful or famous. His highest goal is to rescue and then to protect his children. As a result, we can live close to him now and at his side in the world that will never end.

Christ did not come to be served, but to serve. He who is perfect has given his perfect record to us, and our imperfect record is given to him. In perfect love our *Priest* sacrificed himself to make peace between us and God. Our *King* went all the way to shame and death to protect and rescue his people. Nails didn't hold him to a cross. Love did. Day by day our *Prophet* says: "If you hold to my teaching . . . you will know the truth."

"God has come to help his people" (Luke 7:16). Jesus Christ—our Priest, Prophet, and King—is personally concerned about the eternal well-being of his people. Is it so surprising, then, that he is jealous of the loyalty of his people?

He has revealed his word to Jacob, his laws and decrees to Israel. He has done this for no other nation.

~ PSALM 147:19,20

What advantage, then, is there in being a Jew? . . . Much in every way! First of all, they have been entrusted with the very words of God.

~ ROMANS 3:1,2

Custodians of God's Word

It was never God's plan for the ancient nation of Israel to become a political superpower or to become a world leader in art or in science. The pages of ancient history make it clear that God was willing to let pagan nations enjoy that kind of prominence.

The special distinction God reserved for the chosen nation descended from Abraham was a twofold one. In God's plan, Israel was to be the *cradle of the world's Savior* and the *custodian of God's sacred truth.* Don't draw the conclusion, however, that God wasn't interested in the cultural and scientific achievements of the pagan world under his rule. The Creator was very concerned about the development of the *alphabet* and the widespread use of the *Greek language*, for example, and the building of the *Roman system of roads*. God made good use of all of these when the time came to spread his Word throughout the Mediterranean world.

But what God has been most concerned about throughout all history is his Word. Here is the good news about the great Substitute who exchanged places with sinners under the curse of God. Here is the message of heaven in the language of earth! To put that good news down in writing and to transmit it to future generations was the important task for which God used the people of the promise.

The divine author

If God had wanted to play hide-and-seek with the human race, we would never have found him. But God never plays for fun—always for keeps. From the very first day of the world's history, he established contact with the people he created. He broke the silence and let his voice be heard.

The Bible teaches that God speaks to people in different ways. He speaks through nature:
The heavens declare the glory of God; the skies proclaim the work of his hands.
Day after day they pour forth speech; night after night they display knowledge.
There is no speech or language where their voice is not heard. Their voice goes
out into all the earth, their words to the ends of the world. (Psalm 19:1-4)
You have heard God speak to you in another way—through the voice of your conscience. The Bible teaches that every human being has a natural knowledge of God. When you look at the created world and when you listen to your conscience, nobody has to convince you that there is a God, that's he's powerful, or that you're accountable to him. Saint Paul described this natural knowledge of God:
What may be known about God is plain to [people], because God has made it
plain to them. For since the creation of the world God's invisible qualities—his
eternal power and divine nature—have been clearly seen, being understood from
what has been made, so that people are without excuse. (Romans 1.19,20 TNIV)
But neither nature nor our consciences can tell us everything about God that he wants us to know about him. So through the miracle of inspiration, God put his thoughts toward us down in writing. He shared some of his secrets with us. He breathed into

chosen writers the thoughts and words he wanted them to write down. In the Bible, God has not told us everything about himself that we might like to know, but he has told us everything about himself that we need to know.

The message

Martin Luther once made the statement: "If God had had no more to say to his people than '*la-la-la-la*,' these would be the most wonderful sounds our ears could ever have heard." But when God spoke in his written Word, he did not talk in nonsense syllables. He spoke of the marvelous plan he had for his people, of what they and their ancestors had done to mess up his good plan, and of what his love would do to repair and renew his plan.

God is love not because he is soft on sin but because he found a way to satisfy his need to punish all sin while at the same time sparing the human race. The way God accomplished this rescue amounted to an *exchange* in which God substituted his Son for sinners. God's costly solution effectively gave sinners what his holiness demanded of them. On the basis of the perfect obedience his Son gives them, God has declared that all human beings have met his standards. And on the basis of the innocent death his Son suffered, God has pronounced all human beings forgiven of their sin.

The miracle

How did the several dozen authors God used to put the message of the Old Testament down in writing know what to write down? The apostle Peter tells us: "You must understand that no prophecy of Scripture came about by the prophet's own interpretation. For prophecy never had its origin in the human will, but prophets, though human, spoke from God as they were carried along by the Holy Spirit" (2 Peter 1:20,21 TNIV).

Very simply, the miracle of inspiration is this: The Holy Spirit supervised the sacred writers when they produced the tiny library that we call the Old Testament—a library that includes history, poetry, sermons, and short stories. The Holy Spirit kept the writers from error. He guided them in choosing the words they used. As a result, the apostle Paul could write to Timothy, his young pastor friend, "All Scripture is God-breathed" (2 Timothy 3:16).

Unique writing styles

The miracle of inspiration is sometimes caricatured as the *dictation theory*. But Moses' farewell address in the book of Deuteronomy "sounds different" from one of David's psalms. Does that surprise you? Consider this: Why don't all the pipes in a pipe organ have the same sound? They all utilize the same wind chest for their air supply. The pipes in a pipe organ are of different sizes and shapes and are built differently—some of wood, some of metal, some with reeds. Each vibrates in a slightly different way to produce a unique sound.

In the same way, the Spirit of God used the unique personality and writing gifts of each writer. Through David the Holy Spirit spoke in a different style of language than he did through Isaiah or Zechariah.

Each of the men who wrote the Bible books realized that this was a miracle. Listen to the prophet Jeremiah describe the process that resulted in the book that bears his name:

> The words of Jeremiah son of Hilkiah, one of the priests at Anathoth. . . . The word of the LORD came to me, saying, "Before I formed you in the womb I knew you, before you were born I set you apart; I appointed you as a prophet to the nations." . . . Then the LORD reached out his hand and touched my mouth and said to me, "Now, I have put my words in your mouth." (Jeremiah 1:1,4,5,9)

The opening words of the book of the prophet Micah show that he experienced the same miracle. Seven hundred years before Christ, God used not only Micah's mouth but also his hand and his writing skills to speak to the people of Jerusalem: "The word of the LORD that came to Micah of Moresheth during the reigns of Jotham, Ahaz and Hezekiah, kings of Judah" (Micah 1:1).

Listen to what David said as he wrote his last inspired psalm: "These are the last words of David . . . Israel's singer of songs: 'The Spirit of the LORD spoke through me; *his* word was on *my* tongue'" (2 Samuel 23:1,2).

The heart of the Old Testament

The Old Testament is more than a collection of poetic and historical documents written by ancient Hebrew authors. The Old Testament is the official record of God's early dealings with sinful mankind. The New Testament writers looked upon the Old Testament as a testimony to Jesus Christ (Revelation 19:10). The ancient nation of Israel was not only God's chosen people. They were the people of the promise. The apostle Paul wrote to some first-century Christians: "Scripture foresaw that God would justify the Gentiles by faith, and announced the gospel in advance to Abraham: 'All nations will be blessed through you' [namely, through Abraham's descendant Jesus]" (Galatians 3:8).

Jesus Christ is the heart of the Old Testament. More than just a famous religious teacher like Buddha or Muhammad, he is the fulfillment of all God's Old Testament promises and the only way to the heart and the home of the heavenly Father.

Because of this, the recipients of God's Old Testament revelation treasured the words God had chosen to share with them. One of those recipients put his feelings into words: "How sweet are your [promises] to my taste, sweeter than honey to my mouth!" (Psalm 119:103).

The Old Testament is trustworthy

The believers who first received the Old Testament knew that for the Lord of the universe to bare his innermost heart to them was an act of pure mercy. He didn't owe them his Word. He didn't owe them a thing. Furthermore, they knew that what God had told them in the Scriptures of the Old Testament was true, because God cannot lie. If he made them a promise, he could be trusted to keep it. Jesus described that trust in these words: "Scripture cannot be broken" (John 10:35).

The Old Testament's absolute authority

The message of the Old Testament is supernatural, from Genesis to Malachi. It was revealed by God, not snipped and pasted together from a basketful of folk legends by some religious editors. The Old Testament was God's idea, not ours. It does not tell us everything we might like to know about God or his plans for tomorrow, but it is sufficient for the purpose for which God gave it.

We are not in a position to judge the teachings of the Old Testament with our minds to determine whether or not the Bible sounds correct. It would not be right for us to ask if everything God said makes sense. All we need to know is whether God said it or not. If he said it, that decides it. When a person, or a church, gives up the teaching that the Scripture is the inspired Word of God, then the Bible becomes a wax nose, which anyone may twist to suit his or her particular preference or prejudice.

Preserving the sacred writings

The Bible does not provide detailed information about how God's chosen people preserved the individual documents during the ten centuries during which they were being written down. We also don't know who the person was who gathered into a single collection all the leather scrolls on which the 39 Old Testament books were originally written. Among the Israelites, the first five books of the Old Testament—the five books of Moses—were known as the *Torah* (toe-RAH). This Hebrew name is usually translated as the *Law of Moses* (although the Hebrew word means "teaching"). As Moses approached the end of his life, he gave clear instructions as to what was to happen to the original copies of the five books he had written:

> After Moses finished writing in a book the words of this law from beginning to end, he gave this command to the Levites who carried the ark of the covenant of the Lord: "Take this Book of the Law and place it beside the ark of the covenant of the Lord your God." (Deuteronomy 31:24-26)

Moses realized that these documents were precious. These five books lay the foundation for all of Scripture. Without the information that they supply, we really cannot understand what the rest of the Bible says. Moses therefore commanded that the original copies of these books were to be stored in the Most Holy Place, the innermost room of the tabernacle and, later, of the temple. More specifically, they were to be placed alongside the ark of the covenant, the most sacred artifact the sanctuary contained. But they were not to be just museum pieces. Moses commanded the priests:

> When all Israel comes to appear before the Lord your God [three times each year] at the place he will choose, you shall read this law before them in their hearing. Assemble the people—men, women and children, and the aliens living in your towns—so they can listen and learn to fear the Lord your God. . . . Their children, who do not know this law, must hear it and learn to fear the Lord your God. (Deuteronomy 31:11-13)

The priests played a major role in preserving the sacred books of Moses for the nation of Israel. Later on, so did Israel's kings. Listen again to Moses:

When [the king] takes the throne of his kingdom, he is to write for himself on a scroll a copy of this law, taken from that of the priests. . . . It is to be with him, and he is to read it all the days of his life so that he may learn to revere the LORD his God and follow carefully all the words of this law and . . . [not] turn from the law to the right or to the left. (Deuteronomy 17:18-20)

The scribes

It wasn't enough, however, for God's people to have only the one original, official copy of the books of the Old Testament kept alongside the ark of the covenant. The scattered Jewish communities throughout Palestine needed and wanted their own copies. But since the printing press would not be invented until many centuries later, copies had to be made by hand. We call these *manuscripts* (*manus* is Latin for "hand," and *script* is Latin for "written"). The men who hand copied the books of the Bible were known as *scribes*. If the people of God were to have reliable copies of God's Word, the work of the scribes was critically important. From the first centuries A.D. (not from the Bible itself), we have a list of the rules that regulated the scribes' work, as they made copies of the books of the Old Testament. Here are some of them:

- A scribe had to take a bath before he started his work.
- He was to write only in black ink on scrolls that were the treated skins *(vellum)* of sheep or goats (clean animals).
- The scribe was not permitted to write a single word—not even a single letter—from memory. If he made a spelling mistake, he was not permitted to correct it; he had to start copying the whole page over on a new scroll.
- Sometimes a scribe worked alone. Sometimes several scribes worked together at desks in a room called a *scriptorium*. A *lector* would read the sacred book aloud, and the scribes would all make copies.

Scrolls

People living in Old Testament times would not have recognized the objects we call books with front and back covers and pages in between. They had scrolls—rolled-up sheets of leather treated to form a smooth writing surface. The shortest Old Testament book fits on a single page. If the Bible books were not too long, several could be included on a single scroll. (The five books of Moses were regularly included on a single scroll.) In 1948 a number of scrolls, including some precious Bible scrolls dating to the first century before Christ, were discovered in a cave west of the Dead Sea. These remarkable discoveries are popularly referred to as the *Dead Sea Scrolls.* One of them, containing all 66 chapters of the book of Isaiah, was found wrapped in linen and stored in a clay jar with a lid. This remarkable manuscript was made of 17 sheets of leather sewn together to form a scroll more than 20 feet long.

The Hebrew Bible

In Bible times God's people divided the 39 books of the Old Testament into three categories:

1. the Law of Moses (the *Torah*), the first 5 books to be written.
2. the Prophets, 21 books containing history and prophecy.
3. the Writings, a miscellaneous collection of 13 books of poetry and wisdom literature.

Jesus referred to this threefold division of the Old Testament when he appeared to his disciples the evening of the first Easter Sunday. After having spent several miserable days convinced that Jesus was dead, they were startled to see him alive. And then they heard him say: "This is what I told you while I was still with you: Everything must be fulfilled that is written about me in the *Law of Moses*, the *Prophets* and the *Psalms*" (Luke 24:44).

God chose the descendants of Abraham to be not only the recipients of his Word, but also the custodians of that Word. The pages of the Old Testament offer us considerable evidence that over a period of a thousand years, as each successive book of the Old Testament was written, God's people received it gratefully, studied what it had to say, and added it to the collection of sacred scrolls.

The Law of Moses (the Torah)

Moses wrote the first books of the Bible about 1450 B.C. More than four hundred years later, King David gave this command to his son Solomon, who was about to succeed him as king: "Observe what the Lord your God requires: Walk in his ways, and keep his decrees and commands, his laws and requirements, as written in the *Law of Moses*, so that you may prosper in all you do and wherever you go" (1 Kings 2:3).

Two hundred years later, about 800 B.C., King Jehoshaphat sent priests and Levites out to teach in the cities of his kingdom: "They taught throughout Judah, taking with them the *Book of the Law [Torah] of the Lord*; they went around to all the towns of Judah and taught the people" (2 Chronicles 17:9).

About 600 B.C., copies of the five books of the Law of Moses went with the people of God when they were led off in chains to Babylon. During the years they spent there, they heard God's representatives speak to them. Ezekiel and Daniel reminded them, first of all, that it was their sinfulness that had led God to destroy their homes in Palestine and to lead them into exile in a far-off land. Although many centuries had passed since God had originally given his people his Word through Moses, those documents had not been lost. In distant Babylon, Daniel knew about them; he may even have had a copy. Listen to a prayer he prayed:

The curses and sworn judgments written in the *Law of Moses*, the servant of God, have been poured out on us, because we have sinned. . . . Just as it is written in the *Law of Moses*, all this disaster has come upon us, yet we have not sought the favor of the Lord our God by turning from our sins and giving attention to your truth. (Daniel 9:11,13)

Abraham 2000 B.C.   Moses 1500 B.C.   David 1000 B.C.   Ezra 500 B.C.   Jesus B.C./A.D.

After the Jews had spent 70 years in exile, God mercifully permitted them to return home. He had prepared spiritual leaders to help them recognize that their exile was his discipline on a stubborn and rebellious people. Ezra was Israel's most important leader during that difficult period following the exile. (Many Bible scholars think that Ezra may have been the one who assembled the individual scrolls into the collection that we call the Old Testament.) He is described as "a teacher well versed in the *Law of Moses*, which the LORD, the God of Israel, had given. . . . Ezra had devoted himself to the study and observance of *the Law [Torah]* of the LORD" (Ezra 7:6,10).

When Babylon fell, Persia became the superpower in the Middle East. It was Ezra who asked Persia's King Artaxerxes to authorize a group of exiles to return to Jerusalem. Note the words with which the king granted his request: "I decree that any of the Israelites in my kingdom, including priests and Levites, who wish to go to Jerusalem with you, may go. You are sent by the king . . . to inquire about Judah and Jerusalem with regard to the *Law of your God, which is in your hand*" (Ezra 7:13,14).

A small remnant of the exiles took their families, the few possessions they could carry (including their precious scrolls), and returned to Palestine to reestablish their homes in a land that had been ravaged by war. Then, in the fall of that year, they gathered in Jerusalem to celebrate the Feast of Trumpets: "They told Ezra the scribe to bring out the Book of the *Law of Moses*, which the LORD had commanded for Israel" (Nehemiah 8:1).

By then a thousand years had passed since Moses had originally written the first five books of the Old Testament. During that time copies and copies of copies had been made and preserved and handed down. As a result, day by day God's people could hear God speak to them through his Word of command and of promise. Though ten centuries had passed since Moses wrote, God's people still had the five books of the Torah in their possession—to hear, to read, and to study. God's chosen people remembered that he had called them to be not only the *recipients* but also the *custodians* of his written Word.

The Prophets

We can see the same evidence of God's grace when it comes to the second segment of Old Testament Scripture, *the Prophets*. Day by day, year after year, generation after generation, God's people knew what God had announced through the prophets of previous generations. Look at some of the evidence.

Jeremiah lived about 600 B.C.—at that time God allowed the Babylonian army to invade Jerusalem, smash its walls, and trash the city and its temple. With eyes opened by the Spirit of God, Jeremiah saw this nightmare of judgment coming. He warned the citizens of Jerusalem and their wicked King Jehoiakim—neither of whom appreciated his warning. Jeremiah was arrested and charged with treason—a capital crime. At his trial, however, some of the city elders rose to defend Jeremiah. They said: "A century ago the prophet Micah said the same things Jeremiah has been saying. At that time good King Hezekiah did not put Micah to death." Micah's exact words a hundred years earlier were "Zion will be plowed like a field, Jerusalem will become a heap of rubble, the temple hill a mound overgrown with thickets" (Jeremiah 26:18).

At Jeremiah's time, a hundred years later than Micah, the prophecy of Micah was part of the sacred collection of Old Testament Scripture. A century later Jerusalem's elders had among them some who believed and had read Micah's prophecy. Their believing testimony in the courtroom saved Jeremiah's life.

So as the centuries of the Old Testament passed, alongside the collection of the five books of the *Law* (the Torah), there came to exist a collection of the writings of the *Prophets*. Later prophets quoted from the earlier prophets. When Micah wrote his prophecy about 700 B.C., he included a statement that King David had made three hundred years earlier and which is recorded in the prophetic book of 2 Samuel: "Tell it not in Gath" (Micah 1:10, quoting 2 Samuel 1:20).

The prophet Jeremiah had predicted that Jerusalem would fall to the Babylonian army and that what was left of the Jewish nation would be led off to Babylon as prisoners of war. Still more, Jeremiah had even predicted the exact number of years the Jews would spend in exile: "This whole country will become a desolate wasteland, and these nations will serve the king of Babylon *seventy years*" (Jeremiah 25:11). "This is what the LORD says: 'When *seventy years* are completed for Babylon, I will come to you and fulfill my gracious promise to bring you back to this place'" (Jeremiah 29:10).

More than 50 years after Jeremiah wrote this, when the prophet Daniel was in Babylon, he had with him a copy of Jeremiah's prophecy. After Babylon fell to the Persians, Daniel himself tells us:

> "I, Daniel, understood from the Scriptures, according to the word of the LORD given to Jeremiah the prophet, that the desolation of Jerusalem would last seventy years. So I turned to the Lord God and pleaded with him in prayer and petition, in fasting, and in sackcloth and ashes." (Daniel 9:2,3)

As each additional Old Testament book was written under the miracle of inspiration, God's appointed custodians preserved it and added it to the sacred collection. It seems

Daniel must have taken a collection of the Old Testament books with him when he was led off to Babylon.

When Daniel finished writing down the Bible book that bears his name, God had these instructions for him: "Daniel, *close up* and *seal* the words of the scroll until the time of the end" (Daniel 12:4).

When the famous Dead Sea Scrolls were accidentally discovered in caves west of the Dead Sea, they had been wrapped in linen and placed into large clay jars, which were then sealed. In this way they were preserved until their discovery two thousand years later. God commanded Daniel to close up and seal the prophetic scroll he had just written—not so that it would be *hidden* but so that it would be *preserved* for future generations of God's people to read. Daniel was one of those custodians who helped preserve the Old Testament for us.

The Writings

David's final psalm is Psalm 72, a magnificent hymn praising the great Messiah-King, who would one day come from the family tree of David:

> He will defend the afflicted . . . and . . . crush the oppressor. . . . He will endure as long as the sun . . . through all generations. He will rule from sea to sea. . . . May his name endure forever. . . . All nations will be blessed through him. . . . This concludes the prayers of David son of Jesse. (Psalm 72:4,5,8,17,20)

Three hundred years after David had written his last psalm, King Hezekiah came to the throne of Israel. His first job as king was to undo the damage his unbelieving father, Ahaz, had done during 16 years on the throne. Ahaz practiced Baal worship, offered his own sons as human sacrifices to his false gods, and as a final insult to the true God, shut down the temple in Jerusalem. Although Hezekiah was only 25 when he became king, he spearheaded a reformation. After cleansing and reopening the temple, he gave the order for an impressive service of rededication. "King Hezekiah . . . ordered the Levites to praise the LORD with the words of David. . . . So they sang praises with gladness" (2 Chronicles 29:30).

Centuries earlier, David's psalms, written by inspiration of God, had been part of Israel's worship services. During the reign of wicked King Ahaz, no worship services had been held at the temple. But David's psalms had been preserved, along with the other sacred writings, and now they were reintroduced into public worship by good King Hezekiah.

We're grateful to this godly king for something else he did as one of the appointed custodians of the Old Testament Scripture. "These are more proverbs of Solomon, copied by the men of Hezekiah king of Judah" (Proverbs 25:1). Another Old Testament book that belongs to that third group, the Writings, is the book of Proverbs. These proverbs consist of a collection of sayings, most of them written by wise King Solomon, that make up a kind of instruction manual about living life God's way. Hezekiah saw to it that copies were made and the book of Proverbs was added to the growing collection we know as the Old Testament.

The prophet Malachi, who lived four centuries before Christ, was the last Old Testament writer. Josephus, a famous Jewish historian who lived a generation after Christ, referred to the collection of sacred writings that the Jewish people regarded as the authoritative Word of God. According to Josephus, this collection included books written "from the time of Moses to the time of Artaxerxes" (a Persian king who died in 424 B.C.). The 39 Old Testament books were written from the time of Moses, the first prophet, to the time of Israel's last prophet, Malachi. When Malachi finished writing his book of prophecy, the Old Testament was at last complete.

The Old Testament

Do you see the miracle? Here are several dozen different books, consisting of history and poetry, sermons and short stories, written in different countries by various authors over a period of a thousand years. Yet these different parts fit together to tell a single story of a God who was determined to gather a group of people whom he could love—forever. The love of God described on the pages of the Old Testament was undeserved, it was tough, it was jealous, it was forgiving, and it was persistent.

Genesis
Exodus
Leviticus
Numbers
Deuteronomy
Joshua
Judges
Ruth
1 & 2 Samuel
1 & 2 Kings
1 & 2 Chronicles
Ezra
Nehemiah
Esther
Job
Psalms
Proverbs
Ecclesiastes
Song of Songs
Isaiah
Jeremiah
Lamentations
Ezekiel
Daniel
Hosea
Joel
Amos
Obadiah
Jonah
Micah
Nahum
Habakkuk
Zephaniah
Haggai
Zechariah
Malachi

For Jewish believers, the 39 books of the Old Testament were the Word of God—true and absolutely authoritative. This is the Bible that Jesus read and used. God's chosen people believed its promises; they studied its history and its prophecy. They learned from its Writings. They worshiped with its psalms. And day by day they waited for God to send the Messiah he had promised to their forefather Abraham.

Between the Testaments

The period of about 400 years between the time of the prophet Malachi and the time of Christ is known as the *Intertestamental Period*. The prophet Daniel predicted (chapter 11) that these four centuries would be a difficult period of time for God's believing people who were waiting for the Messiah. The armies of Syria and Egypt took turns tramping through and trampling over Palestine. Although an average Jewish family would have found handwritten copies of the entire Old Testament far too expensive to own, even the poorest could have continued to hear the Old Testament read in their local synagogues. Jews who believed in God's promises hoped to be able to own their own copies at least of the sacred Torah of Moses.

The period from 175–164 B.C. was the most difficult for God's faithful Jewish people who lived during the Intertestamental Period. At that time the throne in Syria was held

by a dynasty of kings who were successors of the Greek world-conquering Alexander the Great. They controlled Palestine, and they tried to force the Jews to accept Greek religion and Greek customs. In 175 B.C. a Syrian tyrant named Antiochus Epiphanes became king and persecuted any Jews who wanted to remain loyal to the truth of the Old Testament. The book of *Maccabees* describes what the Syrian soldiers, under orders from their king, did if they found a Jew who had a copy of any of the Old Testament Scriptures: "When they had torn in pieces the books of the Law which they found, they burnt them with fire. And wherever anyone was found with the Book of the Covenant [the Torah], . . . the king's commandment was that they should put him to death" (1 Maccabees 1:56,57).

The two books of Maccabees are part of a collection of 15 Jewish books known as the *Apocrypha*, written during the last two centuries B.C. and the first century A.D. They were, however, never part of the Hebrew Bible. Martin Luther had this opinion: "Although they are not to be put on a level with the Scriptures, they are valuable to read."

The New Testament period

God mercifully cut short this period of persecution when the Roman army invaded and conquered Palestine. The Roman authorities allowed the Jews to keep their sacred books, to study them, and to conduct their religious affairs without government interference. God's plan was successful. Throughout the centuries of the Old Testament, and into the period of the New Testament, God's people were able, day by day, to hear the voice of their heavenly Father speaking to them through his Word. When Magi from the east came to Jewish King Herod to find out where the newborn King of the Jews could be found, Herod knew where to go for the answer. He asked the chief priests and teachers of the law, the Bible scholars of that day: "What do your Old Testament scrolls say

about where the Messiah will be born?" They answered, "In Bethlehem in Judea, . . . for this is what the prophet has written: 'But you, Bethlehem, in the land of Judah, are by no means least among the rulers of Judah; for out of you will come a ruler who will be the shepherd of my people Israel'" (Matthew 2:5,6).

The authors of the books of the New Testament looked upon the books of the Old Testament as a unit whose author was God. They viewed the entire Old Testament, just as we do, as a testimony to Jesus Christ: the perfect Man who fulfilled God's law in the sinner's place and the Priest, Prophet, and King of whom the Old Testament writers foretold. Listen to the apostle Paul, writing to some early gentile Christians: "You are . . . built on the foundation of the apostles and prophets, with Christ Jesus himself as the chief cornerstone" (Ephesians 2:19,20).

Israel's assignment

We marvel at the miracle. God called human beings, from the bloodline of Abraham, to put his Word down in written form, then to preserve that Word, and then to pass it on down to future generations.

God used generation after generation of Old Testament believers to pass on the gift of truth to people who wouldn't otherwise have had a clue. Humanly speaking, we wouldn't have a Bible today if it weren't for the Jewish people. What a debt we Christians owe to the Jewish people!

Our assignment

Child of God, God used your parents to pass on to you the precious gift of life. You and I have *not* been called by God to put his inspired Word down in writing. (That was the assignment God gave his prophets and apostles.) Nor were we to be eyewitnesses of the Savior's death and resurrection. (That was the assignment Jesus gave his first disciples.) We were not to uncover the gospel from the rubbish of centuries of false teaching. (That was the assignment God gave reformers like Martin Luther.)

But you and I *have* been called by God to listen and learn when God speaks to us through his Word, to put into practice what God has told us, and to pass it on to friends, relatives, acquaintances, and neighbors. That's what it means to be a *recipient* and a *custodian* of God's Word today. "The law from your mouth is more precious to me than thousands of pieces of silver and gold" (Psalm 119:72).

We have found the one Moses wrote about in the Law, and about whom the prophets also wrote—Jesus of Nazareth.

~ John 1:45

A Preview of the Promised Savior

We often speak of the promise God made to the patriarch Abraham. Actually it would be more accurate to speak of the *promises* God made to him. When God called Abraham, he gave him a whole cluster of promises (Genesis 12:2,3):

I will make you into a great nation.

I will bless you.

I will make your name great.

You will be a blessing.

I will bless those who bless you.

Whoever curses you I will curse.

All peoples on earth will be blessed through you.

We can count seven different promises which God gave to the ancestor of his chosen people. Yet it is correct to speak of *the promise* God made to him because the Scripture treats all of the promises God made to Abraham as one. All of them gain their purpose and their certainty from the last and richest promise: "All peoples on earth will be blessed through you."

Through the promised Savior, who would be born from Abraham's bloodline, God would give his greatest blessing: the forgiveness of sin. And he would give it to every human being ever born. God gave Abraham a number of promises, but they all pointed to Christ. Years later, Jesus himself affirmed this when he said, "Abraham rejoiced at the thought of *seeing my day*; he saw it and was glad" (John 8:56). And Saint Paul added a significant commentary: "No matter how many promises God has made, they are 'Yes' *in Christ*" (2 Corinthians 1:20). *In Christ*, God has affirmed and fulfilled all his promises. *Apart from Christ*, God can deal with us only in judgment. Each of the individual promises God gave to Abraham, therefore, can be understood only in the light of God's promise to send the Savior.

Faith in Christ

God regarded faith in any part of that cluster of promises as faith in the last and greatest promise. Take just one example. Abram was 75 years old when God called him (Genesis 12:4); his wife Sarai was 65. Ten years later, when God appeared to him in a vision, 85-year-old Abram told God he was concerned that God's promise wasn't being fulfilled: "What can you give me, since I remain childless? . . . You have given me no children; so a servant in my household will be my heir" (Genesis 15:2,3).

God answered: "This man will not be your heir, but a son coming from your own body will be your heir" (Genesis 15:4). And then follows the significant statement (which Martin Luther called "one of the foremost passages of all Scripture"): "Abram *believed* the Lord, and he *credited it to him as righteousness*" (Genesis 15:6).

Abraham believed the Lord's illogical promise that a son would come from his "good as dead" body and from his barren wife, long past menopause. Through that faith God gave Abraham credit for being righteous, for having met God's holy standard, his demand for moral perfection from every human. Saint Paul emphasized that through faith in God's promise Abraham was justified, pronounced innocent by God (Romans 4:2-5; Galatians 3:6-9).

Does this sound strange to you? Does the Bible teach that if a husband and his wife believe they will have a child, they will be saved?

No, the Bible does not teach that. But God looked upon Abraham's faith in one of the individual, specific promises as faith in the Savior, who was the heart of all of the promises. Abraham was saved by faith in the Savior who was to come, just as you and I are saved by faith in the Savior who has come.

Identifying the Messiah

The promise God made to Abraham contained very little specific information about the coming Messiah. All it told Abraham was that the Savior would be one of his descendants and that, like a king, he would bring blessing to his people. If that's all God had told his Old Testament people, they would have had a tough time identifying the messianic King when he appeared. Were they supposed to judge by what they thought this King should look like? (Twenty centuries later, Pontius Pilate did not recognize that the lowly prisoner standing before him was a king. God surely did not want his people to identify the promised Messiah only on the basis of what he looked like.) Could God perhaps have identified the Messiah by name? (In that case, God's people could have been misled by any deceiver who might come along and call himself by that name.)

God had a better way to help his people identify the Messiah. Over the centuries of the Old Testament, he supplied further information to fill in the picture. God put together a mosaic of the coming Savior, one prophecy at a time. When all these prophecies were put together to form a complete picture, God's people would be able to recognize their Savior-King when he came.

Have you ever noticed how often Jesus connected himself to the prophets and promises of the Old Testament? In his Sermon on the Mount, he said, "Do not think that I have come to abolish the Law or the Prophets; I have not come to abolish them but *to fulfill them*" (Matthew 5:17). The evening of the first Easter Sunday, Jesus told his disciples, "Everything *must be fulfilled that is written about me* in the Law of Moses, the Prophets and the Psalms" (Luke 24:44).

In the Old Testament, God supplied different types of information about the promised Messiah. To enable his people to identify him, God told them in advance about the Messiah's *person*, the *work* the Messiah would do, the *attitude* with which the Messiah would approach his work, and the *results* the Messiah's work would have for us.

The Messiah's person: a human being

In the Garden of Eden, Eve heard God tell Satan, " [*her*] *offspring* . . . will crush your head" (Genesis 3:15). Many a Christmas worshiper has heard this promise: The one who would crush Satan would be a male child, born of a human mother.

Another piece of God's mosaic was the promise he made to Abraham: "I will make you into a great nation. . . . All peoples on earth will be blessed through you" (Genesis 12:2,3). The promised Messiah would be a descendant of Abraham, a Jewish person.

The prophet Isaiah supplied important pieces of the mosaic that gives us an Old Testament picture of the Savior. He would be "a shoot . . . from the stump of Jesse" (Isaiah 11:1). Great King David was the son of Jesse, and the Bible compares David's royal house to a mighty tree. Because of the sin of ancient Israel, however, the axe of God's judgment would have cut that tree down. Humanly speaking, it was impossible for the promised Messiah-King to come from a nonexistent royal line. His birth would be a miracle of God's grace.

Miraculously, he would be born to a pure virgin. "The virgin will be with child and will give birth to a son" (Isaiah 7:14). God had designed the law of human reproduction: Life is passed on from generation to generation by a union of male and female. But, when God sent the promised Messiah to this planet, he chose to suspend that law temporarily. And what was the result? The One who is larger than the universe became a microscopic embryo in the body of a young Jewish virgin. The champion who would conquer his enemies and rescue his people arrived—nine months later—in the humble form of a baby, who depended on his mother for his very existence. But he was a sinless child. Since he wasn't conceived by the union of a father and mother, he didn't inherit sin as you and I did from our parents.

The prophet Micah even pinpointed the place where this miracle birth would take place. It would be Bethlehem, a tiny village six miles south of Jerusalem (Micah 5:2).

In order to meet the demands of God's holy law and also to suffer the curse that God's holy law announced, the Messiah had to be a man. With these prophecies, God informed his chosen people that the Savior on whom their hope centered would be *a member of the human race.*

The New Testament provides positive evidence that these prophecies of the Messiah were all fulfilled. To show that Jesus of Nazareth is a real human being, it gives us not one but two genealogies of Jesus:

1. Saint Matthew provides Jesus' *legal lineage* from Abraham to Joseph and Mary (Matthew 1:1-16).
2. Saint Luke traces Jesus' *bloodline* from Joseph back to Adam (Luke 3:23-37).

The Messiah's person: true God

There are many people—outside and even inside the Christian church—who answer the question "Who is Jesus of Nazareth?" by saying, "He was a human being." Arius, a church leader who lived about A.D. 300, carried half of the members of the international Christian church with him when he taught that Jesus Christ was only a human being.

In the picture that God provided for his Old Testament people, however, there were a number of pieces that show clearly that the Messiah-King would be more than a human being. He would be God in human form.

God told Adam and Eve: "I will put enmity" between you and Satan, and will crush Satan's head (Genesis 3:15). The job of defeating Satan and freeing his slaves is one that only God could do.

Listen to the prophet Isaiah describe the mighty King from David's line: "To us a child is born, to us a son is given, and the government will be on his shoulders. And he will be called Wonderful Counselor, *Mighty God*, . . . Prince of Peace. . . . He will reign on David's throne . . . forever" (Isaiah 9:6,7).

Psalm 45 paints a portrait of the messianic King who brings victory to God's people: "Gird your sword upon your side, O mighty one. . . . Let the nations fall beneath your feet. Your throne, *O God*, will last for ever and ever" (verses 3,5,6). The New Testament letter to the Hebrews tells us that it is the Messiah about whom the psalmist was speaking (1:8).

Why both God and man?

Can you see why it was necessary for the promised Messiah, in addition to being a real human being, also to be truly God? Imagine, for a moment, that you never committed a sin in your whole life. That would mean you were a perfect human being. What would God say to you when you meet him on judgment day? What else could he say but: "Come, my child; your place at my side is ready!"

But what would God answer if you were to ask, "May I take my family along with me?" God would reply: "The fact that you obeyed my law perfectly is enough to save *you*. But your holiness is not enough to cover the sins of *your family*." The psalmist wrote: "No *man* can redeem the life of another or give to God a ransom for him—the ransom for a life is costly, no payment is ever enough. . . . But *God* will redeem my soul from the grave, he will surely take me to himself" (Psalm 49:7,8,15).

Do you see why our Savior had to be more than a human being? To save not just himself but a whole world of sinners, Jesus had to *fulfill the demands* of God's law in our place and *suffer the curse* God's law pronounces on all who disobey.

The picture of the promised Savior that the Old Testament painted showed clearly that he would be both a human being as well as God himself. The Messiah would be the *God-man*, one of a kind, never to be repeated—God's lone bid to redeem a whole history book full of individual sinners.

The Messiah's work: a Servant-King

If you had never seen the portrait the Old Testament paints of the promised Messiah, how would you have expected him to appear to his people? As a conquering king, wearing a golden crown sparkling with diamonds? Riding a warhorse at the head of an army? When God gave his Old Testament people a word picture of the coming Savior, he described him as a different kind of king. He would come as a king but also as a servant. Both pictures are taught in the Old Testament. (Since these descriptions are so different, some Jewish scholars actually thought there would be two Messiahs.)

A servant is a person who has no will of his own. His master's will determines what a servant does. The psalmist David prophesied that the Messiah would have the mind-set of a servant. He quotes the Messiah as saying "Here I am, I have come—it is written about me in the scroll. I desire to do your will, O my God" (Psalm 40:7,8).

The epistle to the Hebrews helps us see that when David wrote those words, he was speaking not just about himself but also about the Messiah: "When *Christ* came into the world, he said . . . 'Here I am—it is written about me in the scroll—I have come to do your will, O God'" (Hebrews 10:5,7).

Of all the Old Testament writers, there is none who pictures the Messiah as God's servant more frequently and more beautifully than the prophet Isaiah. Listen to some of what God told his people through the pen of Isaiah: "Here is *my servant*, whom I uphold, my chosen one in whom I delight; I will put my Spirit on him. . . . He will not shout or cry out, or raise his voice in the streets. A bruised reed he will not break, and a smoldering wick he will not snuff out" (Isaiah 42:1-3).

Isaiah wrote those words long before the Savior ever appeared. When he did appear seven centuries later, Saint Matthew applied Isaiah's words to Jesus:

> A large crowd followed [Jesus], and he healed all who were ill. . . . This was to fulfill what was spoken through the prophet Isaiah: "Here is my *servant* whom I have chosen, the one I love, in whom I delight; I will put my Spirit on him. . . . He will not quarrel or cry out; no one will hear his voice in the streets. A bruised reed he will not break, and a smoldering wick he will not snuff out." (Matthew 12:15,17-20 TNIV)

Many consider chapters 52 and 53 to be Isaiah's most beautiful description of the Messiah as a servant, devoted to carrying out the will of his heavenly Father. Listen to what the Father has to say about him:

> My *servant* will act wisely; he will be raised and lifted up and highly exalted. . . . He had no beauty or majesty to attract us to him, nothing in his appearance that we should desire him. He was despised and rejected by men, a man of sorrows, and familiar with suffering. . . . He was pierced for our transgressions, he was crushed for our iniquities; the punishment that brought us peace was upon him, and by his wounds we are healed. (Isaiah 52:13; 53:2-5)

No other religion on earth—not Judaism, not Buddhism, not Islam—offers this unique combination of a God who is eternal and almighty but who willingly became the lowliest servant. He accepted all the limitations and all the pain of the human beings he had created. He went through the blood and pain of birth to the blood and pain of the cross. Can you see why God pointed this out to his chosen people centuries in advance? God didn't want them to wonder how he felt toward them, and he surely did not want them to miss the only Savior they were ever going to have.

Through his prophets, God also announced that the promised Messiah would be a *king*: "To us a child is born, to us a son is given, and the government will be on his shoulders . . . He will reign on David's throne . . . forever" (Isaiah 9:6,7). "'The days are coming,' declares the LORD, 'when I will raise up to David . . . a King who will reign wisely and do what is just and right in the land. In his days Judah will be saved and Israel will live in safety'" (Jeremiah 23:5,6).

The Messiah whom God promised to send his people would do the work of a king. A king's job is to protect and provide for his people. Jesus was and is the King—now and for all eternity. When he was born, Magi from the east came to Jerusalem asking, "Where is the one who has been born king of the Jews?" (Matthew 2:2).

Five days before he died, the Servant-King entered Jerusalem riding on a donkey's colt "to fulfill what was spoken through the prophet: . . . 'See, your *king* comes to you, gentle and riding on a donkey, on a colt, the foal of a donkey'" (Matthew 21:4,5).

Even the superscription above the Messiah's head as he hung on the cross announced, "Jesus is a king." How sad, how wrong is the picture of the Savior presented by many preachers today: "God so loved the world that he . . ." inspired a Jewish carpenter-teacher to inform his contemporaries that there's a whole lot to be said for loving your neighbor?

That's not the message of the Old Testament. Day by day God reminded his Old Testament saints: "I'm going to send you a King who will conquer your enemies—anyone and anything that could separate you from me. He will keep you safe, so that you can live close to me now and at my side forever."

Normally it's taken for granted that a king lives and works in the nation's capital. That is where the leader lives, along with the people whom he is to protect. We might have expected that when Christ began to preach and to gather a group of followers, he would move to Jerusalem, the political and religious capital of Palestine. The prophet Isaiah had foretold, however, that the Messiah would begin his work, oddly enough, in the far north—in the tribal territories of Zebulun and Naphtali (the region we call Galilee): "In the past [God] *humbled* the land of Zebulun and the land of Naphtali, but in the future he will *honor* Galilee of the Gentiles, by the way of the sea, along the Jordan—The people walking in darkness have seen a great light" (Isaiah 9:1,2).

Saint Matthew described how Isaiah's unlikely prophecy was fulfilled. After his baptism, "Jesus . . . withdrew to Galilee. . . . He went and lived in Capernaum, which was by the lake in the area of Zebulun and Naphtali—to fulfill what was said through the prophet Isaiah: 'Land of Zebulun and land of Naphtali, the Way of the Sea, along the Jordan, Galilee of the Gentiles—the people living in darkness have seen a great light'" (Matthew 4:12-16 TNIV).

Jesus began his ministry in Galilee, and he spent most of his three-year ministry there. That seemed strange to those observing him. Maybe you remember what happened when Philip, a brand-new disciple of Jesus, told his friend Nathanael: "We have found the one Moses wrote about in the Law, and about whom the prophets also wrote—Jesus of Nazareth." Nathanael responded: "Nazareth! *Can anything good come from there*?" (John 1:45,46).

In a way we can understand how Nathanael felt, because there were more unbelieving foreigners living in Galilee than Jews. (It wasn't by accident that Isaiah referred to that northern section of the country as "Galilee of the Gentiles.") But that was one of the clues that God had given his chosen people to help them identify the Messiah. He would be active in Galilee, in a region of Palestine and among people that many Jews looked down on.

The prophet Isaiah provided another piece for God's mosaic picture of the coming Messiah when he wrote: "Your God will come, . . . he will come to save you. Then will the eyes of the blind be opened and the ears of the deaf unstopped. Then will the lame leap like a deer, and the mute tongue shout for joy" (Isaiah 35:4-6).

Years later Jesus referred to this prophecy when John the Baptist sent two of his disciples to Jesus:

> When the men came to Jesus, they said, "John the Baptist sent us to you to ask, 'Are you the one who was to come, or should we expect someone else?'" At that very time Jesus cured many who had diseases, sicknesses and evil spirits, and gave sight to many who were blind. So he replied to the messengers, "Go back and report to John what you have seen and heard: The blind receive sight, the lame walk, those who have leprosy are cleansed, the deaf hear, the dead are raised, and the good news is proclaimed to the poor." (Luke 7:20-22 TNIV)

God had made it clear to his people that one of the fingerprints by which they could recognize the promised Messiah when he came would be that he would perform miracles. He would do what only God can do.

In the ministry of Christ, we see the fulfillment of this promise. His fingers touched sightless eyes, and instantly they could see. His voice told a young man in a coffin: "Get up!" and the man stood up. Christ's power reattached the ear of a man who had come to Gethsemane to arrest him. When he met a man who was being tortured by an evil spirit, Jesus said to the demon that had taken possession of the man's body: "I command you, come out of him and never enter him again!" (Mark 9:25). Whenever Jesus came face-to-face with sin, the evil power had to submit to his authority.

The Messiah's attitude

In the very last book of the Bible, the apostle John calls Jesus "the Lamb who was slain from the creation of the world" (Revelation 13:8 TNIV). It was no secret to Jesus what it would cost him to reconcile a world of sinners to God. As the substitute for sinners, he knew that he would be the heavenly lightning rod that would absorb the fiery lightning bolts of God's anger at sin and at sinners. How very difficult, how heavy a burden—to know in advance that on Calvary he would be forsaken by his own Father! He knew what lay ahead because he had already read the last chapter. What was the Messiah's attitude as he foresaw and foreknew the nightmare that waited just ahead for him?

In the Garden of Gethsemane, the night before he died, Jesus asked his Father if there were another way to rescue sinners. If so, would the Father take this bitter cup of God's judgment from him? But even as he spoke the words, Jesus knew that there was no other way to save the world except for him to trade places with all the people under God's curse. The cross was to be the way. In love for sinners, Jesus told his Father, "Not my will, but yours be done" (Luke 22:42).

Jesus was not forced to be our Savior. He could have refused. But he could bear *our sins* more easily than he could bear the thought of *our eternal hopelessness.* He could endure the dishonor of being damned for sin if it meant we would not be damned for sin. No wonder Satan tried to turn Jesus from his assignment (Matthew 4:8-10)!

Whenever God speaks to us through the voice of his holy law, our ears pick up a double message. God speaks to us about *obedience*, which he demands, but also about *disobedience*, which he forbids. Every human being who has ever lived, except for the Son of Mary, has violated God's law on both counts.

1. We have *withheld the obedience* from God that he demands.
2. We have *flaunted the disobedience* that he forbids.

To satisfy his white-hot anger at sinners, and at the same time to satisfy his merciful heart, God appointed his Son to be the servant who would exchange places with sinners. He would substitute for them in two ways (corresponding to the double message of God's law):

1. He would give God the perfect obedience you and I have withheld from him. He would do what we have not done. (We usually refer to this as Christ's *active obedience*.)
2. He would accept in his own body God's punishment for our disobedience. He would undo what we have done. (We usually refer to this as Christ's *passive obedience*.)

In what spirit did the promised Messiah give his Father that double obedience? All of us know that forced obedience is not genuine obedience. Imagine a father walking into his living room and asking his 12-year-old son, who is watching TV, to wash the family car. The son answers: "But, Dad, this is my favorite program." Then he sees the look in his father's eye and answers, "Oh, all right." He goes outside and washes the car. Gladly? Not exactly. But he'd rather wash the car than suffer some unpleasant consequences.

On the pages of the Old Testament, however, God let his chosen people hear the obedient voice of his Son: "Here I am, I have come—it is written about me in the scroll. *I desire to do your will*, O my God" (Psalm 40:7,8). Christ's obedience to his Father's will was not forced; it was voluntary. Do you see what difference this makes to you?

Imagine that 45 seconds from now a magnificent trumpet sound breaks into your world, and instantly you find yourself looking into those eyes that the Bible describes as flames of fire. When God asks you: "What have you done with the gift of life I gave you? Have you kept my law perfectly?" how are you going to answer?

What a relief—what a delight to be able to answer, "Yes, Father, I have—not personally, but through my Substitute!"

When Jesus said: "Not my will, but yours be done" and "I desire to do your will, O my God," he was doing that in our place, as our Substitute! The Old Testament makes it clear that the Messiah's attitude as he approached his Savior work was one of willing obedience.

Listen to another prophetic passage from the pen of the prophet Isaiah, and see another part of the Messiah's attitude as he contemplated his Savior work:

The Sovereign Lord has opened my ears, and I have not been rebellious; I have not drawn back. I offered my back to those who beat me, my cheeks to those who pulled out my beard; I did not hide my face from mocking and spitting. Because the Sovereign Lord helps me, *I will not be disgraced*. Therefore have I set my face like flint, and *I know I will not be put to shame*. (Isaiah 50:5-7)

The Messiah knew that his life of perfect obedience and his sacrificial death in the place of sinners would satisfy God's justice—both the demands and the threats of God's law. Christ was confident that he would turn the anger of God away from sinners and onto himself. He would crush the serpent's head. He would break Satan's power over the human race. Satan's slaves would be set free to serve God. The price? God's One and Only: dead and damned.

The psalmist David also lets us look inside the mind of Christ as he contemplated being cursed by his own Father. David put these words into the mouth of the Messiah:

> My heart is glad and my tongue rejoices; my body also will rest secure, because you will *not abandon me to the grave*, nor will you let your Holy One see decay. You have made known to me the path of life; you will fill me with joy in your presence, with eternal pleasures at your right hand. (Psalm 16:9-11)

Both Saint Peter (Acts 2:25-28) and Saint Paul (Acts 13:35-37) emphasize that, although David wrote these words, it was the Messiah who was speaking them. As Jesus Christ approached his work, there was no doubt in his mind. He knew what the outcome would be. He was confident that his work would be successful. God wanted his Old Testament people to know that. He wanted them to know that their hope for a happy eternity was not a long shot but a sure thing. It is that for us too. What a God we worship!

Blessings from the Messiah's work

Peace with God is surely the biggest blessing any person can hope for. Adam and Eve needed to know it. It was the biggest blessing God's Old Testament people hoped to receive through the Messiah. Without God's assurance that the blood of a substitute had covered their sin, they could not live. And without the assurance that they were at peace with God, they surely were not ready to die. No wonder God's pledged word through the prophets was so precious to God's people! "The punishment that brought us *peace* was upon him, and by his wounds we are healed" (Isaiah 53:5). "[The Messiah] will be their *peace*" (Micah 5:5).

The main job God gave the kings of Israel was to protect and provide for his people, to keep them safe in body and soul. Sadly, Israel's merely human kings failed to meet God's requirements. The people of Israel lived in constant fear of their hostile neighbors. You can understand, then, why God's promises about the Messiah-King, who would keep his people spiritually safe, were so precious to them. "He will . . . shepherd his flock. . . . And *they will live securely*, for then his greatness will reach to the ends of the earth" (Micah 5:4).

God's promises of the Messiah gave his people confidence as they lived out their lives in an unfriendly world. They had reason to trust him. He had made a covenant with them, a solemn commitment. He had placed himself under obligation to remain faithful to them, and his people knew God could not—and would not—go back on his pledged word. God must tell the truth. "'Though the mountains be shaken and the hills be removed, yet my unfailing love for you will not be shaken nor my covenant of peace be removed,' says the LORD, who has compassion on you" (Isaiah 54:10).

God's Old Testament people knew that their lives would not end at the cemetery. God's promises had convinced them that there is another life in a better world. They knew that through faith in what the Messiah would do for them, they would one day enjoy perfect life with God. That's why they could confidently say with the psalmist: "I will dwell in the house of the LORD forever" (Psalm 23:6).

The last prophetic voice

We have looked at just a few of the prophecies God had the psalmists and the prophets write down for his people as they waited for God to keep his big promise. Down through the centuries of the Old Testament, God made sure that his people got an increasingly clearer picture of the Savior whom he had promised to send. And then, just before the Messiah appeared in public, God did one more thing, so that his people would be sure to make a positive identification of the Messiah. "There was a man sent from God whose name was John. He came as a witness to testify concerning that light, so that through him all might believe. . . . The true light that gives light to everyone was coming into the world" (John 1:6,7 TNIV). God sent John the Baptist to make an important announcement. And what was the announcement? "John saw Jesus coming toward him and said, 'Look, the Lamb of God, who takes away the sin of the world! I have seen and I testify that this is God's Chosen One'" (John 1:29,34 TNIV).

Here was the fulfillment of God's promise to Abraham! All those promises made, and now kept! The reason that Israel could ever be called "God's chosen"—that from their flesh and blood would come the Christ—God had done it! And now this good news could go *to the nations*, so that they too might be God's chosen people.

The heart of the Old Testament

God did not deal with his Old Testament people, just as he does not deal with us, *apart from Christ*. God made it clear that his plan for ancient Israel would be carried out only through the One whom we have learned to know as Jesus Christ. All of the history and the prophecy and the poetry that make up the Old Testament *point to Christ*. The apostle Paul said the same thing when he was on trial before Jewish King Agrippa: "I am saying nothing beyond what the prophets and Moses said would happen—that the Messiah would suffer and, as the first to rise from the dead, would bring the message of light to his own people and to the Gentiles" (Acts 26:22 TNIV).

And as for you, Christian: The person who believes in Jesus Christ understands the message of the New Testament, along with the heart of the Old Testament. The person who refuses to believe in Jesus Christ has lost the message of both the Old Testament and the New.

He who works his land will have abundant food, but the one who chases fantasies will have his fill of poverty.

~ PROVERBS 28:19

A wife of noble character . . . sets about her work vigorously; her arms are strong for her tasks. . . . She . . . does not eat the bread of idleness.

~ PROVERBS 31:10,17,27

Whatever your hand finds to do, do it with all your might.

~ ECCLESIASTES 9:10

Busy Lives

By giving his Old Testament believers information about the coming Messiah, God demonstrated his concern for their eternal happiness. He revealed his fatherly nature to his Old Testament people. But a father is not only concerned about the *long-term* needs of his children. Every father wants to provide also for the *day-to-day* needs of his loved ones. God therefore promised the descendants of Abraham: "Worship the LORD your God, and his blessing will be on your food and water" (Exodus 23:25).

The Israelites trusted their Father's promise. David put his trust into words: "The eyes of all look to you, and you give them their food at the proper time. You open your hand and satisfy the desires of every living thing" (Psalm 145:15,16).

Another of Israel's poets sang: "[The LORD] provides food for the cattle and for the young ravens when they call" (Psalm 147:9).

But cattle and ravens—and people—don't simply walk outside, flop down on their backs, open their mouths toward heaven, and wait for God to drop food into them. Cattle go out into a field and look around for grass to eat. God designed ravens to look for carrion and small mammals wherever they can find them.

That's the way God provides for his *human* creatures too. He has promised to provide whatever his children need for body and life. But his promise was never intended as an excuse for being lazy. Remember what God told our first parents: "By the sweat of your brow you will eat your food" (Genesis 3:19).

Nomads

Abraham, the ancestor of the Jewish people, spent his first 75 years in the city of Ur (northwest of what we today call the Persian Gulf). Ur was a busy commercial center and the capital of ancient Sumer, a port on the Euphrates very close to the Persian Gulf. It was also a center of moon worship. God called Abraham to leave those sophisticated surroundings. For the remaining century of his life, Abraham and his wife Sarah lived as nomads, wandering from place to place, caring for flocks of sheep and goats. So did their children and their grandchildren.

They lived in the sunny south of Palestine, known as the *Negev* (Hebrew for "hot, dry south land"). Their homes were tents made of goat's hair. They made their living from their sheep and goats, which provided them with food and clothing. Although the Negev is rugged, it offered adequate grazing land for much of the year, provided the rains came. Besides, it was sparsely settled, and that reduced the likelihood of friction with native herdsmen.

As nomads, Abraham and his household moved their tents from place to place, always looking for grassland and for a water supply. Genesis 26:12-25 describes the problems Abraham's son Isaac had in providing water for his household and his flocks. A generation later, Jacob's sons led their flocks to Shechem, 50 miles north of their home in Hebron, to find pasture. Jacob was concerned about his sons and sent Joseph there to visit his brothers and bring back a report. When he got there, Joseph learned that they had traveled *another* 15 miles farther north to graze their cattle. (Imagine, they had led their flocks 65 miles from their home—just to find green grass!)

This nomadic period of Israel's history came to an end when God relocated the members of Jacob's family to Egypt. There they spent the next several centuries. It was in Egypt that Jacob's offspring grew into the nation of Israel.

Settlers

When the right time on God's calendar arrived, God led his people out of Egypt to the new homeland he had promised them. Once the Israelites occupied Palestine, their day-to-day life changed. Instead of living as nomads in a land belonging to strangers, they could now settle down in a country of their own.

God described their new homeland as "a land flowing with milk and honey." Ancient Palestine was a land where they could raise the flocks and the crops they needed to stay alive. It never was, however, a land of lavish abundance. God's chosen people had to work hard to provide for their daily needs. As they waited for the Messiah to come, they lived busy lives.

Farmers

Almost all Israelite families lived on little farms. When the Israelites entered their new homeland, they discovered that they had to follow a different set of rules than they had become accustomed to in Egypt. Ancient Egypt was known as "the gift of the Nile." Each year the snowmelt from mountains in central Africa caused the Nile River to flood, depositing fertile soil downstream. The Nile Valley is a ribbon of breath-taking fertility in a land that is practically rainless. During the many years the Israelites lived in Egypt, they grew accustomed to an agricultural way of life that depended on irrigation.

This changed when God led them to their new homeland. The land occupied by the 12 tribes has only two seasons: a "winter," which is the rainy season, and a rainless, sunny summer.

The early rains came in what we call autumn and made it possible for the farmer to plow the rain-softened ground. From about December to February, Palestine receives 75 percent of its rainfall. The latter rains came in what we call spring and brought the barley and wheat crops to ripeness. The Israelite farmer soon learned that he and his family were totally dependent on the Lord's blessing. If the rains did not come at the right time, fields turned brown and famine was not far away. God used this rainfall pattern to train his chosen people to depend on him to provide for the necessities of everyday life. For fertility and fulfillment, a heavenly Father had to give the word.

An unusual element in God's training program for this nation of farmers occurred every seventh year—the so-called *sabbatical year*. At Mount Sinai, God announced: "For six years you are to sow your fields and harvest the crops, but during the seventh year let the land lie unplowed and unused. Then the poor among your people may get food from it. . . . Do the same with your vineyard and your olive grove" (Exodus 23:10,11).

As a result, every seventh year farmers couldn't work their land. They could pick grapes from their vineyard to eat, but they couldn't harvest the crop. No raisins and wine this year. To make it easier for his people to obey, God pledged: "I'll give you such abundant crops in the preceding years that in the sabbatical year your family won't starve. That's a promise!"

Animal raisers

Israelite farmers used three animals to help them do their field work: the donkey, the mule, and the ox. (In Bible times, horses were primarily animals of war.) Of the three, the ox was most valuable for plowing the heavy soil. "Where there are no oxen, the manger is empty, but from the strength of an ox comes an abundant harvest" (Proverbs 14:4).

The Lord taught his people to show concern for their farm animals. It's been said: "If a man is a Christian, even his dog will know it." The Bible agrees: "A righteous man cares for the needs of his animal" (Proverbs 12:10). A farmer could work his ox and his donkey six days in a row, but every seventh day, the Sabbath, he had to permit the animals to rest.

After the farmer had harvested his wheat crop, he would place the sheaves on a flat piece of ground known as the threshing floor. There he would drive an ox back and forth over the sheaves. The animal's hooves (or the threshing sledge he was pulling) would cut the stalks, separating the wheat kernels from the straw. While the ox was doing this, God instructed the farmer: "Do not muzzle an ox while it is treading out the grain" (Deuteronomy 25:4). It was only natural that, while threshing the grain, a hungry ox would want to stoop down and take a mouthful. The farmer was not permitted to put a muzzle on him, as if to say "Wait until you're finished working, and then I'll give you something to eat."

Herders

After farming, caring for flocks of animals was the next most common occupation in ancient Israel. At that time people's wealth had four legs. When Jacob's family came down to Egypt to escape the famine in Palestine, they brought their flocks with them.

When Joseph introduced his brothers to the Egyptian pharaoh, he told him: "The men are shepherds; they tend livestock" (Genesis 46:32).

Sheep—the variety with a fat tail—were kept in almost every part of the hill country on both sides of the Jordan. They provided milk, meat, and wool, as well as the sheepskin coats so necessary to protect a shepherd from the cold. (Later the leather was used to make scrolls.) Sheep have no natural defenses—no horns, no claws, no fangs. They are helpless; they need a shepherd.

Goats were often raised along with sheep, although they were able to range farther into the desert and survive on a more varied diet. Goats were kept for the same products as sheep. Their black hair was also used for spinning into yarn and weaving into the heavy black cloth used for tents.

Like the life of the farmer, the day-to-day life of a shepherd was hard. Listen to Jacob describe to his father-in-law, Laban, the 20 years he spent shepherding his flocks: "I did not bring you animals torn by wild beasts; I bore the loss myself. . . . The heat consumed me in the daytime and the cold at night, and sleep fled from my eyes" (Genesis 31:39,40).

The Old Testament describes a number of other difficulties the shepherd had to contend with: danger from wild animals (1 Samuel 17:34,36), danger from hit-and-run attacks by desert raiders (Job 1:13-15), and the ever-present threat of famine if rain didn't fall (1 Kings 18:5; Jeremiah 14:4-6).

When the sun went down, therefore, several shepherds might lead their flocks into a large sheepfold for the night. This was a sheep pen made of fieldstone, open to the sky, with four walls and a single entrance. A casual observer might look at the hundreds of animals and wonder how the shepherds could separate their individual flocks the following morning. The hundreds of animals looked indistinguishable. But at sunrise each shepherd, in turn, would stand at the entrance to the sheepfold and call his sheep by name. Almost miraculously, his sheep would respond to his voice and would follow him out (John 10:3-5). The Palestinian shepherd did not drive his flocks; he led them.

Camel teamsters

The camel was by far the largest animal in Palestine. The Israelites usually did not own camels, because camels ("the ship of the desert") do best under hot, dry living conditions. At the time the Israelites were slaves in Egypt (a country which is largely desert), God sent a disastrous plague on the livestock of the Egyptians. All the camels in the country were killed (Exodus 9:3,6). Job, the greatest man in the Middle East, owned three thousand camels (Job 1:3). He lived in Uz, in the land of Edom (south and east of the Dead Sea). At the time of the judges, the Midianites, a desert tribe who lived east of the Sinai Peninsula, terrorized the Israelites when they attacked with a camel-mounted cavalry (Judges 6:5).

Since a camel can carry four hundred pounds and a rider more than 20 miles in a day, it was the basic means of transportation in the desert. Camel caravans were the convoys and teamsters of the Old Testament era. They moved freight from Asia to Africa, and from Africa to Europe, through Israel's land bridge between those three continents.

In his preaching, Jesus twice mentioned the size of the camel. Jesus once had a disappointing experience with a rich young man who had left him because his money was more important to him than Jesus. To emphasize how impossible it is for a person with such an attitude to be saved, Jesus drew this striking contrast: "It is easier for a camel to go through the eye of a needle" (Mark 10:25).

In his final sermon to the people of Jerusalem, Jesus accused the Pharisees of straining out a gnat but swallowing a camel (Matthew 23:24). They strained their wine before drinking it to avoid a speck of dust, but they swallowed whole and without even blinking the false teachings that dishonored Christ and blasphemed God.

Fishermen

The Sea of Galilee is actually a freshwater lake (6 miles wide and 12 miles long) that supported a thriving fishing industry. In Jesus' time Galilee's shores were dotted with villages whose inhabitants made their living by catching fish. After a long night on the lake, they could say, as the disciple Peter once did: "We've worked hard all night" (Luke 5:5).

Israeli fishermen still push their boats out onto the Sea of Galilee every evening in search of the fish that are considered a delicacy. These are probably the same kind of fish that Jesus once used to feed thousands of people (John 6:5-13) and in whose mouth Peter once found a coin which, at Jesus' command, he used for paying the temple tax (Matthew 17:27).

Palestine's fishermen also provided the smoked and pickled fish that were considered luxury items in the international trade of the day.

Other occupations

In Bible times the people who occupied Palestine knew how to work with metals. Archeologists call the period from the time of Abraham to the time of Moses "the Middle Bronze Age," because people at that time relied on tools and weapons of copper and bronze. The Hittites, who came from the land we know as Turkey, had discovered the secret of smelting iron, which requires a much higher

temperature than smelting copper, but they kept that information to themselves. Later the Philistines managed to learn the secret and held a monopoly on iron implements.

> Not a blacksmith could be found in the whole land of Israel, because the Philistines had said, 'Otherwise the Hebrews will make swords or spears!' So on the day of the battle not a soldier with Saul and Jonathan had a sword or spear in his hand; only Saul and his son Jonathan had them. (1 Samuel 13:19,22)

When David conquered the Philistines, their iron-smelting formula became public knowledge. In the cities of Israel, blacksmiths and metalworkers fashioned and repaired farm implements and tools and weapons and musical instruments and household utensils. There were also craftsmen who worked with precious metals and jewelry.

Of all the craftsmen in an Israelite town, the potter was surely among the most important. Day after day he could be seen working at his wheel, turning out the pots and dishes and cups and water jars and oil lamps every household needed.

Woodworkers manufactured furniture and yokes for oxen. You even know the names of two carpenters who lived and worked in Nazareth. Our Lord grew up smelling lumber and sawdust.

While the field crops were ripening, farmers would cut down stalks of flax for their fibers used in making linen cloth, fishing nets, and lamp wicks. Textile workers included those who spun flax into linen and wool into yarn. Others wove yarn into fabric. Still others dyed it with a red or purple dye manufactured from *murex* mollusk shells found along the Mediterranean coast. Cloth dyed this color was very expensive and was worn only by kings and rich people. The rich man who ignored Lazarus, the beggar at his gate, is described as "dressed in purple and fine linen" (Luke 16:19). After Pilate ordered Jesus to be crucified, the soldiers took Jesus into their barracks to have some private fun at their prisoner's expense: "They put a purple robe on him. . . . And they began to call out to him, 'Hail, king of the Jews!'" (Mark 15:17,18).

On his second missionary journey, the apostle Paul met Lydia, "a dealer in purple cloth" (Acts 16:14). The Lord opened Lydia's heart to respond to Paul's message. She was baptized, along with the other members of her household.

The homemaker

One of the busiest people in any town in ancient Palestine was the Hebrew homemaker. Even apart from her most important job—making her home a godly center for her family—her plate was really full. Her day's work usually began

with grinding wheat or barley into flour so she could bake the flat loaves of bread that were an important part of her family's diet. In homes of the wealthy, a ceramic firebox served as an oven. But, for the average homemaker, her "oven" was a pair of flat stones placed on a fire she had kindled outside.

Another important part of her day-to-day activity was to take the big clay jar to the town well to get the family's water supply for the day. Do you remember the directions Jesus gave his disciples on the first Maundy Thursday to help them find a room to celebrate the Passover? "As you enter the city, a *man* carrying a jar of water will meet you" (Luke 22:10). Those directions may not seem unusual to us, but they must have sounded very strange to the disciples. They must have wondered: "Did we hear right? 'A *man* carrying a jar of water?'" That job was always done by hardworking women.

The final chapter of the book of Proverbs summarizes (in the form of beautiful poetry) the day-to-day duties of a Hebrew homemaker:

> She selects wool and flax and works with eager hands. She gets up while it is still dark; she provides food for her family. Her lamp does not go out at night. She watches over the affairs of her household and does not eat the bread of idleness. Her children arise and call her blessed; her husband also, and he praises her. . . . Give her the reward she has earned, and let her works bring her praise at the city gate. (Proverbs 31:13,15,18,27,28,31)

The Old Testament tells us about some impressive and heroic acts of our ancestors in the faith. But it also records the unglamorous, unspectacular, sometimes unpleasant things they had to do. They lived out their day-to-day lives in the land of promise, waiting for the Messiah to come.

God's plan for us includes work

God called his ancient people of Israel, as he has called us, to lead lives that are busy. He has called us to work and to do our work "with all [our] might" (Ecclesiastes 9:10). Really, who has more reason to excel at what he or she does than a Christian? We live in a society and a culture that often views work as a necessary evil. You've met people who believe that if you're smart, you'll try not to work any longer or any harder than you have to.

This kind of twisted thinking shows how deeply sin has infected our lives. From the very beginning, even before sin polluted God's perfect world, God gave his people work to do for him. He gave our first parents a beautiful garden home and ordered them "to work it and take care of it" (Genesis 2:15). Honest labor has an immense dignity in the eyes of the Lord. Anybody who doubts that needs only to visualize the carpenter shop in Nazareth where the almighty Son of God perspired over a workbench with a saw or a hammer in his hand. God takes our humble labor and uses it to accomplish his purposes: God blesses our daily labor with income to provide for the physical needs of our loved ones. God places his sons and daughters in offices or shops, in kitchens or classrooms, so that with their daily activity they can serve as good advertisements for the Lord, whose name they bear. The apostle Paul encouraged Christian workers to be faithful, absolutely trustworthy, "so that in every way they will make the teaching about God our Savior attractive" (Titus 2:10).

In Old Testament times, day by day, God's chosen people lived lives that were busy. That's true of God's New Testament people too.

The world we live in is full of emotional "babies," crawling over each other, screaming: "*Mine*! This I *want*, and this I'm *going to have*, and never mind what it does to anybody else!" Rather than making a difference, such people make only a salary. God has much better plans for us. Every time we look in a mirror, we see two persons. First, we see a sinner, a failure, a promise breaker. But we also see a prodigal child wearing a white robe, with God's ring on his finger and the Father's kiss on his cheek. And then we hear the Father's voice: "Whether you eat or drink or whatever you do, do it all for the glory of God" (1 Corinthians 10:31). "It is good and proper for a man to eat and drink, and to find satisfaction in his toilsome labor. . . . Moreover, when God gives any man wealth and possessions, and enables him to enjoy them, to accept his lot and be happy in his work—this is a gift of God" (Ecclesiastes 5:18,19).

As God's Old Testament people waited for the Messiah to come, they didn't sit twiddling their thumbs. They were busy. It's much the same with God's New Testament sons and daughters. The Lord doesn't ask just for a share of your life, implying that you may do what you want with what's left. He asks you to dedicate to him *all* your life—all that there is of you. That makes being a Christian a full-time job. God couldn't ask for more. And he won't settle for less.

Know then in your heart that as a man disciplines his son, so the Lord your God disciplines you.

~ Deuteronomy 8:5

Do not make light of the Lord's discipline, and do not lose heart when he rebukes you, because the Lord disciplines those he loves.

~ Hebrews 12:5,6

Disciplined by God

The Old Testament history of God's people does not always make for easy or pleasant reading. Think of God's first two children, our first parents. When Adam and Eve listened to Satan's filthy whispering—worse yet, when they believed it—their lives changed for the worse. God cursed the earth from which they made their living: "By the sweat of your brow you will eat your food" (Genesis 3:19). They soon found out what thorns and thistles are. Drudgery, restlessness, and dissatisfaction became a part of their lives. They discovered what pain is. They learned what heartache is when they had to bury their son, murdered by his own brother. Do you suppose that during his life Adam ever wondered (and he had more than nine centuries to wonder about it): "Now that we've rebelled against God, *do we really matter to him*?" They were in "bondage to decay" (Romans 8:21).

Imagine you are one of Abraham's descendants. You grew up hearing about God's covenant of grace and about all the wonderful promises he had made to your famous ancestor—promises that centered on the coming Savior. But then your people had to spend several centuries in Egypt, where slave masters oppressed them with forced labor and where "the Egyptians used them ruthlessly" (Exodus 1:14). Your questions about whether Yahweh really cared about his promises seemed to be answered when he rescued you from Egypt and led you through the Red Sea.

But then, what lay ahead? Forty years of wandering in a wild and barren wasteland, "the vast and dreadful desert, that thirsty and waterless land, with its venomous snakes and scorpions" (Deuteronomy 8:15). A whole generation of your people died in that desert and never made it to the Promised Land. Every day for 40 years your people were busy covering graves and digging dozens of fresh ones. Would you have wondered: *"Do we really matter to God?"*

Finally you reached your new homeland. Under great King David, the enemies on all sides were defeated, and you could finally live in peace. But then what happened? In 930 B.C., after David's son and successor died, a civil war tore your country in two. Two hundred years later the breakaway nation—10 of the 12 tribes—was crushed on the field of battle. It disappeared into the Assyrian captivity and was never heard from again. Now only a small remnant—Judah—was left of what, under King David, had once been a powerful nation. And it wasn't long before that remnant no longer lived in Palestine, but in exile a thousand miles away from home. By the rivers of Babylon you and your people wept when you remembered Jerusalem (Psalm 137:1). You wondered: *"Does God really care about us?"*

The facts seem to indicate that God had no particular love for the nation descended from Abraham. On the surface it might seem that he discarded that nation on the junk heap of history, along with a bunch of other ancient nations. But appearances can be deceiving. Over thousands of years of Old Testament history, God had a plan—a good plan—for Abraham's descendants. He had made a covenant, a solemn contract, with Abraham and his family, and he stuck with it. God's promise had to do with Jesus Christ,

Abraham's offspring. The apostle Paul once asked the question: "Did God reject his people?" His answer: "By no means!" (Romans 11:1).

There are two messages every child must hear from his or her parents:

1. "I love you more than you can possibly understand. You are precious to me."
2. "Because I love you, I must teach you to obey me. This is the only way I can protect you from things that could hurt you."

If earthly parents feel this way toward their children, is it so strange, then, that a heavenly Father also feels this way? God's primary goal for his chosen people had never been just to give them a homeland in Palestine. God was never interested just in giving his people what they wanted. He had something much better in store for them. God wanted to change them. He wanted to help them grow to spiritual maturity. God wanted to teach them to live close to him in order to get them ready to live forever in his presence around the throne of the Lamb.

God's discipline

When, however, the people of Israel resisted his good plan for them, or when they were indifferent to it, God had to intervene. A loving God could do no less. His love for his chosen people was not a flabby love. It was a strong love, a tough love, which often had to tell them: "No, not that way! This way! Don't forget, the Messiah is coming!" God therefore disciplined his chosen people to help them grow spiritually. There are hundreds of examples in the Old Testament of how God disciplined the nation of Israel. Let's look at a few of them.

At Mount Sinai

During the year that the Israelites camped at Mount Sinai, Moses often climbed up the mountain to receive from God the law he was to share with the people. One time he was gone from the camp for about six weeks, and the Israelites grew impatient. The outward splendor of the idolatry they had observed in Egypt had created an appetite in them that wasn't satisfied with the spiritual worship God designed for them. They asked Aaron, Moses' brother, to make them *a god they could see*. He made them a calf of gold. The bull calf, admired for its power and virility, had been a familiar icon in Egypt.

The following day, when Moses came down the mountain with the two stone tablets of the Sinai law covenant in his hands, he heard sounds of singing and dancing. "Moses saw that the people were running wild and that Aaron had let them get out of control" (Exodus 32:25). He smashed the stone tablets on the ground and suddenly the singing and dancing stopped.

Moses commanded the Levites to strap on their swords and kill anyone taunting the Lord, daring him to stop what they were doing. In a short time three thousand bloody corpses littered the campground. And then Moses burnt the golden calf, ground it to powder, and scattered it in the stream that provided drinking water for the Israelites

(Deuteronomy 9:21). God sent a message to his people loud and clear: "Your behavior is an insult to me. By it you degrade yourself. You imperil the promise of the Savior. Furthermore, such behavior will only destroy you. I cannot and I will not tolerate it!" God disciplined his disobedient people.

In the Promised Land

Forty years after they left Mount Sinai, the Israelites entered the Promised Land. God's instructions to them were very clear: "The people who live in Canaan worship false gods, and I don't want you infected. When you enter the land, therefore, I order you to annihilate the occupants. Break down their altars, and destroy their idols!"

Under the leadership of Joshua, the army of Israel broke the back of Canaanite military resistance. After that it was up to each individual tribe, as it entered its new tribal territory, to wipe out whatever Canaanite resistance remained.

But now, in Judges chapter 1, read of how the various Israelite tribes responded repeatedly to the Lord's command:

"The *Benjamites*, however, failed to dislodge the Jebusites, who were living in Jerusalem" (verse 21).

"*Manasseh* did not drive out the people of Beth Shan or Taanach or . . . Megiddo and their surrounding settlements, for the Canaanites were determined to live in that land" (verse 27).

"Nor did *Ephraim* drive out the Canaanites living in Gezer, but the Canaanites continued to live there among them" (verse 29).

"Neither did *Zebulun* drive out the Canaanites living in Kitron or Nahalol, who remained among them" (verse 30).

"Nor did *Asher* drive out those living in Acco or Sidon . . . " (verse 31).

"Neither did *Naphtali* drive out those living in Beth Shemesh . . ." (verse 33).

The Israelites' disobedience was flagrant. They permitted Canaanite inhabitants to continue to live in the land. They intermarried with them; they joined them in worshiping their gods. In response, the Lord disciplined his people in a way that hurt.

I brought you up out of Egypt and led you into the land that I swore to give to your forefathers. I said, "I will never break my covenant with you, and you shall not make a covenant with the people of this land, but you shall break down their altars." Yet you have disobeyed me. . . . Now therefore I tell you that I will not drive them out before you; they will be thorns in your sides. (Judges 2:1-3)

In the face of their stubborn disobedience, God disciplined his people by withdrawing his helping hand. Canaanites who should have been put to death instead lived to fight another day and to make the lives of the Israelites miserable. A persistent refrain in the book of Judges is "[The Israelites] groaned under those who oppressed and afflicted them" (Judges 2:18).

Civil war

The period of the Judges lasted for more than three centuries (about 1380–1050 B.C.). That was not a happy period in Israel's history. The reason is found in the closing verse of the book of Judges: "In those days Israel had no king; everyone did as he saw fit" (Judges 21:25).

The Israelites had forgotten that God had chosen them to belong to him, to be his special people, ruled by the Lord God himself, children of God waiting for the Messiah. "I have redeemed you; I have summoned you by name; you are mine . . . the people I formed for myself that they may proclaim my praise" (Isaiah 43:1,21). "They are . . . the work of my hands, for the display of my splendor" (Isaiah 60:21).

Unfortunately, the Israelites thought the reason for their national and international problems was that they had no king, as did the other nations around them. They therefore asked for a king, and God granted their request. The period of Israel's united kingdom lasted a little more than a century (1050–931 B.C.). Under three kings—Saul, David, and Solomon—Israel enjoyed brief moments of glory. But shortly after Solomon died, civil war tore the nation apart. The group that broke away consisted of ten northern tribes. The smaller remnant to the south—Judah—consisted of the tribes of Judah and Benjamin. We're especially interested in Judah, since Christ came from that tribe. Jesus was later named "the Lion of the tribe of Judah" (Revelation 5:5).

Exile

The breakaway northern kingdom lasted only about two hundred years (931–722 B.C.). Again, the reasons are not hard to find. Although the Lord sent prophets to call his people to repent, they ignored his prophets. "[The people of Israel] commanded the prophets not to prophesy" (Amos 2:12). The Lord disciplined Israel, but they ignored his discipline. Listen to a message proclaimed by the prophet Amos, and see if your ears can pick out a sad refrain:

"I gave you empty stomachs in every city and lack of bread in every town, *yet you have not returned to me*," declares the LORD. "I also withheld rain from you. . . . People staggered from town to town for water but did not get enough to drink, *yet you have not returned to me*," declares the LORD. "Many times I struck your gardens and vineyards, I struck them with blight and mildew. Locusts devoured your fig and olive trees, *yet you have not returned to me*," declares the LORD. "I sent plagues among you as I did to Egypt. I killed your young men with the sword, . . . *yet you have not returned to me*," declares the LORD. . . . "Therefore this is what I will do to you, Israel, . . . prepare to meet your God, O Israel." (Amos 4:6-12)

Whoever refuses to meet God as the *Savior* had better get ready to meet him as *Judge*. God's harsh discipline for the ten northern tribes came when the Assyrian army invaded their land, hammered them into submission, and led the survivors off to Assyria in chains, where they became lost to history. We still speak of the lost ten tribes. "The king of Assyria deported Israel to Assyria. . . . This happened because they had not obeyed the LORD their God, but had violated his covenant" (2 Kings 18:11,12).

Conditions were not much better in the southern kingdom of Judah. Listen to the prophet Isaiah describe the people to whom God sent him to preach: "These are rebellious people, deceitful children, children unwilling to listen to the LORD's instruction. They say to the seers, 'See no more visions!' and to the prophets, 'Give us no more visions of what is right! Tell us pleasant things . . . and stop confronting us with the Holy One of Israel!'" (Isaiah 30:9-11).

C. S. Lewis remarked that there are really only two kinds of people in the world: those who tell God: "*Your* will be done!" and others to whom God says: "*Your* will be done! Have it *your* way! You wanted to be without me; now be without me!"

God's chosen nation needed God's hard discipline. It was either that or death. The promise of the Messiah had to be kept, for God cannot go back on his word.

Results of God's discipline

God's discipline produced two different kinds of results in the nation of Israel: Some of the people rejected God's discipline and fell under his judgment. Some of the people repented and returned in faith to the family of God.

We have an example of the beneficial results of God's discipline in a prayer recorded for us in Nehemiah chapter 9. It gives us glimpses of the Lord's patient discipline during the entire period of Israel's history. The time was about 445 B.C. Fewer than 50,000 Jews had returned to Jerusalem from the Babylonian captivity. As they celebrated the Feast of Tabernacles, the Levites led the assembly in this prayer:

"You are the LORD God, who chose Abram. . . . You made a covenant with him. . . . You have kept your promise because you are righteous. But they, our forefathers, became arrogant and stiff-necked, and did not obey your commands. They refused to listen and failed to remember the miracles you performed among them. . . . But you are a forgiving God, gracious and compassionate, slow to anger and abounding in love. . . . But they were disobedient and rebelled against you; they put your law behind their backs. They killed your prophets, who had admonished them in order to turn them back to you; they committed awful blasphemies. So you handed them over to their enemies, who oppressed them. But when they were oppressed they cried out to you. From heaven you heard them, and in your great compassion you gave them deliverers. . . . In all that has happened to us, you have been just; you have acted faithfully, while we did wrong." (Nehemiah 9:7,8,16,17,26,27,33)

Because of God's patient, firm, loving discipline throughout the history of Israel, a faithful remnant of people remained loyal to him. Through these faithful believers, the chosen nation preserved God's Word. They stood up for the truth, and they let their voices be heard. And a new generation memorized God's ancient promises.

God disciplines individuals

God usually doesn't deal with people in crowds. He has always been more interested in individual people than he is in nations. The Bible tells us that Jesus preached to crowds of people, that he miraculously fed crowds, that on one occasion he wept over a crowd. But the Bible never records that Jesus saved a crowd. God deals with people one at a time. Throughout the Old Testament when God lovingly disciplined his chosen people, he disciplined not only the nation; he disciplined individuals.

God did not settle the men and women descended from Abraham in Palestine simply to give them what they wanted. He had something better than just food to keep them alive, a family to share it with, and the freedom to enjoy it all. God planted his chosen people in the Promised Land to give them an opportunity to grow to spiritual maturity. God trained them to become more like him, to get them ready for the time when his Son would return in glory and they would live with him forever.

Spiritual growth happens almost as slowly as physical growth, but it does not happen as automatically. In every person's neck is a pituitary gland, which drives and regulates physical growth in children and which shuts down the growth process when the body has reached adult size. Nobody has to choose to grow. Physical growth just happens.

Spiritual growth is different. It doesn't happen by itself, automatically. God creates trust in our hearts, and then he nourishes that faith with his promise, so it can grow strong. If God sees a pattern of behavior in you that will be harmful to your life of faith, his tough love will call that to your attention. Look at a couple examples from Israel's history.

Moses, a reluctant leader

Moses was a chosen servant of God, whom God wanted to use to help carry out his good purpose of saving the world. While the Egyptian king was planning to kill off all the Hebrew boy babies, God was planning to use Moses as his instrument to set his people free. He rescued baby Moses so he was not drowned in the river Nile, as Pharaoh had ordered. Instead of being drowned, the baby was found by the princess, who took him to his own mother to nurse him. During the years that Moses' mother cared for her child, she did more than just give him food and change his diapers. She let him know he was not an Egyptian but a beloved child with whom God had made a covenant in Christ. Before Moses returned to the royal palace to live as the son of the Egyptian princess, he had learned about God's wonderful promises to Abraham.

We're not surprised, therefore, when the Bible tells us: "By faith Moses, when he had grown up, refused to be known as the son of Pharaoh's daughter. He chose to be mistreated along with the people of God rather than to enjoy the fleeting pleasures of sin. He regarded disgrace for the sake of Christ as of greater value than the treasures of Egypt" (Hebrews 11:24-26 TNIV).

As the adopted son of the Egyptian princess, "Moses was educated in all the wisdom of the Egyptians" (Acts 7:22). His curriculum may well have included natural science, math, astronomy, history of the Middle East, architecture, law, and government—an excellent educational background for a man who would be God's leader of the new nation of Israel. God had a lot invested in this man Moses.

Then the time arrived on God's calendar to put his plan for Moses into action. At a burning bush, God shared his plan with Moses:

"I am the God of your father, the God of Abraham, the God of Isaac and the God of Jacob. . . . I have indeed seen the misery of my people in Egypt. I have heard them crying out because of their slave drivers, and I am concerned about their suffering. So I have come down to rescue them. . . . So now, go. I am sending you . . . to bring my people the Israelites out of Egypt." (Exodus 3:6-8,10)

During all the time Pharaoh was trying to exterminate Israel, God was working out his own plan to rescue them. Christ must come!

Moses' objections

You would think Moses would have felt honored that God chose him to help in carrying out his good plan. But, instead, Moses had a whole string of objections (Exodus 3:11–4:13):

"Who am I to bring the Israelites out of Egypt? (3:11). Why should the Israelites trust somebody who received his training in the palace of the enemy? Besides, in Egypt I'm a fugitive from justice."

"Who shall I say sent me? (3:13). After what the Israelites have suffered, they won't believe that the God of their fathers has come to help them."

"What if they don't believe me? (4:1). The Israelites aren't used to hearing prophetic messages from God."

"I'm not eloquent in speech (4:10). I can't think fast enough or talk well enough to stand up to a king."

"Please send someone else (4:13). God, you picked the wrong man."

God's discipline

Up to now the Lord had been patient in dealing with Moses' reluctance to do a job he didn't want to do. But now "the LORD's anger burned against Moses" (Exodus 4:14). The Savior-God dealt lovingly but firmly with this reluctant, willful child. He didn't simply say: "Shut up, and do what I tell you!" God rebuked Moses' littleness of faith and promised to help him carry out his important assignment. God equipped Moses to be what he had called him to be. Then he restated Moses' call and sent him on his way.

Elijah, a discouraged prophet

The prophet Elijah was another child of God whom God called to serve him in a special way. He lived in the early and middle 800s B.C. He was a wonderfully privileged man. In all of history only two people have been permitted to escape death; Elijah was one of the two. God called Elijah to speak for him at one of the darkest periods in Israel's history—when Ahab was king of the breakaway northern kingdom. Listen to the capsule description the Bible gives us of that wicked king: "There was never a man like Ahab, who sold himself to do evil in the eyes of the LORD, urged on by Jezebel his wife. He behaved in the vilest manner by going after idols" (1 Kings 21:25,26). "Ahab . . . did more evil in the eyes of the LORD than any of [the kings] before him" (1 Kings 16:30).

Together with his wicked queen, Jezebel, he made Baal worship the state religion of the northern kingdom. It is against that dark and difficult background that we meet Elijah, a man God called to serve him as prophet.

Against that dark background God chose to display his amazing grace. In the half-dozen chapters that record Elijah's ministry, the phrase occurs again and again: "The word of the LORD came to Elijah" (1 Kings 17:2; 18:1). In that dark hour of Israel's history, God refused to let his Word become extinct. Instead of giving the fickle people and their wicked royal family the silent treatment, he continued to speak to them. He let them hear the message of his law and the message of his love.

God gave Elijah still further evidence of his mercy. He supported Elijah's preaching with miraculous signs and wonders. While God has performed miracles at all periods of the world's history, there were three periods in history when miracles occurred so frequently that people considered them almost commonplace.

1. One of those times was the exodus from Egypt and the conquest of the Promised Land.
2. The second period was the time of Elijah and his successor, Elisha.
3. The third was the time of Jesus' ministry and the establishment of the Christian church.

When God sent Elijah to live at the home of a widow in a time of famine, God miraculously *put bread on her table*. When her young son died, Elijah *raised the child to life*—the first instance of that miracle in Bible history. At the sacred showdown with Baal's prophets on Mount Carmel, God supported his prophet by *sending fire down from heaven* to consume his sacrifice. Through these miracles God trained Elijah, shaping him into God's kind of man for a very difficult kind of world. They would reassure God's prophet, especially when he was tempted to be discouraged and disheartened.

But the miracles Elijah performed also served as rebukes for wicked King Ahab and Queen Jezebel. They would be eye-openers for the unlearned and the pagans. Finally, Israel was to observe and worship.

Elijah's response

Now get set for a disappointment. When King Ahab returned to his palace from Mount Carmel, he told his wicked queen about the contest with Baal's prophets in which her god Baal had come out second best. When she learned about Elijah's remarkable victory, she was furious and sent a threatening message to the prophet. And the result? "Elijah was afraid and ran for his life" (1 Kings 19:3).

Without the Lord's permission and against the Lord's will, Elijah resigned from the ministry. He ran away from the assignment God had given him. My, how he ran! He traveled first to Beersheba in the far south of Palestine—one hundred miles away from the region and from the people to whom God had called him to preach. Even there he didn't stop. He went another day's journey into the desert, where he prayed: "I have had enough, Lord. . . . Take my life" (1 Kings 19:4).

God's discipline

Now observe how God disciplined his wayward prophet. God answered Elijah's prayer the way a mother answers the request of her two-year-old daughter who sees her working with a sharp knife and asks to play with it. The mom gives her something better—a wooden spoon or maybe a cookie. When Elijah woke up from a nap, "there by his head was a cake of bread baked over hot coals, and a jar of water" (1 Kings 19:6)—served to him by an angel! What gentleness on God's part!

But get set for another disappointment. "Strengthened by that food, [Elijah] traveled forty days and forty nights until he reached Horeb" (1 Kings 19:8)—a mountain more familiar to us by the name Mount Sinai. Can you believe that? This discouraged prophet headed still farther south into unfriendly desert country. He was now three hundred miles away from where God had called him to live and to preach. He climbed into a cave and had a private pity party.

It's clear that Elijah wanted to die. His prayer, "Lord, take my life!" was clearly outside of the will of God. Elijah had sinned by running away from God. Now he found himself arguing with God, trying to justify an action he knew deep down was wrong. The Lord asked him an embarrassing question, "What are you doing here, Elijah?" In plain English: "Elijah, I gave you some important work to do for me three hundred miles up north. What business do you have coming down here?"

Elijah answered: "I have been very zealous for the Lord God Almighty. The Israelites have rejected your covenant, broken down your altars, and put your prophets to death with the sword. I am the only one left, and now they are trying to kill me too" (1 Kings 19:10).

It is said that if you stick your nose in Limburger cheese, the whole world stinks. That was Elijah's problem here. "God, everything is lost. The whole nation has turned to idolatry, and you don't seem to be doing anything about it. I'm the only faithful child you've got left in all of Israel. There's no reason for me to go on with my life." Elijah was so depressed that he overlooked the evidence God had shown him in recent weeks that he wasn't the only believer left. How about the widow and her son? Elijah was forgetting that when God sent down fire on his sacrifice on Mount Carmel, the people enthusiastically acknowledged the Lord as the one true God.

Maybe Elijah misinterpreted the Lord's patience with him during his three-hundred-mile trip south, as though that indicated the Lord's approval. But God did not approve of what Elijah had done. Instead he rebuked him. He corrected Elijah's false notion of how he ought to do his work. God told Elijah to go out of his cave and stand on the mountain. God had something to show him.

A *powerful wind* of tornado force tore the mountain apart. It dislodged rocks and sent them crashing down the mountain. God's second display of power took the form of an *earthquake*. The mountain, which had shuddered when the tornado struck, now shook even more violently. Cracks opened up in the crust of Mount Sinai. People who have experienced an earthquake say that few experiences cause terror quite like having the earth move beneath your feet. After the earthquake, God sent a *fire*. Elijah seemed to be surrounded by flames, like an animal trapped in a forest fire.

No doubt Elijah would have been very happy if God had seen fit to use any one of those three destructive forces on Queen Jezebel. He would have considered it appropriate if a tornado blew her to kingdom come or if an earthquake scared the daylights out of her and shattered any inclination ever again to persecute one of God's prophets. Maybe the best idea of all would be if fire from heaven could reduce her to a little pile of charcoal.

But Elijah was not thinking God's thoughts. After each of the three terrifying power displays, a significant statement is made: "The Lord was *not in the wind.* . . . The Lord was *not in the earthquake.* . . . The Lord was *not in the fire*" (1 Kings 19:11,12).

Those three were terrifying phenomena of judgment, all right, but that's not how God does his real work. His real work is showing himself to people in his Word of promise, winning their hearts, making them his children, and keeping them in his family. Sometimes God uses some pretty forceful methods. (Calling down fire from heaven on Mount Carmel is pretty spectacular, by any definition.) But that's not the Lord's customary way of winning people for his family. They are, at most, heavenly two-by-fours that God uses to get people's attention. Jesus Christ came not to *destroy* people's lives but to *save* them. He is, after all, the Savior not the slayer.

After trembling before the powerful wind, the earthquake, and the fire, Elijah heard "a gentle whisper" (1 Kings 19:12). God reminded Elijah (as he often reminds us): "My child, I haven't ever overwhelmed anybody into my family with my awesome power, and I'm not about to start now." The power by which God saves sinners lies in a quiet word, which people like Ahab and Jezebel can oppose and shout down and outlaw and overrule and force underground.

When Elijah heard that soft voice, he got up and stood at the entrance to his cave. God continued to discipline his prophet, who was discouraged when he had no business being discouraged. "What are you doing here, Elijah?" he asked again (19:13). For the second time Elijah recited his little piece about how he'd been zealous for the Lord but that now he was the only one left.

God's instruction

Instead of sympathizing with Elijah, God gave him marching orders: Elijah was to head north again and to anoint three people into new jobs (1 Kings 19:15,16):

1. "Anoint Hazael king of Aram" (Israel's neighbor to the north). This new king would attack King Ahab and make life miserable for him. Great is the Lord even outside the borders of Israel!
2. "Anoint Jehu . . . king over Israel." Jehu would be the instrument ("hatchet man" would be a more accurate term) that the Lord would use to wipe out Ahab's whole royal family and to destroy Baal worship in Israel. God rules the unbelieving and vicious king and queen.
3. "Anoint Elisha . . . to succeed you as prophet." Elijah's work as prophet was not a failure, and God wanted it to continue through Elisha. God rules his church of believers, even if we can't see it.

Do you see how the Lord disciplined Elijah? He found him when he tried to run away from the Lord. He rebuked him for his stubborn disobedience. He reminded him: "Elijah, I'm in control of the forces of evil in the royal palace about which you're so concerned, and I'm going to deal with that." And, finally, God authorized Elijah to anoint his successor so that the important job of letting God's voice be heard could continue in northern Israel, even after Elijah had gone to heaven.

God also said to Elijah (whose cheeks must have been burning). "Oh, and one more thing, Elijah. You imagine that you're all alone. You've told me twice that you're the only loyal believing child I've got left in all of Israel. Your eyes are playing tricks on you, Elijah. You're not all alone. *I have seven thousand in Israel whose knees have not bowed to Baal.* But those seven thousand people need a pastor, Elijah. Now I want you to get back up north where you belong." The Lord disciplined his prophet. The result was that Elijah left his cave and headed back up to northern Israel to resume the work he had abandoned.

God's discipline was successful

We've looked at how God disciplined two of his Old Testament people—Moses and Elijah. Did God's discipline accomplish in these two men what God intended?

The New Testament gives an interesting answer to that question. Centuries after these two Old Testament prophets lived, Jesus was about to bring God's plan for our redemption to completion. A couple weeks before he headed to Jerusalem on what we call his death journey, he took three disciples up on a mountain. "As he was praying, the appearance of his face changed, and his clothes became as bright as a flash of lightning" (Luke 9:29).

A couple weeks later those same three disciples were going to see Jesus looking considerably different—kneeling in the dust of Gethsemane—as he struggled with his Father in prayer, his sweat falling to the ground in large drops, like blood. And so, weeks in advance, on the Mount of Transfiguration, Jesus gave them a glimpse of the majesty he possesses as the Son of God. But there on that mountain Peter, James, and John saw something else. Let Saint Luke tell the story: "Two men, Moses and Elijah, appeared in glorious splendor, talking with Jesus. They spoke about his departure, which he was about to bring to fulfillment at Jerusalem" (Luke 9:30,31).

The same two famous Old Testament prophets whom God once disciplined appeared with Jesus on the Mount of Transfiguration. They discussed with Jesus what he was about to accomplish in Jerusalem—his death, his resurrection, and (when his work on earth was finished) his majestic ascension to heaven. As Moses and Elijah saluted their captain, they spoke about his *exodus* in Jerusalem, through which he would accomplish what they could only talk about. Because of that great Substitute, the Father's plan could be carried out.

Did God's discipline of Moses and Elijah accomplish what God wanted it to? Yes, it did. They recognized their sinfulness, their stubbornness, their self-will, and returned in faith to the Savior, whom they met and spoke with on the Mount of Transfiguration. In this unusual way, Moses and Elijah gave the three disciples—and us—an unforgettable glimpse of the God-man.

God's discipline today

You and I were not *born* into the world fully grown. Neither were we *reborn* into God's family fully grown. From our parents we each inherited the devil's disease. We want to be more than God created us to be. We don't like to live under him (in a master-and-servant relationship). Instead, we insist on living alongside him, with the right to disagree with him. We challenge God's will for our lives. We question his ability to care for us. Sometimes we even dare to question God's claim when he says, "I love you!"

Every one of those wrong choices has painful consequences. A person who eats only fried foods and Twinkies exposes his body to certain health risks. The same is true of smoking, misusing God's gift of sex, or taking illegal drugs. These all have direct and painful consequences. A loving Father must step in to protect us.

This may be God's reason for stepping into our lives with discipline. When your father scolded or spanked you as a child, the reason was that you had done something a loving parent could not tolerate. Your future was at a crossroads.

But the Bible teaches clearly that the discipline God permits to enter our lives is not necessarily the result of our bad behavior. Sometimes God disciplines to build us up. The Bible gives us a good example of this in the story of a man named Job. He was a prominent and well-to-do man, "the greatest man among all the people of the East" (Job 1:3). God himself described Job as a devoted child of his, who "feared God and shunned evil" (Job 1:1).

The introduction to the book of Job lets us eavesdrop on some of the supernatural goings-on in this universe—things that Job didn't know, things that happen in the spiritual world which are ordinarily hidden from our eyes. It tells us that Satan had accused Job before God:

> "Does Job fear God for nothing?" Satan replied. "Have you not put a hedge around him and his household and everything he has? You have blessed the work of his hands, so that his flocks and herds are spread throughout the land. But stretch out your hand and strike everything he has, and he will surely curse you to your face." (Job 1:9-11)

God's purpose in disciplining Job

God knew, of course, that Satan's accusations were a lie. To defeat Satan—to show him what a *liar* he is and what a *loser* he is—God permitted heartache and heartbreak to enter the life of this pious man, this beloved child of God. Thousands of his cattle and camels were stolen by desert raiders, and suddenly he was no longer a rich man. His seven sons and three daughters were killed when a tornado leveled their house, and Job and his wife were left childless. Finally, a terrible disease robbed Job of health, leaving him helpless and in constant misery.

Job's immediate response was to say, "The LORD gave and the LORD has taken away; may the name of the LORD be praised" (Job 1:21).

But as dreary, difficult days and weeks passed, Job's faith began to sag. Some of his friends came to visit. They tried to convince him that his suffering was God's punishment for something he had done. Job knew these accusations were not true, but his anxious cries show that his trust in God's love was shaken: "I cry out to you, O God, but you do not answer; I stand up, but you merely look at me" (Job 30:20). Can you hear what Job is saying? "God, you're hiding!"

Listen to Job again: "[God] has denied me justice" (Job 27:2). "He destroys both the blameless and the wicked" (Job 9:22). Can you hear what Job is saying? "God, you're unfair!"

Those accusations were not only an insult to God, they were attacking Job's faith, and God had to step in. He disciplined this beloved child of his—to help him, to teach him, to strengthen him.

God does not play hide-and-seek

As we read the Old Testament, we notice that God frequently intervened in the affairs of his chosen people. Earlier in this chapter we traced how God made his presence known in the lives of Moses and Elijah. God is always present, always active.

But sometimes God seems to pull back, to hide himself. While he was suffering, Job felt that God was absent when Job wished he would be active. Job wanted to see evidence that God still loved him. When he didn't see this, he concluded that God had withdrawn himself. Day by day as Job lived in his nightmare of grief and pain, his sinful nature led him to imagine that he was alone, that God had abandoned him.

But the Holy Spirit was also active in the heart of Job during the dark night of his grief. The Spirit works through the Word of God: the words we *read*, the words we *hear*, and the words we *remember*.

A struggle between faith and unbelief

We have heard some of Job's bitter complaints about how God was hiding himself and about how he was treating Job unfairly. But scattered among those tortured expressions of Job's aching heart are some beautiful statements in which Job's faith showed itself. Have you ever stood on an ocean shore on a windy day and watched someone swimming? You can see him, and then suddenly waves will block your view of the swimmer, and he disappears from your sight. That's sort of the feeling you have when you read Job's speeches. In some of them we can't see Job's faith; we sense only his bitterness and his loneliness. But often in the very next breath, Job would say something that showed how the Spirit of God was at work in his suffering child, guiding him and disciplining him. "Though he slay me, yet will I hope in him" (Job 13:15). "He knows the way that I take; when he has tested me, I will come forth as gold" (Job 23:10).

God's purpose for our lives

The book of Job makes it clear what God's purpose for us is. God's primary purpose for us is not that we enjoy a comfortable life, that we make a name for ourselves, that we accumulate a pile of money, or that we get a job where we can push people around. Pure and simple, God's primary purpose for our lives is for us to bring glory to his name by kneeling before his one and only Son. He'll do in our lives whatever is necessary to produce this result. God has never promised that tornadoes will skip over Christians' houses while on the way to destroy an unbeliever's house.

During Job's long weeks of suffering, three of the friends that came to visit Job reminded him over and over again: "Job, God hates your sin and must punish it. Your suffering is God's punishment for your sin. Repent, and God will get off your back." You can understand why that kind of advice was no comfort for Job.

In chapter 32 of the book of Job, we get to meet a fourth friend, a man named Elihu. What he had to say was considerably different from what the other three had said. When Job complained that God was *hiding* and God was *silent*, Elihu answered: "God does speak . . . to turn man from wrongdoing and keep him from pride, to preserve his soul" (Job 33:14,17,18). When Job complained that God was unfair, Elihu responded: "Far be it from God to do evil. . . . It is unthinkable that . . . the Almighty would pervert justice" (Job 34:10,12). "God is mighty, but does not despise men. . . . [He] gives the afflicted their rights . . . and exalts them forever. . . . Those who suffer he delivers in their suffering" (Job 36:5-7,15).

What God's discipline taught Job

Did God's discipline accomplish in Job what God wanted to accomplish? Listen to Job speak in the closing chapter of the book: "I spoke of things I did not understand, things too wonderful for me to know. . . . I despise myself and repent in dust and ashes" (Job 42:3,6). Through God's discipline, Job learned:

- God is a holy God, who hates sin (Job's friends made that very clear).
- God is a compassionate God, who can be trusted. If he chooses not to remove evil from our lives, he will make it serve our good.
- God is an incomprehensible God, who doesn't explain all his actions to us. We don't know the answers to all our questions, but we trust that he does know. All his loving promises will find their fulfillment in Christ.

In the closing chapter God shows how successful his discipline of Job was: "The LORD made him prosperous again and gave him twice as much as he had before. . . . The LORD blessed the latter part of Job's life more than the first" (Job 42:10,12).

God shows himself in Christ

Christians are not exempt from the problems and tragedies of life any more than Jesus was. When life is difficult and we're hurting and we ask God to step in and do something about our hurts, does he hide himself? A father whose son was killed in the Korean War in the 1950s asked his pastor: "*Where was God* when my son was killed on the battlefield?" The pastor thought for a moment and then answered: "I don't know. I suppose he was in the same place he was when *his* Son was killed on Calvary."

A pretty good answer, wouldn't you say? *Where is God* when things go wrong for us and life is hard? He's *at work in us*, molding and shaping the will of some people whom he has claimed as his children. He reminds us of what he has done and is still doing to transform evil into good. God does not just sit idly by and watch us suffer by ourselves. Twenty centuries ago he actually became one of us.

[Jesus] being in very nature God, did not consider equality with God something to be used to his own advantage; rather he made himself nothing by taking the very nature of a servant, being made in human likeness. And being found in appearance as a human being, he humbled himself by becoming obedient to death—even death on a cross! (Philippians 2:6-8 TNIV)

When you're hurting and, with tears in your eyes, you ask "Doesn't God care about me?" there's only one answer to that question. Jesus is the answer. Although he may not answer my question about *why* a certain thing happened to me, I can learn how *God* feels about it. Jesus gives God a face, and that face is streaked with tears. Remember that, dear child of God. A God with tears! A Savior with a heart!

Isn't this something to remember when you're suffering and it seems as though God is not doing anything about it? In the womb of a young Jewish woman, the eternal God became one of us. Jesus went through the entire human experience, from the blood and pain of birth to the blood and pain of death. *Because of Jesus*, we no longer have to wonder about how God feels toward us or what he's like. In a stable in Bethlehem, God took on a human form—a shoe size, a sleeve length. In Jesus, God has joined us. He hurt and bled and cried and got tired and shed tears and was misunderstood and fell asleep on a boat cushion and lived a single life and suffered and died.

"No other religion—not Judaism, not Hinduism, not Buddhism or Islam—offers this unique contribution of an all-powerful God who willingly takes on the limitations and suffering of his creation."*

God's discipline in our lives

The questions that bothered Job still bother Christians today. Is God *hiding?* No, he's not. Listen to Jesus, and you'll hear God speak: "You did not choose me, but I chose you" (John 15:16). "I am the way and the truth and the life. No one comes to the Father except through me" (John 14:6). "I am with you always, to the very end of the age" (Matthew 28:20). Is God *unfair?* No, he's not. God took the worst thing that could possibly happen—the damning of his own Son—and turned it into final victory over sin and death. Jesus showed that h*e would rather go to hell for you than go to heaven without you.*

From Calvary we can hear God calling out: "I love you! I care about you!" This voice of God transforms our pain so that it actually becomes God's instrument to discipline us, to teach us, to strengthen us. Is God unfair? Well, was it fair for God to forsake his Son? Was it necessary? Was it to be expected? Was it love?

The Bible's overwhelming message *about God* is that he is personal and intimate. The Bible's overwhelming message *about people* is that you matter to God. If God has to choose between your personal comfort and your eternal safety, which do you hope he chooses? God is more interested in giving you what he knows you need than he is in giving you what you think you want. "One thing God has spoken, two things have I heard: that you, O God, are strong, and that you, O Lord, are loving" (Psalm 62:11,12).

Philip Yancey, Where Is God When It Hurts, page 225.

These are the last words of David . . .
Israel's singer of songs: "The Spirit of the
LORD spoke through me; his word was on
my tongue."

~ 2 SAMUEL 23:1,2

[The LORD] put a new song in my mouth,
a hymn of praise to our God.

~ PSALM 40:3

My lips will shout for joy when I sing praise
to you—I, whom you have redeemed.

~ PSALM 71:23

A Song on Their Lips

Many of God's creatures can sing. Every spring, when you hear the song of the first robin, you have to marvel at the lovely ability God gave his little feathered creatures.

But the ability to put words and music together is a special gift God has reserved only for his highest creatures. When God had finished his work of creation, "all the angels shouted for joy" (Job 38:7). The same thing happened the night the Savior was born. When God wrapped himself in human flesh and blood in order to trade places with sinners under his curse, angel choirs sang, "Glory to God in the highest heaven, and on earth peace to those on whom his favor rests" (Luke 2:14 TNIV).

God's human creatures sing

The only other creatures of God who have the ability to put words and song together are God's human creatures. At creation God reserved that very special gift for his angels and for his children. Unfortunately, like all of God's gifts, this gift can be abused. Many of the songs that you hear on the radio today speak messages that do not give glory to God. Would it surprise you to learn that there are songs like that in the Bible too? The oldest poem recorded in the Bible was written by Lamech, one of Cain's descendants. Lamech's song glorified the spirit of revenge (Genesis 4:23,24).

Centuries later, as Moses walked down Mount Sinai holding the two stone tablets of the law, he heard singing in the camp of Israel. The Israelites were singing, but with their songs they were praising a false god—a golden calf. You can be sure that any songs that praise revenge or glorify idolatry do not originate with the Spirit of God; those songs are spawned in hell. When you listen to them, you can almost hear the serpent hiss. Satan uses songs like that to mislead people about what life is all about.

God's people sang

Day by day God put a song on the lips of his chosen people. And why shouldn't they sing? They knew they mattered to God. The Old Testament is full of their songs. Fifteen centuries before Christ was born God opened a path through the waters of the Red Sea to permit his people to escape their slavery in Egypt. After his people had passed through the sea safely, God closed the waters again when Pharaoh's armies tried to follow. As Moses stood on the far shore and looked back at the floating corpses of what had been Egypt's finest, he sang: "I will sing to the LORD, for he is highly exalted. The horse and its rider he has hurled into the sea. The LORD is my strength and my song; he has become my salvation. The LORD is a warrior; the LORD is his name" (Exodus 15:1-3).

Five hundred years later a Hebrew lady named Hannah had spent her best childbearing years slender, with arms that were empty and a heart that ached for a child. She shared her heartache with the Giver of life, and he answered her prayer. Nine months later, as she held her little Samuel in her arms, Hannah sang. Her song reminds us of the song Mary later sang when she learned she was going to be the mother of the Savior (Luke 1:46-55): "My heart rejoices in the LORD. . . . I delight in your deliverance. There is no one holy like the LORD; there is no one besides you; there is no Rock like our God" (1 Samuel 2:1,2).

The book of Psalms

God is very much interested in the songs his people sing. Day by day during the time of the Old Testament, God put songs on the lips of his chosen people. Many of those songs are found in one Old Testament book that Jesus, as well as the New Testament writers, quoted more often than any other. That's the book of Psalms.

We sometimes think of the book of Psalms as the hymnbook of the Old Testament. It was that, and psalms found their way into Israel's public worship (1 Chronicles 16:7-36). But the book of Psalms is much more. It served not only to help God's people worship but also to teach them. There's much that you and I can learn from the Psalms. As we look at some of these songs, we'll understand better why the New Testament writers quoted from this book so frequently.

The language of praise

"Shout with joy to God, all the earth! Sing the glory of his name. . . .
Say to God, 'How awesome are your deeds!'" (Psalm 66:1-3).

The writer of Psalm 104 takes us on a tour of the wonderland of God's creation. He summarizes what happened on each of the six creation days and calls us to praise the Creator:

"O LORD my God, you are very great. . . . He wraps himself in light as with a garment" (Day 1: verses 1,2).

"He stretches out the heavens like a tent and lays the beams of his upper chambers on their waters" (Day 2: verses 2,3).

"He set the earth on its foundations; it can never be moved. You covered it with the deep. . . . At your rebuke the waters fled. . . . You set a boundary they cannot cross; never again will they cover the earth" (Day 3: verses 5-9).

"The moon marks off the seasons, and the sun knows when to go down" (Day 4: verse 19).

"How many are your works, O LORD! In wisdom you made them all; the earth is full of your creatures" (Days 5 and 6: verse 24).

Day by day God put a song on the lips of his chosen people, and those songs still today teach us the language of worship and praise. When the scientific community today tries to convince you that life is the product of time-plus-chance, that life may have originated in the scum on some prehistoric pond, that the universe is just debris from a huge explosion billions of years ago, or that human beings developed from lower forms of animal life, Psalm 104 can teach you the language of praise. The universe and everything in it was not an accidental development; it was God's creative design, and we praise him for that.

Everything good and beautiful and true in the universe comes from the hand of an unbelievably generous Creator. He gave you a body made up of 75 trillion tiny building blocks called cells. At least 100,000 genes in the nucleus of those cells passed on your father's hair color to you, or your mother's intelligence, or your grandmother's musical ability. "Sing for joy! Clap your hands!" the psalms command us. Just as infants learn how to talk by listening to their mothers, so the psalms *help us to learn the language of praise.* "I praise you because I am fearfully and wonderfully made; your works are wonderful, I know that full well" (Psalm 139:14).

Christ in the Psalms

Ever since God promised to send one of Eve's descendants to be the Savior of sinners, God's people waited for him to keep that promise. Down through the centuries God kept their faith alive by repeating his promise and supplying additional information about the coming Savior. He told Abraham that the Savior would be one of his descendants. He gave David the same promise. In the psalms of David, God pulled the curtain back and gave his people much additional information about the coming Savior.

True God

Although the promised Messiah would be a descendant of David, he would also be David's Lord (Psalm 110:1). In other words, in addition to being a human being, he would be true God. Listen to David address the Savior in one of the messianic psalms: "Your throne, *O God*, will last for ever and ever" (Psalm 45:6).

The King

In another messianic psalm, David described the coming Savior as a King who would rule over the whole world and whose reign would never end:

[The King] will endure as long as the sun, as long as the moon, through all generations. He will rule from sea to sea . . . to the ends of the earth. All kings will bow down to him and all nations will serve him. . . . All nations will be blessed through him. (Psalm 72:5,8,11,17)

The suffering Substitute

David's psalms make it clear exactly how his great descendant would rescue a world of sinners from the consequences of their sin. David's greater Son would take their place under the curse of God.* In another messianic psalm, David described the suffering Christ would undergo as our Substitute. He did so in language so vivid that it almost seems the poet was an eyewitness to the scene on Calvary:

My God, my God, why have you forsaken me? Why are you so far from saving me, so far from the words of my groaning? All who see me mock me; they hurl insults, shaking their heads: "He trusts in the LORD; let the LORD rescue him." . . . A band of evil men has encircled me, they have pierced my hands and my feet. They divide my garments among them and cast lots for my clothing. (Psalm 22:1,7,8,16,18; referring to Matthew 27:46 and Mark 15:24-34)

*John F. Brug, Psalms 1–72, *The People's Bible commentary series*, pages 10,11.

David's psalms showed God's people the depths of the suffering the Messiah would endure in order to earn pardon for guilty sinners: "Even my close friend, whom I trusted, he who shared my bread, has lifted up his heel against me" (Psalm 41:9; referring to John 13:18). "I looked for sympathy, but there was none, for comforters, but I found none. They put gall in my food and gave me vinegar for my thirst" (Psalm 69:20,21; referring to Matthew 27:34,48).

The victorious Champion

The songs God put on David's lips made it clear that the Messiah's work would not end in defeat and death. David quotes the Messiah as saying to his Father:

My heart is glad and my tongue rejoices; my body also will rest secure, because you will not abandon me to the grave, nor will you let your Holy One see decay. You have made known to me the path of life; you will fill me with joy in your presence, with eternal pleasures at your right hand. (Psalm 16:9-11; quoted in Acts 2:26-28)

The psalms taught God's Old Testament people that although the Messiah would be rejected by the nation's religious leaders, he would be successful in carrying out his Father's assignment. A world of sinners was saved, and that is something to be happy about:

The LORD is my strength and my song; he has become my salvation. The stone the builders rejected has become the capstone; the LORD has done this, and it is marvelous in our eyes. This is the day the LORD has made; let us rejoice and be glad in it. (Psalm 118:14,22-24)

Songs of forgiveness

God had led David from his father's sheepfold to the throne of Israel. Still more, he had raised David from sin and shame to be "Israel's singer of songs" (2 Samuel 23:1). David remembered a time, however, when the melody of his life was nothing but clashing discord. When he tried to run his life *his* way, he produced dreadful disharmony. David showed no love for God or man when he had a sleazy affair with Bathsheba, the wife of one of his army officers. And then he had her husband killed to keep him from learning that his wife was going to bear David's child. For the next months David was not "Israel's singer of songs." He stubbornly refused to admit that his sin was an insult to God. His attitude was "Hey, so who's perfect?"

But the Spirit of God is not easily discouraged. He convinced David that what he and Bathsheba had thought was "mature entertainment"—you know, "for adults only"—was adultery. We can see the Spirit at work in several psalms David wrote at that time:

When I kept silent, my bones wasted away through my groaning all day long. For day and night your hand was heavy upon me. . . . Then I acknowledged my sin to you and did not cover up my iniquity. I said, "I will confess my transgressions to the LORD"—and you forgave the guilt of my sin. (Psalm 32:3-5)

Have mercy upon me, O God, according to your unfailing love; according to your great compassion blot out my transgressions. Wash away all my iniquity and cleanse me from my sin. Restore to me the joy of your salvation. . . . O Lord, open my lips, and my mouth will declare your praise. (Psalm 51:1,2,12,15)

David's psalms describe not only a painful spiritual journey but also the path to spiritual healing. God led a murderer and an adulterer to become Israel's shepherd-king, the pattern for the Messiah (also called the Son of David). That's what God's grace can do.

Because great David's greater Son exchanged his perfect life for our sinful ones, a holy God can look upon us as having obeyed his law. And because Christ suffered the punishment for sin that you and I should have suffered, a holy God can consider that the penalty for our sin has been paid. God doesn't invite us to a bargaining table and ask, "What have you got to offer?" An African Christian remarked: "God gives to you. He will not trade with you." The person who believes that will sing the song of forgiveness. Day by day God put that song on the lips of his Old Testament people.

The Psalms taught Luther

Martin Luther's only ambition was to be rid of his sin. As a young monk, he read the statement in Saint Paul's letter to the Romans that the gospel shows us God's *righteousness* (Romans 1:17). At first he understood that to mean that the gospel shows us Jesus as the *perfect example of the holy life* God demands from each of us. But that offers us no comfort at all when our consciences condemn us.

But Luther's study of the Bible, including especially the book of Psalms, opened his eyes to see that Jesus did not come just to *set an example*; he came to *trade places with sinners*. In Psalm 31, for example, David prayed, "In you, O LORD, I have taken refuge; . . . deliver me in your righteousness" (verse 1).

If God's righteousness delivers us, then it cannot be a holiness that he *demands from us*. He demands it from us, but we cannot deliver. Rather, the righteousness of God is the right standing with God that Christ *earned for us* and that he gives us through faith. The book of Psalms put a good-news song on Luther's lips, and when he learned to sing that song, the Reformation was born.

Songs for us

The psalms teach us to sing that gospel song too. The God whom we have learned to know through Jesus Christ is merciful, even when we don't deserve his mercy. He makes life worth living, and that calls for our thanksgiving. One short psalm preaches to us: "Know that the LORD is God. It is he who made us, and we are his; we are his people, the sheep of his pasture. Enter his gates with thanksgiving and his courts with praise; give thanks to him and praise his name" (Psalm 100:3,4).

The psalms in the Bible, however, are not all happy songs sung by Old Testament people of God on sunny days when everything was going well. There are also psalms that express the writer's despair:

> Why, O LORD, do you stand far off? Why do you hide yourself in times of trouble? (Psalm 10:1).
>
> Hear me, O God, as I voice my complaint. (Psalm 64:1).
>
> Why have you rejected us forever, O God? Why does your anger smolder against the sheep of your pasture? (Psalm 74:1).
>
> How long, O Lord? Will you hide yourself forever? How long will your wrath burn like fire? O Lord, where is your former great love, which in your faithfulness you swore to David? (Psalm 89:46,49).

When Israel's poets wrote the psalms, they were not composing hymns for Israel's book of worship. They were writing down their conversations with God. The psalms were not primarily written for other people but for God. And they were not written by professional poets but by ordinary people who sometimes had difficulty making sense out of life. Abraham's grandson Jacob, for example, wrestled with God in prayer at a difficult and dangerous time in his life (Genesis 32:24-28). As you read many of the psalms, it's like listening in on the emotional back-and-forth of a believer who is wrestling with God. God's people struggled to make sense out of life. They often had difficulty harmonizing what they knew about God with what they experienced in life. Very often what we believe from God's written Word seems to be contradicted by the information we receive from our five senses.

The oldest psalm in the Bible is Psalm 90, written by Moses. In that psalm Moses shared these thoughts with God: "The length of our days is seventy years—or eighty, if we have the strength; yet their span is but trouble and sorrow, for they quickly pass, and we fly away" (verse 10).

The fact that our lives are short and filled with trouble is not a particularly happy thought to include in one's prayer to God. But that thought led Moses to pray, "Teach us to number our days aright, that we may gain a heart of wisdom" (Psalm 90:12).

Do you see, as Moses did, that only if God gives us a heart of wisdom can we sin-blinded creatures acknowledge the power of God's anger and flee to his steady love for deliverance?

Some of the most beautiful psalms were written at a time when a child of God was hurting. In Psalm 102 a man weakened by pain catalogs his suffering. He feels abandoned by his friends, and even by God:

> Hear my prayer, O LORD; let my cry for help come to you. Do not hide your face from me when I am in distress. . . . Because of my loud groaning I am reduced to skin and bones. All day long my enemies taunt me; . . . I eat ashes as my food and mingle my drink with tears because of your great wrath, for you have taken me up and thrown me aside. (verses 1,2,5,8-10)

David wrote Psalms 34 and 56 when the Philistines had taken him captive. They had the man who had killed their champion Goliath. David realized his life was in danger. He wrote Psalm 59 when King Saul had sent men to watch David's house in order to kill him. Both situations seemed hopeless, and his psalm spoke to God about that: "Deliver me from my enemies, O God; protect me from those who rise up against me. Deliver me from evildoers and save me from bloodthirsty men" (Psalm 59:1,2).

Many psalms are the words of Old Testament believers who struggled to believe in a gracious God, while the world they lived in was collapsing about them.

Help, LORD, for *the godly are no more*; the faithful have vanished from among men. Everyone lies to his neighbor; their flattering lips speak with deception. (Psalm 12:1,2)

I see *violence and strife in the city*. Day and night [the wicked] prowl about on its walls; malice and abuse are within it. Destructive forces are at work in the city; threats and lies never leave its streets. (Psalm 55:9-11)

Read Psalm 74, and you will learn how one of Israel's poets reacted as he stared at the smoldering ruins of what had once been the beautiful temple in Jerusalem. This was the sacred place where God chose to make his dwelling among the people of the promise. You can almost hear the bewildered child of God choke back his sobs, as he describes the behavior of the attacking Babylonian soldiers in 586 B.C.:

Your foes roared in the place where you met with us. . . . They behaved like men wielding axes to cut through a thicket of trees. They smashed all the carved paneling with their axes and hatchets. They *burned your sanctuary* to the ground; they defiled the dwelling place of your Name. . . . How long will the enemy *mock you*, O God? (verses 4-7,10)

But the people who wrote the psalms do more than just give us the painful details of how their world was collapsing about them. Reading the psalms is not at all like watching 30 minutes of bite-sized human tragedy on the evening TV news. God had put a song on the lips of his chosen people, and we hear that song—even in those psalms which describe the terror and tragedy that threatened to shake their faith.

When the Philistines took David captive and his life was in danger, we learn from 1 Samuel chapter 21 that David pretended to be insane. He made marks on the doors of the gate and even drooled saliva down his beard. As a result, the Philistines released him.

Now listen to how, in Psalm 34, David *gave God the credit* for rescuing him: "This poor man called, and the LORD heard him; he saved him out of all his troubles. The angel of the LORD encamps around those who fear him, and he delivers them. Taste and see that the LORD is good; blessed is the man who takes refuge in him" (verses 6-8).

After giving us a description of how the enemy mocked God by trashing his beautiful temple, in Psalm 74 the poet *declared his faith:*

Remember *the people you purchased of old*, the tribe of your inheritance, whom you redeemed. . . . You, O God, are my king from of old; you bring salvation upon the earth. The day is yours, and yours also the night; you established the sun and the moon. It was you who set all the boundaries of the earth; you made both summer and winter. Do not hand over the life of your dove to wild beasts; do not forget the lives of your afflicted people forever. *Have regard for your covenant*, because haunts of violence fill the dark places of the land. Do not let the oppressed retreat in disgrace; may the poor and needy praise your name. (verses 2,12,16,17,19-21)

Psalm 55 gives us a frightening description of the violence and the evil a child of God observed on the streets of ancient Jerusalem. But instead of being disillusioned, his reaction was to entrust himself to God's care. And then he actually found words of praise:

But I call to God, and the LORD saves me. Evening, morning and noon I cry out in distress, and he hears my voice. He ransoms me unharmed from the battle waged against me, even though many oppose me. Cast your cares on the LORD and he will sustain you; he will never let the righteous fall. (verses 16-18,22)

The Psalms speak to our situation

What do the children of God think, what do they say, when their world seems to be falling apart in front of their eyes? What do you say? Do you sometimes think: "God, where are you?" "God, are you hiding?" From the songs God put on the lips of his Old Testament believers, we can see that they asked these same questions. But they did more than ask the questions; they answered them.

Lonely?

When King Saul learned that God had rejected him as king and had appointed David to take his place, he tried to kill David. For months David was on the run like a hunted rabbit. He fled to at least a dozen different places, trying to escape Saul's sword. On one occasion, when he was hiding from Saul in a cave, David felt terribly alone: "No one is concerned for me. I have no refuge; no one cares for my life" (Psalm 142:4).

What's the answer to the loneliness a child of God may feel today? David knew that the Lord was constantly present. Though he may have felt lonely, he knew he was not alone:

O LORD, you have searched me and you know me. You know when I sit and when I rise; you perceive my thoughts from afar. You discern my going out and my lying down; you are familiar with all my ways. . . . All the days ordained for me were written in your book before one of them came to be. (Psalm 139:1-3,16)

Confused?

You don't have to be a rocket scientist to see that something is terribly wrong with life on our planet. We live in a world where people are hurting and where hurting people are hurting other people. Martin Luther often remarked that as God governs the world, he remains a hidden God. If you judge by appearances, you'll draw one of two conclusions: either that God doesn't see the bad things which are taking place and everything in the world happens by accident, or that God does see and is powerless to do anything about it. Either God is a fool, who neither sees nor knows what's going on, or he's a rascal, who knows about it but doesn't do anything to prevent the evil.

The people who wrote the psalms were just as bothered by the bad things they saw in their world as you and I are by the bad things we see in our day-by-day life. "Look, the wicked bend their bows, they set their arrows against the strings to shoot from the shadows at the upright in heart. When the foundations are being destroyed, what can the righteous do?" (Psalm 11:2,3).

What *can* the righteous do when they see believing children of God suffering, while the enemies of God seem to be getting away with murder—and God seems to be doing nothing about it? What can the righteous do? You can share your confusion with the Lord in prayer. That's what God's Old Testament believers did. You can remember that the Lord has made a covenant with you. He has given you a solemn promise, and he cannot lie. No matter how puzzling God's world government may seem to you, you can put your money where God's mouth is, because he cannot go back on his word. He promised that Christ would come, and Christ will make it right.

> I will sing of the LORD's great love forever; with my mouth I will make *your faithfulness* known through all generations. I will declare that *your love* stands firm forever, that you established your faithfulness in heaven itself. You said, "I have made *a covenant* with my chosen one." (Psalm 89:1-3)

Overwhelmed?

Like Israel's poets, we have days when God seems very close and we can sing. But also like those poets, each of us has dark days when life is hard and God seems very far away. When we feel we can't take it anymore, isn't it comforting to know that other people of God have felt that way? What did they say to God when life threatened to overwhelm them? Listen to them: "You are a shield around me, O LORD, my Glorious One, who lifts up my head. . . . I lie down and sleep; I wake again, because the LORD sustains me" (Psalm 3:3,5). "The LORD is my rock, my fortress, and my deliverer; my God is my rock, in whom I take refuge. . . . The cords of death entangled me; the torrents of destruction overwhelmed me. . . . The snares of death confronted me. In my distress I called to the LORD; I cried to my God for help. From his temple he heard my voice" (Psalm 18:2,4-6).

Martin Luther once expressed the opinion that without troubles it's impossible for a human heart to think about God. It's better for a person to be sorrowful than overconfident. Can you see the truth of that statement?

When things in our lives are going well and we're on top of every situation, Satan tempts us to be proud and overconfident. But it's *in our weakness* that God shows his strong love. God has a perfect blueprint for our lives, and he's building according to its specifications.

A matter of trust

In Psalm 91 an anonymous poet wrote, "If you make the Most High your dwelling— even the LORD, who is my refuge—then *no harm will befall you*" (verses 9,10).

Oh, really? How about the babies massacred in Bethlehem by King Herod? How about the 2,800 people who were killed when hijacked airliners slammed into the World Trade Center? Why did more Christians die for their faith in the 20th century than in all the other centuries combined?

What was the poet thinking when he wrote, "No harm will befall you"? Was he exaggerating? No, he wasn't. The apostle Paul once wrote, "We know that in all things God works for the good of those who love him" (Romans 8:28). Some well-meaning people twist this passage to make it say, "Only good things will happen to those who love God." But God never said that. He never promised that life would be soft and easy.

When the poet assures us, "No harm will befall you," he is not denying that in this sinful world, sickness and pain and problems and trouble and heartache will enter the lives of God's faithful. (You may remember that Satan even quoted Psalm 91:9-12 to prove that it was safe for Jesus to jump off one of the towers of the temple. Check out Matthew 4:6.) When God promises "No harm will befall you," what he is saying is "*I am in control* of the evil in the world. When something painful enters your life and you don't know whether you can stand up under it, *trust me to protect you*—in one of two ways: I may remove the evil, or I will make it serve your good."

God put a song on the lips of his Old Testament people. Many of the psalms are beautiful expressions of the trust they had in our Lord's protection. Honestly, now, did God save you so that you could worry? Would he teach you to walk so that he could laugh at you when you fall? Would he allow himself to be hammered to a cross and then disregard your prayers? The psalms are not teasing us when they teach us: "He will command his angels concerning you to guard you in all your ways; they will lift you up in their hands, so that you will not strike your foot against a stone" (Psalm 91:11,12).

Your song

There is no singing in hell. We have Jesus' word for it that in hell there is only "weeping and gnashing of teeth" (Matthew 13:42).

There is singing in heaven. The very last book of the Bible describes seven visions God gave the apostle John. In one of them he got a glimpse of heaven. Listen to what he saw and heard:

> I looked and heard the voice of many angels, numbering thousands upon thousands, and ten thousand times ten thousand. . . . In a loud voice they sang:
> "Worthy is the Lamb, who was slain, to receive power and wealth and wisdom and strength and honor and glory and praise!" (Revelation 5:11,12)

Thomas Carlyle, a well-known English historian, has called Christianity "a creed of sorrow." Why would he make a statement like that? What led him to misread Christianity so completely? Was it because the Christians he came in contact with looked as if their religion had given them a headache? Did the Christians he observed day after day give him the impression that Christianity is something to be *endured*, rather than something to *be enjoyed*?

Child of God, the *promise* of heaven is yours already here on earth. The *glory* of heaven is something we'll have to wait to experience. But already now we have the same joy that the angels in heaven sing about: "Worthy is the Lamb, who was slain!"

The God whose holiness will not permit him to accept me for what I am is a God whose mercy has accepted me for what Jesus is. Day by day, God's Old Testament people thought that was something to sing about. In *rough* times the psalms helped them trust God. In *pleasant* times the psalms helped them thank God.

Dear Christian, that's something for you to sing about too. God has put a gospel song on your lips!

"I will ransom them from the power of the grave; I will redeem them from death. Where, O death, are your plagues? Where, O grave, is your destruction?"

~ HOSEA 13:14

You hold me by my right hand. You guide me with your counsel, and afterward you will take me into glory.

~ PSALM 73:23,24

I will dwell in the house of the LORD forever.

~ PSALM 23:6

[Abel, Enoch, Noah, and Abraham] were still living by faith when they died. They did not receive the things promised; they only saw them and welcomed them from a distance, admitting that they were foreigners and strangers on earth. People who say such things show that they are looking for a country of their own. . . . They were longing for a better country—a heavenly one.

~ HEBREWS 11:13-16 TNIV

A Future Life in a Better World

An English farmer noticed that every autumn a tragedy is played out in his corn fields. All summer long families of field mice make their homes among the growing plants. They eat and sleep, they work and play and raise their families. They imagine that those green fields belong to them. And then one day, at the end of the summer, the mouse community gets an awful shock. The farmer enters those fields with his harvesting machinery. And all of a sudden those comfortable summer homes and the food pantries that the mice have enjoyed come crashing down on their heads.

Can you see any similarity here between field mice and people? Maybe you know people who look upon this world as their home. This is where they belong. Day after day they work and play, earn money and fall in love, get married and have children—imagining that this world is their home and will always be their home. If you think of the mice, you might ask such people: "Are you remembering that this world is just a temporary place to stay . . . that harvest day is nearly upon us? Are you making plans for living in *another* world?" If you ask that question, they might look at each other, roll their eyes, and change the topic of conversation.

People don't like to think about death or about the end of this world or even about the existence of another world beyond the one we can see. They are willing to pay doctors high salaries to keep death away. Our society is willing to pay professional athletes and entertainers even more, because they distract us. They keep our minds off of things we'd rather not think about. If their lives are meaningless, people would rather not be reminded of it. Thornton Wilder, an American author, offered this advice to his readers: "Don't ask: 'Who am I? Where did I come from? Where am I going?' Just enjoy your ice cream while it's on your plate."

Some people flat-out deny that there is another world in addition to the one we can see. At Jesus' time, some of his opponents were the Sadducees, who claimed "that there is no resurrection, and that there are neither angels nor spirits" (Acts 23:8). There are people like that today. There are people who argue: "There is no other world 'out there.' This world is the only heaven or the only hell anybody is ever going to see."

Some people are convinced that pollution will choke out life on this earth. According to another scenario, the world we live in is going to self-destruct, and the entire planet, with all of its people, will end up as a gigantic thermonuclear fireball. As a result, the very grim possibility exists that all of us may be "cremated equal."

Can that be true? At some time in the future, is everybody and everything our world has achieved in its long history going to be buried under the debris of a universe in ashes? No, that is *not* true. God did not design life on earth to be meaningless, to come to a dead end, to end up at zero. God taught his Old Testament people that there is another world and another life besides this one. The writer of the book of Ecclesiastes put it this way: "[God] has also set eternity in the hearts of men" (Ecclesiastes 3:11).

This has always been God's plan. In his letter to Titus, the apostle Paul emphasized that the hope of a future life in a better world is not some new religious notion but something that God promised back in eternity. Saint Paul spoke of "the hope of eternal life, which God, who does not lie, promised *before the beginning of time*" (Titus 1:2).

God made that promise clear with his words, and he made it clear with his actions.

God's words

At the time the people of Israel were slaves in Egypt, God appeared to Moses in a burning bush. There he commissioned Moses to deliver the chosen people from slavery. Listen to the words God used to identify himself: "I am the God of your father, the God *of Abraham*, the God *of Isaac* and the God *of Jacob*" (Exodus 3:6).

Fifteen centuries later, Jesus explained the significance of those words: "Moses *showed that the dead rise*, for he calls the Lord 'the God of Abraham, and the God of Isaac, and the God of Jacob.' He is not the God *of the dead*, but *of the living*" (Luke 20:37,38).

At the time Moses stood in front of the burning bush, Abraham had been dead and buried for five hundred years. Yet God considered him alive. Abraham's personality did not cease to exist when, at age 175, he stopped breathing. His dead body was buried alongside his wife Sarah's, but his soul and his spirit were alive and well in the Savior's protecting care. He was resting, until one day he would hear the Savior call: "All right, Abraham! Nap time is over! Time to get up!"

It's interesting and instructive to see how the Holy Spirit describes the death of God's believers on the pages of the Old Testament. Look at several of the "death notices" God wrote for some of his people:

Abraham breathed his last . . . and he was *gathered to his people.* (Genesis 25:8)

[Isaac] died and was *gathered to his people.* (Genesis 35:29)

The LORD told **Moses,** ". . . you will die and be *gathered to your people.*" (Deuteronomy 32:48,50)

Ever since God first promised Adam and Eve that he would send a Savior, in every generation God raised up people who believed in that Savior. When those believing sons and daughters of his died, God looked upon them not as dead and gone but as still living—in another life, in another world. When he later had his Word put down in writing, the death notices of his believing children recorded that they were joining their believing ancestors.

The death notices God wrote for other people, however, were different. Ahaz was an idolatrous king who "did not do what was right in the eyes of the LORD. [He] even sacrificed his son in the fire, following the detestable ways of the nations the LORD had driven out before the Israelites. He offered sacrifices and burned incense at the high places" (2 Kings 16:2-4).

Now read the death notice God wrote for him: "Ahaz *rested with his fathers* and was buried with them in the City of David" (2 Kings 16:20).

The expression "[he] *rested with his fathers*" is immediately clarified by "he was *buried with them* in the City of David." In other words, in the royal cemetery in Jerusalem. Nothing is said about Ahaz' joining his believing ancestors around the throne of the Lamb. King Ahaz wasn't interested in a Savior who was going to trade places with sinners under God's judgment. During his life he made it clear that he preferred to live apart from that Savior. When he died he got to experience what he wanted.

About 800 B.C. in the northern breakaway kingdom of Israel, a prince named Ahab became king. He not only worshiped idols but actually made the filthy fertility cult of Baal the state religion of Israel. Listen to the description the Bible writer gives us of him: "Ahab . . . did more evil in the eyes of the LORD than any of those before him" (1 Kings 16:30).

Now check out his death notice: "Ahab *rested with his fathers*" (1 Kings 22:40). These are the same words the Bible uses when describing the death of the other kings of the northern kingdom. All were wicked, all worshiped idols, and when they died the Bible records only that they were buried in the same cemetery as their royal ancestors.

Once again, compare this with the way the Bible describes the death of one of God's believers, and you'll see the difference: "[Jacob] breathed his last and *was gathered to his people*" (Genesis 49:33).

Remember that Jacob was living in Egypt when he died. He was not buried until several months later, when his funeral procession traveled to the land of Israel. There Jacob was laid to rest in the family burial plot Abraham had once purchased for Sarah. But already at the moment of his death in Egypt, he "was gathered to his people." Although months would elapse before Jacob's mummified body joined Abraham's and Sarah's and Isaac's and Rebekah's and Leah's in the family burial plot, God announced that Jacob had joined his ancestors in another life in a better world. God announced that *with words*.

God's actions

And God spoke also *with actions*. Genesis chapter 5 tells us of a godly man named Enoch, who "walked with God" (verse 24). The New Testament adds the information that he lived at a time when unbelieving people wanted to live independently of God. Enoch warned his contemporaries: "The Lord is going to return to this world!" God showed that he approved of Enoch's godly life by making an exception to the rule (first announced in the Garden of Eden) that all people must die: "He was no more, because

God took him away" (verse 24). "By faith Enoch was taken from this life, so that he *did not experience death*" (Hebrews 11:5).

God crowned Enoch's difficult ministry by taking him from this earth without seeing death. This miracle reassured the faith of the early believers (the descendants of Noah's son Shem) that there is another life awaiting God's people. There is another world besides the one we now inhabit. Martin Luther commented: "Enoch was taken from this world by God himself. This is the comfort that relieved the power of death for Old Testament believers."

With his prophet Elijah, God repeated this miracle in an even more dramatic fashion. Elijah was God's spokesman during one of the darkest periods in Israel's history. Disgusting idolatry had such a grip on the nation God had called for himself that Elijah actually thought he was the only believer left. One day Elijah's difficult ministry came to a sudden end. At God's command, Elijah had anointed Elisha to succeed him as prophet. And then, as the two of them were walking along and talking together, "suddenly a chariot of fire and horses of fire appeared and separated the two of them, and Elijah *went up to heaven in a whirlwind*" (2 Kings 2:11).

Elijah was taken directly out of this world into the presence of God. Although on that occasion God did not speak a single word, can you hear what he was saying with his actions? "There is another world and another life besides this one!"

God's prophecies

On the pages of the Old Testament, God kept reminding his Old Testament believers that there is another world, an unseen world, on the other side of the cemetery. He did this not just through an occasional miracle or through the death notices he wrote for his people. Through his prophets, God described life in the new world. Listen to the message one of God's prophets brought to God's people: "Your *dead will live*; their *bodies will rise*. You who dwell in the dust, *wake up* and shout for joy. Your dew is like the dew of the morning; the earth will give birth to her dead" (Isaiah 26:19).

"I will raise the dead!"

Israel's heathen neighbors had a much different idea of what happens after a person dies. For them the afterlife was a shadowy existence in a dark, depressing, murky underworld. "Don't you believe it," God told his Old Testament people through his prophets. "Your dead will rise to a new life in another world! Your dead will live!"

God did not then—just as he does not now—answer all the questions raised by the Bible teaching of the resurrection of the body and the life everlasting. When Abraham and Isaac and Jacob and Moses died, did they know that they had not ceased to exist?

The Bible doesn't answer that question. Is an unborn child in her mother's womb alive? Why, yes. Does that unborn child *know* she's alive? No. After that child is born, is she alive? Yes, of course. Does a 3-month-old child *know* she's alive? No, not necessarily, that awareness does not come until later.

That's sort of how it is at the other end of life too. When you die, do you cease to exist?

In other words, are you as a person *gone* forever? No, you're not. God's Old Testament people understood that just as well as you and I do. When you die, your body returns to dust, but your personality, your soul—the real you—continues to live on. Jesus told the penitent criminal: "Today you will be with me" (Luke 23:43). Listen to the prophet Daniel's majestic prophecy of the resurrection of the dead on the Last Day: "Multitudes who sleep in the dust of the earth will awake: some to everlasting life, others to shame and everlasting contempt. Those who are wise will shine like the brightness of the heavens" (Daniel 12:2,3).

From this prophecy Old Testament believers learned that as God's people, they would be raised to life, where they will shine forever in heavenly brightness. The "multitudes" of the dead who will be raised to life on the Last Day will include every one of God's believing people, but not only his believers.

The all-knowing God is aware of the fact, however, that throughout all history multiplied millions of people have attempted to dethrone him, to annihilate him. If God were to tolerate this, he would not be God. "Righteousness and justice are the foundation of your throne" (Psalm 89:14).

No government simply tolerates terrorist attempts to overthrow it. God's love is not spineless and flabby. It's strong; it's a love of integrity and justice. If people have spent all their lives trying to *avoid* God's fellowship, they're not suddenly going to *seek* that fellowship just because they have died. "Shame and everlasting contempt" is the real and horrible consequence of a life spent saying no to God. Such people will not be annihilated (Matthew 25:41) or simply discarded on some cosmic junk pile. They will retain the awful ability to experience God's eternal rejection.

"I will restore my creation to its original perfection!"

To kindle in the hearts of his people a longing for the blessings awaiting them at the end of the world, God spoke several fascinating prophecies through the prophet Isaiah: "I will create *new heavens* and a *new earth*. The former things will not be remembered, nor will they come to mind" (Isaiah 65:17). "The LORD Almighty will prepare a feast of rich food for all peoples, a banquet of aged wine—the best of meats and the finest of wines. . . . He will swallow up death forever" (Isaiah 25:6,8).

On the pages of the Old Testament, God promised his people that when he takes this planet apart permanently, he will restore heaven and earth to their original perfection. The world we live in now is only a pale reflection of the beautiful and perfect world that a wise and loving Creator originally designed as the first home of Adam and Eve. Every evening the world's misery is served up to us in living color: poverty and famine and global warming, violence and wars and terrorist threats. And, lurking in the shadows, is the ultimate terrorist: death. The British author George Bernard Shaw called death "the ultimate statistic: one out of one dies." Death mocks all human strength, beauty, achievement, wealth, and honor. Death will come for us too.

God promised to change that, however, and he kept reminding his Old Testament people of this. He would restore his creation to its original perfection.

"I will right the wrongs!"

Listen to God's spokesmen describe another facet of the miracle God will perform when he returns in glory: "I will ransom them from the power of the grave; I will redeem them from death. Where, O death, are your *plagues?* Where, O grave, is your *destruction?*" (Hosea 13:14). "The Sovereign LORD will wipe away the *tears* from all faces" (Isaiah 25:8). "Gladness and joy will overtake [the ransomed of the LORD], and *sorrow* and *sighing* will flee away" (Isaiah 35:10).

God assured his Old Testament believers that in the new world that was waiting for them he would right all the wrongs. He would undo all the painful results of sin that were complicating their lives. He promised to change their sinful bodies into perfect, forever bodies. In the new life and the new world, they would be free from the temptation to sin, and they would be free from the consequences of sin. It's almost too much to believe, isn't it? Saint John assures us that we will be like God (1 John 3:2). We'll never sin again, never stumble again, never feel lonely again, never doubt again.

God's people were confident that the Savior whom God had promised to send would surely come. He would come as a King, to ransom his people. Remember that God's job description for Israel's king was to be a shepherd. The king's job was to protect God's people from anyone or anything that would harm them. He was to provide for his people's daily and deepest needs. God's Old Testament people knew that their Messiah-King would be seated at the right hand of God, as Lord of all creation. They trusted that when the Messiah returned in glory to take his believing people to live at his side, their future life would be totally different from their present life.

In their future life in a new world, they would no longer be subject to death and anxiety and fear and suffering. Sin and evil would be a thing of the past. Can you imagine how precious a thought that was to people for whom day-to-day life was a struggle? The results of sin back then were much the same as the results of sin today. Because of sin, some babies have no daddies and some wives no husbands. Because of the sin that lives in human hearts, the young are abused and the elderly, forgotten. Because of sin, God is cursed and God's creation is worshiped. Because of sin, fellowship with God and his church is scorned, while entertainment and even drugs are worshiped. As we read the pages of the Old Testament, we realize that life back then was not all that much different from life today.

In the face of all this, God sent his people a message of hope. In the new world that lies ahead, in the new life that's waiting for God's believing people, sin will have no power! Sin will not even be present!

Day after day, century after century, a gracious God kept reminding his Old Testament believers that there is *another world* and *a better life* besides this one. They heard his voice:

"I will raise the dead! I will have a family after all!"

"I will live with you!"

"I will restore my creation to its original perfection and right the wrongs in your life!"

God's people responded in faith

How did God's believing people react when God promised them a new life in a new world? Although they couldn't see the fulfillment of what God promised, they accepted what he promised on faith. They knew, above all, that the God who had promised to send the Savior had entered into a covenant of love with them. They trusted that God's loving concern for them would not come to an end when they left this world. They had heard God say: "Can a mother forget the baby at her breast and have no compassion on the child she has borne? Though she may forget, I will not forget you!" (Isaiah 49:15).

God's believing people knew in faith that the God who in Christ had entered into a solemn contract with them would continue to love them in a life that extends beyond the grave. Many years later, the apostle Paul put this into words as he stood before a Jewish king named Herod Agrippa: "It is because of my hope in what God has promised our ancestors that I am on trial today. Why should any of you consider it incredible that God raises the dead?" (Acts 26:6,8 TNIV).

God's Old Testament people knew that life extends beyond the grave into another world. They were on their way from earthly struggle to eternal peace.

God's people expressed their hope

The first reference in the Bible to eternal life (yes, it is an indirect one) is found in the name Adam chose for his wife. Picture the setting. Adam and Eve had believed another word besides their Father's; they had questioned God's love and thrown disobedience in his face. God first announced his judgment on their unbelief. "Dust you are and to dust you will return." After hearing God pronounce this withering curse, Adam and Eve knew they had only death ahead of them. But then God revealed his fatherly heart. He made it clear that a great descendant of Eve would restore life to a lost world. Now listen to Adam after he heard God's promise: "Adam named his wife *Eve*, because she would become the mother of all the living" (Genesis 3:20).

The name Adam chose for his wife was Eve (Hebrew: *HAHV-vah*, "life"). Martin Luther had this interesting comment about that choice of name:

> Adam believed and understood the saying concerning the woman's Seed who would crush the head of the serpent. In choosing a name for his wife ("life") he gave support to the hope in the future Seed. If he had not been aware of the future life, he would not have assigned so pleasing a name to his wife. He called her Eve to remind himself of the promise through which he himself also received new life, and to pass on the hope of eternal life to his descendants.

God's Old Testament believers realized that life was not over for them just because their earthly journey would now inevitably come to an end. They knew they were heading toward their true home, and sometimes their words expressed their homesickness. Listen to what Abraham's grandson Jacob said on his deathbed: "I look for *your deliverance*, O LORD" (Genesis 49:18).

God's people believed God's promises of a new life in a new world, and they looked forward to the day when they would enjoy the fulfillment of those promises. The apostle tells us that Jacob's grandfather Abraham had felt the same homesickness his grandson did: "By faith [Abraham] made his home in the promised land like a stranger in a foreign country. . . . For *he was looking forward to the city with foundations*, whose architect and builder is God" (Hebrews 11:9,10).

Think of Job, that child of God who lost all his possessions, whose ten children were killed when a tornado struck their home, and who finally was stricken with a life-threatening illness. In the Bible we meet him sitting on a pile of ashes, covered with painful sores from the soles of his feet to the top of his head, and tears streaming down his cheeks. And then we hear him speak:

"I know that my Redeemer lives, and that in the end *he will stand upon the earth*. And after my skin has been destroyed, yet *in my flesh I will see God; I myself will*

see him with my own eyes—I, and not another. How my heart yearns within me!" (Job 19:25-27)

Job's heart longed for his new life in his new home with his heavenly Father. Here on earth we Christians can never be completely satisfied. Not because we're greedy but because God has planted a hunger in us for something which cannot be found on earth. Only God *can* satisfy that hunger, and he promised his Old Testament people that he *will*.

Listen to David declare his trust in the new and better life God had promised: "In righteousness *I will see your face*; when I awake, I will be satisfied *with seeing your likeness*" (Psalm 17:15). David looked forward to the day when he would see God face-to-face. Think of what that will be like!

Here on earth our view of God is often distorted—perhaps by our ignorance, perhaps by tears. Saint Paul said, "Now we see only a reflection as in a mirror; then we shall see face to face" (1 Corinthians 13:12 TNIV). The mirrors used at Paul's time were pieces of polished metal that gave only an indistinct image.

In his Word God lets us see him, but not completely. We often experience that he is a "hidden God" (as Martin Luther called him). Looking at God now is like looking at a person in a mirror. When you do that, you don't get a complete picture. You don't see the person from all sides, but only from one side. That's going to change when, in the new world, God's people get to see him face-to-face. "God himself will be with them and be their God" (Revelation 21:3).

Can we be sure of this? Listen again to the poet: "Surely goodness and love will follow me all the days of my life, and *I will dwell* in the house of the LORD forever" (Psalm 23:6).

Notice, David doesn't say: "I surely *would like* to dwell in the LORD's house forever." He doesn't say: "I surely *hope* I dwell in the LORD's house forever." He says: "*I will dwell* in the house of the LORD forever."

How could he say that? Because, as Martin Luther reminds us, "Every promise God makes *includes Christ.* If a promise is separated from the Mediator, God is not dealing with us at all."

Because God's promised Substitute *supplied the perfect obedience* that God's holiness demands, and because he *suffered the punishment* that God's justice demands, the way to the Father's house is open. The door is open not just a crack, but it's wide open. That's what the Savior has promised, and God keeps his promises. "Not to us, O LORD, not to us but to your name be the glory, because of your love and faithfulness" (Psalm 115:1).

Many prophecies fulfilled

Was it a long shot for God's Old Testament people to look forward confidently to a new life in a future world? Anyone can make a lucky guess about the future. People *do* pick winning lottery numbers, despite the fact that the odds are overwhelmingly against them.

A single correct prediction about a future event is one thing. But dozens and hundreds of prophetic predictions are found on the pages of the Old Testament, written down by different people over several thousand years of history. The most important of these have been fulfilled in the life and death and resurrection of Jesus Christ. Can anyone say this is just a lucky coincidence?

Many important prophecies of Old Testament Scripture have not yet been fulfilled. God's believing people in Bible times trusted God would keep every one of those promises, and they looked forward to the day when he would. So do we. We have "a faith and knowledge resting on the hope of eternal life, which God, *who does not lie*, promised" (Titus 1:2).

So what?

So what difference does this make to you today? You're not a lost creature—a product of time and chance, a highly evolved animal who grew unguided from a blob of mud somewhere or from some space dust. You are a one-of-a-kind creation of the Most High God. You are redeemed by his Son's blood. You are made over into a Christian by his Holy Spirit. As a believing child of God, you have heard your Father speak to you about what lies ahead, just as he spoke to his Old Testament believers during the many centuries before Christ was born.

The news gets even better. Saint Paul emphasizes that since we are children of God, we are also his heirs (Galatians 4:7). Being God's heirs is almost too much for our minds to grasp. A child born in a millionaire's family stands to inherit his or her father's millions. But what are all those millions compared to what you and I will inherit when the Lord, who owns heaven and earth, calls us to join him at his side forever?

When God promised to take his people to a new and different life in a better world, he wasn't speaking only about Abraham and Sarah and Moses. Saint Paul wrote to some Christians in ancient Rome: "Everything that was written in the past was written to teach us" (Romans 15:4).

The Bible stakes God's reputation on his ability to conquer evil and to restore to his children a perfect life and a perfect home around his throne, just like his first two children had in the Garden of Eden. He has given you the solemn promise that he's going to lead you *not around death*, bypassing it somehow, *but right through death*. And the reason he can promise you that is Jesus Christ. Jesus Christ is the reason why we hope for a future life. He suffered the blood and the pain and the terror of death so that we wouldn't have to fear dying. Because of our connection with Adam and Eve, we're each going to die. We're going to walk through the dark valley of the shadow of death. Our bodies will have to go back to dust. But because of our connection with Jesus Christ, we believers are going to live forever. By volunteering to die, he broke death's power, so we don't have to fear it. Our bodies will rise and be reunited with our souls.

Our Kinsman-Redeemer

What God has to say to you, he has said in Jesus Christ. When Job said: "I know that *my Redeemer* lives" (Job 19:25), he used a name for the Savior that describes a close relative, a next of kin. In Bible times, God gave a kinsman-redeemer some very special assignments. It was his special duty to *ransom a poor relative* who had had to sell himself into slavery to pay his debts; to *pay off a poor relative's mortgage*, so the family wouldn't be dispossessed; to *marry the childless widow* of a kinsman, so the dead man's line and family name wouldn't die out; and to *avenge the murder* of his next of kin.

To many people, Jesus of Nazareth is no more than a carpenter-teacher who taught people to love one another and who died as an unfortunate martyr. Through the Word of God, the Holy Spirit has taught you to know that Jesus Christ is more. Like Job, you have learned to know Jesus as your Kinsman-Redeemer. He spent nine months inside the womb of a human mother so that he could become a human being like the rest of us.

Jesus Christ hurt and cried and suffered and died and rose again so we could be sure that our place in the incredibly beautiful home that he has promised awaits us. He was yesterday, he is today, and he remains our Savior into the grave and back out of it.

That's why we don't have to be afraid of walking through the valley of the dark shadow. Three out of four people in this world don't have a clue as to how to connect with God. You know. You have a Kinsman-Redeemer who has already taken the trip through that dark valley. He has promised to walk alongside you today and next week and until the Last Day and into eternity. Because he has not told us everything we might like to know, there is much about the future that is hidden from us. Our comfort rests in knowing that Jesus, who has defeated death, now rules all creation, including what lies in the future. What God has promised you, he has promised *in Jesus Christ*.

The night before he died, Jesus told some of his followers: "My Father's house has plenty of room; it that were not so, would I have told you that I am going there to *prepare a place for you*? And if I go and prepare a place for you, *I will come back and take you* to be with me" (John 14:2,3 TNIV).

A little bit later that same evening, Jesus spoke these words to his Father: "Father, I want those you have given me *to be with me where I am*, and to see my glory" (John 17:24).

That's God's promise to you in Jesus Christ. His reputation is our guarantee. If his rising from the grave were a hoax, if it were not true—if there were no future life—then it wouldn't really matter whether anything else was true or not.

Our present existence as passengers on a revolving planet is not our permanent existence. We're just "passing through." Christ has promised: "I have something better in store for you—a future life in a perfect world . . . with me!"

Does this sound too good to be true—a delicious self-delusion? Life in this world is not a "giant bowl of cherries." People who live in broken homes, who have known abusive parents, who are trapped in pain, or who have loneliness for a constant companion may find it difficult to imagine the totally different life that awaits God's believing people. There simply are no words to describe the life God has prepared for those who love him. The bodies we now have get tired and sick and old. Worst of all, they're constantly being ambushed by our sinful nature. Our bodies don't at all resemble the glorified bodies we will have one day. You could never guess what a tomato looks like by looking at a tomato seed. You'll never get a glimpse of your future body by looking at the body you now have. The new life God's heirs will receive on the other side of the curtain will be utterly unlike the life we now have. It will be what God originally designed life to be. You've got God's promise on that.

Your attitude

You know that the big things in life—like being born and dying and standing before God—are things that you have to do *all alone*. So what will *you* do when the sun turns black and the stars fall from the sky like overripe figs and the earth as we know it disappears and every dime you own is taken from you?

The Bible tells us that when it happens, many will call out to the mountains and rocks: "Fall on us and hide us from the face of him who sits on the throne and from the wrath of the Lamb! For the great day of their wrath has come, and who can withstand it?" (Revelation 6:16,17 TNIV).

So what will *you* do when God's magnificent trumpets break into our world and announce the end of life on this earth? Jesus has told us what to do: "When these things begin to take place, *stand up* and *lift up your heads*, because your redemption is drawing near" (Luke 21:28).

When people are defeated or ashamed, they *hang* their heads. Those who are confident and unashamed (1 John 2:28) in Christ can *lift up* their heads. On that day you will know, just as you know today, that Jesus Christ, your Kinsman-Redeemer, lived the kind of life you should have and died the death you deserved. At the moment when time stops and eternity begins, you can say, just as Old Testament people of God could say: "This is the great day of the Lord, and this is the greatest day of my life! I know I'm going to heaven, and I know how to get there—through the Messiah whom God promised and sent." Listen to a hymn that was part of the worship of Old Testament Israel:

No man can redeem the life of another or give to God a ransom for him—the ransom for a life is costly, no payment is ever enough—that he should live on forever . . . *But God will redeem my [soul] from the grave; he will surely take me to himself.* (Psalm 49:7-9,15)

We believe that promise, and we look forward to the new life in the new world that God has told us lies just ahead.

Martin Luther suggested that Christians learn to live with one foot on earth and one foot in heaven. That might not seem like the most *graceful* way to walk through this life, but it is the only *safe* way.

God never said that our journey to his side would be easy, but he did say that it would be *worthwhile*. Jesus Christ is the only one who makes life worthwhile.

"I am the resurrection and the life. Anyone who believes in me will live, even though they die; and whoever lives and believes in me will never die. *Do you believe this*?" (John 11:25,26 TNIV)

A

Abraham 6, 9, 10, 15-22, 127, 128, 139, 180
Adam 58-60, 97, 185
Adonai (the Lord) 3-5
Ahab 36, 156-158, 181
Ahaz 109, 121, 181
altar 70, 71, 75, 76, 79
Ammon 37-39
Apocrypha 123
Arabah 33
Aram 37, 159
ark of the covenant 76, 77, 116, 117
Asherah 72, 73, 109
Assyria 8, 38, 103-105, 153
atonement cover 77, 87

B

Baal worship 71-73, 121
Babylon 38, 79, 80, 103, 104, 119, 120
barley 35, 36, 45-47, 90
beer 46, 47
blood sacrifice 26, 70, 85-88
bread of the Presence 76
bronze basin 75, 79
burnt offering 20, 70, 85, 109

C

calendar
  agricultural 45
  sacred 88-91
cherubim 77
circumcision 17
covenant 16
  Abrahamic 15-22
  Sinai 22-27
curtain 76

D

Daniel 104, 118, 120-122, 183
date palm 48
David 77, 78, 83, 108, 109, 169-174
Day of Atonement. See Yom Kippur
Dead Sea 29-33
Dead Sea Scrolls 117, 121
desert 33

E

'el (God or a god) 9-13
Edom 38, 39
Egypt 31, 32, 38, 89, 90
Elijah 156-160, 182
Elohim (God) 2, 3, 7, 8
El Shaddai (God Almighty) 9, 10
Enoch 181, 182
Eve 58-60, 97, 128, 130, 185
Ezekiel 104, 118
Ezra 119

F

farming 34-37, 44-49, 56, 140, 141
fellowship offering 85, 86
Fertile Crescent 29-31
figs 47, 48
fishermen 49, 143
foods
  clean 50, 51
  unclean 50, 51
foreshadow 95, 96

G

Galilee, Sea of   30, 49, 143
Gilgal 74, 88
gospel 55, 62-67, 102
grace 17
grain offering 69, 90
Great Rift Valley (Arabah) 33
guilt offering 87, 88

H

Haggai 81
Hezekiah 109, 110, 121
Holy Place 76, 78
homemaker   144, 145

I

idolatry   57, 58, 71-74
Immanuel ("God with us") 10-13
incense, altar of 76
inspiration, miracle of   113-116, 119-122
Intertestamental Period 105, 122, 123
Isaiah 103, 104

J

Jehoshaphat 39, 118
Jeremiah 104
Jerusalem 74, 77-80
Jesus Christ 10-13, 112, 113, 127-136, 163, 164, 172
Job 161-163, 186
Joel 61, 104
Jonah 8, 105
Jordan River 29-31, 33
Josephus 121, 122
Joshua 4
Jubilee Year 40
Judges 106, 151, 152

K

kings 106-111
Kinsman-Redeemer 190

L

lampstand 49, 76
law (See also Torah) 55-62, 66, 67, 102
Levites 81-83, 98, 99
Levitical cities 98
Luther, Martin 12, 13, 59, 62, 91, 114, 123, 127, 171

M

Maccabees, book of   123
Malachi 121, 122
manna 44
manuscripts 117
Mediterranean Sea 24, 29, 32, 37
Mesopotamia 30-32
Messiah ("Anointed One")   128-136, 169, 170
Micah 104
midbar (See also desert) 33
Moab 37, 38
Moses 101-103, 154-156, 160, 180
Most Holy Place 76-78

N

Nahum 105
Negev 46, 139

O

Old Testament 115-122
olives, olive oil 49, 76
origin 2

P

Palestine 29-41
passive obedience (of Christ) 133-135
Passover, Feast of 49, 88-90
Pentecost 90
Philistia, Philistines 37, 108
priests 81-83, 97, 99
prophets 102-107,
Prophets, the 120-123
Proverbs 121, 145
Psalms 167-176

Q

quail 43, 44

R

resurrection 179-190

S

Sabbath 17, 18, 84, 88, 144
sabbatical year 40, 140, 141
Samaritans 80
Samuel 88, 103, 106, 107
scapegoat 65, 66, 87
scribes 117
scroll 117, 121
Sea of bronze (of cast metal) 79
Sea of Galilee 30, 49, 143
shepherds 141, 142
Shiloh 74
sin 59-62
sin offering 84-87
Substitute, substitution 63-67

T

tabernacle 74-77
Tabernacles, Feast of 88, 90, 91
temple, second (Zerubbabel's) 80, 81
temple, Solomon's 77-80
theocracy 105, 106
Torah (teaching) 116-122
Transjordan 33
Trinity, triune 3

U

Unleavened Bread, Feast of 88-90

W

Weeks, Feast of (See also Pentecost) 88, 90
wheat 45, 46, 140, 141
wine 45-47
wisdom literature 118
Writings, the 118, 121

Y

Yahweh (the LORD) 5-8, 17
Yom Kippur (Day of Atonement) 65, 66, 86, 87

Z

Zechariah 81, 140
Zerubbabel 81